FORSAKEN

A Novel of
Terror and Recompense In a Flyover Town

by
SEBASTIAN GERARD

UrbisMedia-Ltd. 2020

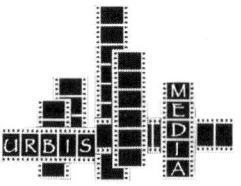

UrbisMedia-Ltd.com

Designed by Laura A. Rodil
www.sophella.com

Cross photo by Peter Marquis-Kyle
Stoneman photo by the Author

ISBN 978-1-09832-430-8

For My Cousin Monica

Other Books By The Author

The River Dragon's Daughters (2019)

The Babo Gospels: Essays and Parables on Faith and Reason (2018)

Stumbling Blocks & Stepping Stones, A Novel of Coming of Age Catholic (2016)

For Goodness Sake, A Novel of the Afterlife of Suzie Wong (2008)

Lifelines (2004)

CONTENTS

PART ONE

I

Thoughts and Prayers

The starlings that hung in the crisp autumn air rising above the Upstate New York town, and the crows that had already appropriated the cross pieces on the telephone poles, had already sensed that's the bustle of activities taking place in the streets below would likely render leftovers for them to scavenge. For the present there was too much activity and they would have to bide their time above the fray.

The flashing lights of police cars and the emergency response vehicles, and the broadcast towers from media trucks had become familiar warnings, even to people in small towns that were usually off the national media radar. As were the blaring sirens and shouts, and even screams, from the confused assembly of people in the late morning overcast light. Only the leftovers mattered to the anxious avians.

At ground level the ribbons of yellow crime scene tape fluttered in the light breeze and were mostly ignored by reporters and the cameramen still arriving for the imminent press conference. The hastily assembled public address system squawked and screeched with feedback as Sheriff Cavanaugh stood straight in his starched white and militarily creased shirt with four golden stars on each epaulet, checking his notes in front of the microphone. Two burly deputies were behind his left shoulder and the Mayor and Pastor Thorne of the local African-American Baptist church were on his right flank. The tech support guy from Palatine High School finally got the PA system to settle down.

"Good morning everyone . . . Well I guess good morning is not really an appropriate greeting given the reason that we are all here. This has been a terrible morning."

Jerry Cavanaugh, still sporting his US Marine Corps buzz cut and his slightly blurry USMC symbol and *Semper Fi* tattoos on his forearms, affected the reluctant demeanor of someone who preferred not to be doing a press conference. But in fact, although he admitted it only to himself, he rather enjoyed this little stage to display his military bearing and his civil authority. Whatever it was, it was all sort of an act, a performance, as most every elected public official had come to appreciate. In fact, nationally, these performances were getting to be rather commonplace.

"At 9:18 this morning a shooter came onto the campus of Palatine High and entered the classroom building by the east door. He was armed with an AK47 and five clips of ammunition. He was also carrying a loaded .38 revolver and a bayonet. He shot and killed campus security officer, Mr. Bouscaren, who was stationed outside the main entrance of the building."

Bouscaren, aged 53, a large portly man, had been wearing a Kevlar vest, but was shot once in the neck and once in the head. A large coffee mug and a glazed donut were found under his body. His Glock 9mm pistol was still in its holster.

The Sheriff did not mention these details. "According to statements we have been taking, the shooter then entered the building and began firing his weapon at any target and yelling something in a foreign language. The shooter forced his way into three classrooms and one office, firing at random according to witnesses. Four students, one teacher and one staff member were killed and thirteen students injured. There might be three more students who were lightly-injured and managed to escape the building. We are still assembling this information. Names of the victims are being withheld at this time.

"The shooter is dead and we are establishing his identification as we speak. I know that you must have many questions, as do we at this point. Please be patient and there will be another conference in about an hour, at which Mayor Vreeland will speak."

Karen Gagan-Kemp of FOX News 5, who had forced her way to the front of the media scrum, immediately shouted, "Sheriff Cavanaugh, how many?"

The Sheriff, who was familiar with the attractive, impeccably-coiffed local evening news anchor, cocked his head and pursed his lips in frustration. "Later, Karen," he said, leaning back toward the mic "your patience will be appreciated."

"Just one question," she insisted. The other reporters let her take the lead.

Cavanaugh ignored her. "Reverend Thorne of Redeemer Baptist Church has asked to lead us in a prayer for now. Thank you."

Gagan-Kemp glared at the Sheriff, and pushed her way back through the scrum before the very large clergyman could get the mic adjusted to his height. Thorne, six-foot-five in height and near 300-pounds wrapped in an expensive black suit and a bright maroon silk shirt beneath a starched clerical collar, loomed like a Protestant church unto himself, as imposing as an Old Testament prophet. Ironically, he did not possess a prophet's stentorian voice, but a squeaky high-tone that made one wonder if it was coming from elsewhere.

"My brothers and sisters in Christ," Thorne presumptuously began, "we implore our blessed Savior to receive the souls of those lost to us today in this senseless and Satanic act of murder, into his welcoming embrace." Beads of sweat were already forming on his forehead beneath Thorne's processed and pomaded hair. "Lord Jesus, we take comfort in that your sacrifice on that Roman cross has redeemed those who have taken you into their hearts."

Off to the side, nearly blotted out from the view of the television cameras by the mountainous Thorne, Pastor Carson "Pearly" Gaites, of the Lutheran-affiliated Congregation of the Risen Savior leaned uncomfortably on his single crutch. Out of professional courtesy, if not Christian charity, Thorne might have allowed Gaites to precede him, but theirs was not a relationship of apostolic fraternity, but of competitors for the limited souls in Palatine and its hinterland. Someone aware of their rivalry mumbled that Gaites was waiting his turn for those who did not want to end up in "Black heaven." Gaites, was a "specialist" in preaching about heaven because he had a near death experience and said he was actually in paradise for over an hour while EMT staff were cutting him out of his crunched automobile and "brought him back" to life because Jesus had more work for him to do." His congregation's enrollment surged for a while, but tapered off after his reference to the heaven he experienced as being a place free of "Jigaboo music."

Gagan-Kemp reached the FOX 5 remote truck and her assistant. "Pastor blowhard will be going on for a while. He seems in usual funeral oration form. Listen, somebody said that there was a civilian involved in stopping the shooter. Right now, there's no information coming out of the Sheriff, so see if you can find out if there's anything in the usual sources of communication. I think there have been some family members of victims that have been notified, but the police are keeping press away from them for present. I need to find someplace to take care of what that double latte and bran muffin is doing to me. I don't want to be following the nationals once they get here."

Those listening to Reverend Thorne drone on with his recitation of scriptural references thinned to a couple dozen, mostly Black, Jesus-praising devotees. But the general scene began to thicken again with the arrival of more concerned parents and friends as well as the usual snooping onlookers. There were scattered shouts of jubilation and tears of joy as parents discovered their children were unharmed. There were hugs and those looking for someone to hug, names called out, and seemingly everyone else on a cell phone. Stand-ups from a half-dozen television stations were being set up, trying not to be in each other's shot.

In the middle of a cluster of Sheriff's Department vehicles, their flashing colored emergency lights generating an almost carnival midway atmosphere, a young man is being interviewed by Cavanaugh and a couple of plainclothes officers, alerting Gagan-Kemp's reporter's nose that something significant or newsworthy might be involved. Thinking it might be one of the students who had information she made her way over, but was intercepted by a Sheriff deputy.

"Sorry ma'am, no press at the moment." He knew who she was, the most popular local evening news anchor. The cops referred to her as "Lady Blah-Blah."

"Can you just tell me who the young man is that the Sheriff is talking to?" she asked, using her best girlish 'wouldn't you like to fuck me' look that actually got her the news anchor job and might get her a move on up to the network. KGK, as she had come to be known, started out as the "weather girl," a good spot to show off the Barbie Doll figure. But it bugged her that her anchor job got her called what the British termed a "news reader." She had the itch to be, or at least be seen to be, a real journalist, a reporter with credentials earned right where history was happening, and where she could be the author of its "first chapter." Like those BBC women reporters in the Middle East, or Paris, or Beijing; then maybe graduating to *60 Minutes*, or a Pulitzer for a book, somebody that everybody would raise a glass to at any Foreign Correspondents Club, or be asked to keynote one of those Washington Press Corps affairs. But that required more than perfect legs and tits, and the Chiclet smile she was giving the deputy.

"Just his name? Officer . . . Carney," she said, reading the name plate below his shield. KGK's breathy voice always carried a hint of moan.

"Don't know. Just that he's not a student. He's a teacher."

"A teacher?" she repeated.

"Yeah, but he's gonna be a hero."

"A hero? Why?"

"That's the guy they are saying took down the shooter."

"Really? I thought it was a law officer?"

"Not what I've heard; a civilian," he assured her.

"Thanks," KGK said and made her way around the perimeter until she came upon a small group of students. She approached the only one that was not on her cell phone. The girl had obviously been crying, but the reporter ignored that.

"Excuse me, miss . . .

"I can't talk right now, I'm too . . ." the girl said.

"I understand, KGK replied. "I'm just trying to find out the name of that teacher over there talking to the Sheriff. Do you know his name?" She pointed.

"That's Mr. Greco."

"Mr. Greco. Do you know his first name?"

The girl turned and interrupted one of the other girls to ask if she knew.

The other girl frowned, but then said, "Marius. Or maybe Marcus."

"Do you happen to know what he . . . ?" KGK began to ask, but one of the other girls on a phone burst into tears and they all turned to hugging one another.

KGK made her way back to their remote truck and asked her assistant to get into the school's website and find out what she could about Mr. Marius, or Marcus Greco.

Pastor Gaites had replaced Thorne and was now droning on, relating the now boring cliched story of how he had stood before the "pearlescent gates of heaven" but was snatched back before entering by the EMT because God had more work for him to do before he would return to be reunited with those who were "called" by their creator with terrorist bullets. That interpretation of the morning's events elicited a couple of audible groans and a wrenching sob from some bereaved family member. By the time KGK had returned from one of the Port-o-Pottys that had already been ranked at the site, the assistant met her with some information.

"Your Mr. Greco has been teaching urban anthropology here for the past year and a half. He's from California, master's degree from UCLA, also assistant wrestling coach, thirty-one, single. Cute, too, in a James Franco sort of way, but looks taller by the photo on the school website."

"I'll have to confirm that," KGK said. But when she returned to where her subject had been involved in conversation with the Sheriff, he was gone. Maybe there will be more at the next press briefing, she thought. She headed back to the remote truck her mind screaming that Rev. Pearly Gaites "shut the fuck up."

<hr>

Two evenings before the morning of the school shooting, at midnight, Marius Greco made a call to LA.

"Nine PM, exactly," Chamsi answered. "How are things in...what's the name of that place?"

"Palatine. Nothing very exciting happens here," he responded. "How about there? How is she doing? Last time I called, things didn't sound too good."

Chamsi could sense the impatient worry in his voice. "Dr. Rong scanned her again last week and ran some other tests.

He's not optimistic Marius, and you know how she is; she doesn't want any bullshit, just straight talk. And I can't stop her from insisting that she is a burden living at our house."

His heart sank. "What about the list?"

"There's not much hope with anything soon on that. Anyway, it's not in our hands. And there's always the possible discrimination factor," she said.

"How about you, Cham? How's school going?"

"It's a struggle, but I can't complain, particularly when I see what she is going through. At least I am learning stuff that can help matters. I can now install pick lines for her IVs when she needs them and keep check on her vitals at home."

"You're getting a little over my head here," Marius said.

"But I'm also getting some experience in the OR, which is where I want to specialize. Your mom has been great. She's always bringing stuff over. We're becoming addicted to Mexican food. She does laundry and cleans. She's a saint, Marius."

"So are you, Cham. I feel so damn helpless here." He paused. "What about those cousins? Any more trouble with them?"

"Not since my cousin, Ali, put a gun against the forehead of one of them when he came to the door about a month ago. My cousin doesn't like those guys from their school days. But it makes their sister nervous. She thinks somebody is going to get hurt, or killed."

"Maybe I should come back, Cham . . .".

"No, Marius," she interrupted. "Really, that would only inflame them more. They are never going to stop blaming Jazmeen for her brothers being in prison. At least she is safe from them. Just stay where you are for now and take care of your work. It's the best we can do for now."

"Well, I made another deposit to your account. Use it as you see fit. At least let me help that way. Okay?"

"Okay."

"And give our girl a hug for me."

"I will. And I'll tell her it's from you."

Marius could feel his throat tightening with emotion. "Okay," he croaked. "Next time, Cham; same night, same time?"

"Yes. Good night, Marius."

———

KGK had just finished refreshing her makeup and gathering her stuff for the 4 o'clock press briefing when her assistant handed her a couple sheets of paper. "here, I got a little further information from California," she said. KGK stuffed them into her bag and set out for the briefing.

Sheriff Cavanaugh adjusted the mic up from Rev. Gaites' height and cleared his throat. "I want to thank the Reverend for his thoughts and prayers as we have been gathering information about this morning's tragic events. Since then several members of national press have arrived and I am told that the BBC and *Telemnudo* are on their way." The Sheriff paused to look at some notes. The sun glinted off the four silver stars on the wings of his collar. "At approximately 8:47 this morning shooter entered the main classroom building by the north door. He was carrying an AK47 assault rifle and several magazines of additional ammunition. We have subsequently learned that he was also armed with a .38 revolver and a bayonet. Before entering, he shot Mr. Bouscaren, the Security Officer. Mr. Bouscaren died immediately, having received two gunshot wounds to his back and the back of the head. The perpetrator then proceeded through the halls, apparently looking for any target of opportunity. He did not seem to be seeking out any particular persons. He almost immediately shot two female students at their lockers. They had heard the shots that killed Mr. Bouscaren, but did not take them as sounds of gunfire. We know this because both girls survived being shot and are in the hospital, one in critical condition."

"Thank you, Jesus," a woman in the crowd shouted. A reporter beside KGK mumbled, "For what, the Second Amendment?"

Sheriff Cavanaugh briefly looked up from his notes with a frown. "She is in surgery as we speak," he continued.

"And in our thoughts and prayers," the same woman shouted.

"Please," Cavanaugh said through an anger-constricted voice, "this is a press conference. You will have ample time and opportunity for . . . ah . . . ah, other expressions, later. I'll thank you to allow me to continue without interruption. People have been waiting patiently for this information."

"Christ, why doesn't Mother Theresa shut up and go and light a candle at the shrine," the reporter beside KGK grumbled again, referring to the assemblage of signs, balloons, teddy bears and candles forming at the campus gate.

KGK recognized the Boston accent and said, "People here are in shock. We should make allowances." She realized that that really didn't sound like her, that level of empathy.

Yeah," he replied ambiguously. "Maybe I've covered too many of these. And they are all seeming to follow the same cliché script. Thoughts and prayers." His reply was actually closer to her cynicism about these events.

Beads of sweat has begun to appear on Sheriff Cavanaugh's forehead just below his hairline and the armpit areas of his crisply ironed shirt were also dark with perspiration. "From the sequence of events that we have been able to reconstruct, it appears that the perpetrator next encountered Mr. Parker, a mathematics teacher, who was about to enter his classroom. Mr. Parker died in the hallway from three gunshot wounds to his torso. I am told that Mr. Parker was scheduled to retire at the end of this term." The Sheriff decided not to add that

Mr. Parker had been his math teacher when he attended this same high school. Sentimentality must not intrude upon professionalism. He continued, an image of a slumped Mr. Parker, lingering in the background of his thoughts. He noticed that Mayor Vreeland had arrived, taking a place behind him on the steps that served as a dais.

"Mrs. Ramirez, the administrative office secretary, was wounded when the perpetrator fired through the office window. The bullet missed her but she received several cuts from the flying glass. She should be released from hospital soon."

"God bless you, Mrs. Ramirez," someone shouted in celebration of the woman whose job often involved bad news but was nevertheless much beloved by both students and faculty. "Go Esperanza," someone else yelled.

Cavanaugh just ignored this outburst, not wanting to appear disrespectful to the sweet-tempered woman he remembered. "The perpetrator then proceeded down the hallway seeking targets. But by this time most of those in the building had been alerted by the gunfire and either left by the southside door, or followed drills to secure themselves in classrooms. Unfortunately, the Chemistry Lab was not locked and three students working early on experiments were shot. Two were killed almost instantly according to another student that hid below a lab table. That student also had the presence of mind to quickly dial 911 on her cell phone, which was the first alert that the school was under attack."

"We're not going to have much of a story if they don't start giving us some names," KGK grumbled.

"Standard operating procedure for these kinds of things," the Brooklyn reporter responded. "The answer I got at one of these events, the one out in San Bernardino I think, was that the cops can't be sure that there were not specific targets that the perpetrator was after, and so they don't want them identified."

"Thanks," KGK replied, "For saving me from looking like a complete rookie."

"My pleasure. Maybe you can help on some local details later. Any decent bars in this burg?"

"Only indecent ones."

They had missed a couple of sentences from Cavanaugh; his description of four other students being wounded that the shooter had discovered running down a side corridor. All were wounded. Conklin commented that the perpetrator did not seem interested in finishing off his victims, perhaps intent on finding someone in particular.

"We may never know the answer to that question," Cavanaugh added. I want to turn things over now to Mayor Vreeland who will take things from here at this point."

It was obvious to several of the local press that Vreeland must have made it clear to the Sheriff that he wanted to relate the juiciest part of the emerging story.

"Firstly, I want to say that my thoughts, prayers and condolences go out to the victims and families and friends who have been affected by this heinous act of terrorism. We have seen too many of these tragic events in the news, but we never expect that we will be visited by one of them in our own community. But no place is exempt in the world in which we live today, a world of globalization in which no community has secure borders against those who hate our Christian democracy."

"There's a first, what the hell is a Christian democracy?" mumbled the Brooklyn reporter. "Isn't that a contradiction in terms?"

KGK quietly wondered whether there was any possibility this guy would be able to file an objective story.

"We have four dead citizens of Palatine and several in critical condition in the hospital. Our once quiet, law-abiding community has been thrust into the post-911 world because we can no longer control our national borders."

KGK had heard Vreeland on this subject before. She had actually interviewed him when it was first mentioned that the small-town mayor might be a good Republican candidate for Governor. Polished and always well-dressed, he probably was a millionaire a few times over from his farm equipment sales and rental business, he had ticked almost all of the conservative boxes except never having served in the military. That did not prevent Vreeland from being militaristic, which he expressed through his service on the Draft Board during the Vietnam War.

"Fortunately, we still have courageous Americans willing to stand up and risk der lives for der fellow citizens," the Mayor said with an accent still slightly flavored by his Swedish background. Some of you have already heard that it was a teacher at Palatine High who single-handedly put a stop to this terrorist attack. Were it not for this brave young man, the count of victims might have been many times higher. I can tell you that the Sheriff has informed me that the attacker still had two remaining magazines for his AK-47 assault rifle, the same type of weapon that was used by the Vietcong and the Army of North Vietnam."

Vreeland motioned to the tall, lean, young man who have been standing down off the steps to the side, seemingly had hiding himself behind a burly sheriff's deputy. At first, the young man made no response, perhaps not having heard or been listening to mayor. When the mayor called him by name he looked slightly startled and hesitant to come up and join him at the microphone.

KGK immediately recognized him as the young man sheriff deputies had been conversing with. She already knew that he was Marius Greco, the anthropology teacher. The Mayor then introduced him to the assembly of media locals, composed of parents, students, and the curious, saying that he would be allowed to take a few questions. Immediately there was a burst of shouts and cheers, cameras snapping photographs, and jostling to get closer to the front. "Way to go! Mr. Greco," shouted somebody, and it got repeated to falling almost into a chant. Vreeland, who had remained close by at Greco's shoulder to maintain control of the proceedings, and also insure his inclusion into photographs that were likely to go not just statewide, but national, and viral on the Internet, asked the crowd to calm down as it was not an occasion for cheering.

Greco appeared to be staring off into space.

A local newspaper reporter spoke up first." Firstly, I think I can speak on behalf of all the people of the town of Palatine, thanking you for your courageous act, which I am sure has saved many lives. Can you tell us how you managed to stop the terrorist?"

Greco took a few breaths. He seemed rather diffident, but when he finally spoke it was in a rather composed, sonorous tone. "I cannot say that it was something that I intended to do. I had been locked in my classroom with nine of my students, hoping that we would not be noticed and that he—the attacker—could not manage to breach the door. When the gunfire stopped I thought that he might have moved out of our hallway and I took a chance to open the door and look there so that we might all escape from the building. When I got out there—our classroom door is near to the corner of an intersecting hallway—and I looked around the corner and immediately saw the gunman. He was right there, kneeling down, apparently trying to get a fresh magazine into his rifle. I was surprised he didn't hear me approaching. He immediately looked up and saw me, just as I heard the magazine click into place. I had no choice; I just dove on him. In another instant he could've shot me at point blank range. I'm bigger, and probably stronger than him, and I used to wrestle in high school. I got on him, twisted him around and got a chokehold around his neck. I don't know how long I choked him, but after a while he just went limp. I let go, grabbed the rifle and the deputy arrived. That's all."

There was a cacophony of questions immediately from the media scrum. Greco just stood there making no response. Vreeland stepped in and said he would select the questions to keep order. He immediately recognized KGK.

"How long did it take for the police to arrive to you, Mr. Greco?" she asked.

"I don't really know, a moment or two, maybe more. Time gets a little warped when you are in stress mode."

"And then what happened?" She followed up immediately.

"Stress also makes you a little stupid, too, I think. I should have slid that rifle down the hall and got back into my classroom with the students because a police officer saw me with the rifle and almost mistook me for the shooter. He fired one shot from his rifle that passed me and I threw the rifle towards him and flattened myself on the floor. He was actually beginning to put handcuffs on me, even though the shooter was unconscious right beside me all dressed up like a ninja. Maybe he thought there were two shooters. Anyway, we quickly cleared it up, but I was lucky that I didn't end up a victim of, . . . of . . . ah . . ."

"Friendly fire," somebody yelled.

"Yeah, friendly fire," Greco repeated, almost inaudibly.

"What about the perpetrator?" Another reporter yelled without waiting for recognition from the mayor. "Did you kill him?"

Greco winced. His voice dropped down noticeably. "No. I think he's okay. Well, not okay, I must have hurt him pretty good. But I did hear the paramedics say that he had a pulse. Then they took him away. So, I don't know any more about his condition."

"Were you trying to kill him?" another reporter asked.

"I think I was just trying to keep him from killing me, and more of us, and did what I had to do to, ah, neutralize him, actually the only thing I could do."

"Have you had any military training, Mr. Greco?"

"Army. I had a deployment in Iraq."

Vreeland cut in front of the mic. "Okay, just a couple more questions for now. There'll be another briefing tomorrow morning from both law enforcement and medical staff." He did not say that the Coroner would be giving a report as well.

The reporter next to KGK asked what the name of the shooter was, but the Sheriff stepped in to say that that information was being withheld temporarily for safety and investigative purposes.

"Dumb upstate rubes," he growled.

A woman in the back shouted out: "Mr. Greco, we are having a prayer meeting and candlelight vigil at the gate this evening. I hope you will join us in giving thanks to the Lord. Please allow us to thank you in person as well."

Some other reporters shouted questions, but Greco made no reply, just giving an ambiguous slight nod of his head and quickly turned back toward the school building and disappeared inside. The sheriff adjourned the press conference.

Hello, Mr. Greco, this is Karen Gagan-Kemp of WPAL8 News," the voice on Marius Greco's phone message said. "I was at your press conference this afternoon. I'm calling to ask if you would do an interview segment on the news with me tomorrow evening. The community is very anxious to receive more information about today's tragic events, a story in which you have become an important and inspirational element. Please give me a call back at 737-0888, extension 23, tomorrow morning at your earliest convenience. Thank you very much."

Marius had already told the two uniformed sheriff deputies that had been assigned to guard his residence—just a couple of days the Sheriff had insisted because the shooter might have relatives or accomplices who might want to take revenge on him—that he did not want to be disturbed by the media whose trucks were already parking in his street. At least KGK had not called him a "hero." The evening paper already had his photo with the word, and all the broadcast media and Internet were using it. Marius knew media, but even he was amazed at how quickly it latched onto something novel and newsy and, in its instantaneousness, there emerged what was being called a "new normal." Ironically, there was no longer a "normal." "Jesus, I'm their shiny new thing," he mumbled as he slipped his favorite Bill Evans CD into the player, and then a frozen pepperoni pizza into the little countertop oven.

His phone rang again.

He ignored it.

In three Bill Evans tunes, the pizza was ready and Marius substituted his video DVD for his nightly movie. He had already made his selection: *Network*, but fell asleep on the couch during a love scene between William Holden and Faye Dunaway.

The following morning Marius was up early and quickly changed into his running gear. The media were up early too. When he looked out the front window they were all over the sidewalk and lawn, brandishing their microphones and cameras, and he had a quick mental image of the townspeople in the *Frankenstein* movie, pitchforks and torches in hand, surging up the hill to attack the monster. He quietly slipped out the back door, tapping the sheriff deputy on the shoulder on the way, hurdled the back fence and through the neighbor's yard into the street behind. There, waiting to greet him, leaning against her BMW and sipping her Starbucks latte, was KGK.

"You didn't answer my phone message last night," she said with the familiar tone of a young couple.

"Yeah, and now you are going to impart some embarrassing information you obtained from that spy camera you have my shower?"

She ignored the riposte. "You slipped out the back way of the school yesterday, so I thought that rear exits might be a habit of yours. Seems I guessed right," she said with her cute smile.

"So, two data points constitutes a habit with you media people, huh? Three times must be a tradition. How many for a paradigm?"

"That's too big a word for the evening news," she responded, taking a sip of latte.

"I guess that disqualifies me, then."

"No, no, not at all. We expect such language from academics. Certifies them."

"I'll need my run to consider it. The oxygen helps to clarify my thinking. Back in forty minutes. He paused while pulling up one of his socks. "By the way, nine."

"What nine?" she said, with a frown on her face.

"Nine iterations, for a paradigm," he explained with mock solemnity.

"You're just making that up," she said. "anyway, iterations is too big a word, too. I think 'pattern' would work better."

"Sure, dumb down the language. That's the job of today's broadcast media."

"Then I'll try to keep it high-toned in tonight's interview. People will think that they've tuned into PBS."

"You'll have to change your hair then," he said with a smile, turning to start his run.

"I suppose my dress, as well," she yelled after him. Marius just waved without looking back.

Neither noticed the other, but they were both smiling. Some kind of a connection had been made between them, something in that little playful riff of conversation that clicked. It felt like snappy dialogue between Cary Grant and Rosalind Russell in *His Girl Friday*. Otherwise, Marius would never have considered KGK as interesting. Attractive, certainly; but interesting? Not from what he had assumed about her when he had seen her anchoring the local evening news. Now, even her appearance, altered by the little facial expressions, shrugs, and postures that never entered into broadcasts, made her a more appealing encounter, a little (he searched for the apt word), "arousing."

He hurdled a fresh pile of dog shit that would have ruined his morning run. "Jesus, I should be all 'mad as hell and I'm not going to take it anymore' and I'm more like a guy in a news anchor a focus group with an electrode attached to his pecker," he mused.

KGK was still smiling when Marius called her cell phone in an hour to say he would do the interview. He voiced one condition: she could not call him a hero. She had a few hours to do some background on her interview subject. Her producer consented to committing a half-hour following the news broadcast in which there would be an announcement at the top and bottom and a scroll underneath any news dealing with the shooting.

Marius was being powdered, mic-ed and sound-checked in the nearby studio that had been given a crisp *60 Minutes* ambience. If she handled this interview well, it might be moved on up to the national network, which was already interested in giving the interview a wider audience.

The newspapers had already disclosed the basic information about Marius Greco. Born and educated in Southern California. Father immigrated from Sicily, worked in the wine industry above San Francisco, and married a Mexican-American woman. Marius had a Bachelor in liberal arts; one tour of military duty (Army) in Iraq; Masters in urban anthropology from UCLA; taught one and half years of high school in LA before accepting position at Palatine High.

When they were seated opposite one another, Marius noticed that KGK had slipped in to her serious-faced journalist demeanor. She was proving to be a rather protean character. There weren't any little warm-up niceties. She was all business. He thought maybe she was just a little nervous.

"Good evening Mr. Greco. I want to thank you on behalf of WPAL and National Broadcasting for agreeing to do this interview on such short notice and at the time that our community is only beginning to do its grieving over the horrific events that took place just days ago." The camera that was focused on Marius only registered a slight nod.

"Before we begin I should announce that we now have the name of the perpetrator. He is Mr. Khalid Aziz, age seventeen, who was a student at Palatine High. We have not been allowed to release information about the residential or family information of Mr. Aziz, only that he is now a resident of an intensive care unit at a local hospital and is in critical condition. We have also been informed that he is in no condition to make any kind of statement regarding his assault. As is now probably well-known, at least locally, a stop was put to that assault by my guest, Mr. Greco, a teacher of urban anthropology at Palatine High. I know Mr. Greco that you prefer not being referred to as a "hero," despite the courage you demonstrated in taking on a heavily-armed perpetrator who apparently excepted no one as a target. I hope you won't mind if I ask you to briefly repeat your statement of yesterday afternoon about your role in putting a stop to the carnage."

"I would hardly call it a "role". I was trying to determine if he was no longer in the hallway so that I might get my students out of the building when I literally stumbled on him while he was re-loading his rifle. He was having trouble with the mag . . . the magazine of ammunition, and I was able to get the jump on him. Nothing heroic about it; I am bigger and stronger."

"Of course, we know now that Mr. Aziz is in a coma. You were asked at the press conference whether you tried to kill Mr. Aziz and you were a little vague in your response, saying that you were just trying to stop him from killing anyone else. Subsequently, we have learned that Mr. Aziz had actually been a student of yours. Is that why you decided against killing him? You certainly had cause to do so."

Marius clearly didn't like the tenor of the question, but he struggled to keep his face from betraying his annoyance that she seemed to be going somewhere with this line of questioning. "I'm afraid your information is rather incomplete," he responded in a stony tone. "Mr. Aziz was briefly in my class on the "American Cinema as Social History" but dropped it after a couple of weeks.

"Why did he drop your class?"

"I asked him the same question when I was signing his drop card. He was pretty straightforward with his response. Too many Jews, he said."

"Too many Jews? That's an odd response. What could he mean by that?"

"I knew exactly," Marius responded. "The early years of the American cinema were very influenced by immigrant Jews. Most of the so-called Hollywood moguls were the sons of East European Jewish immigrants—sons of rabbis, businessmen and even peddlers. In fact, Jewish peddlers were the first distributors of early films to the bars, social clubs, and other venues where films were first shown in the eastern seaboard cities. Apparently, that was too many Jews for Mr. Aziz, who said he wasn't an anti-Semite, but anti-Zionist."

"Could your awareness of that have made any difference in your decision not to finish Mr. Aziz?"

"What? I don't understand your question, Ms Gagan-Kemp. That there are too many Jews in early American cinema? Or, that Mr. Aziz is only anti-Zionist?" Marius was clearly becoming irritated. The thought crossed his mind that since he insisted on not being regarded as a hero, KGK might be trying to posture him as something less than heroic. "I was just trying to prevent Mr. Aziz from harming anyone else. I just wanted to incapacitate him, and I did enough to do that.

"May I ask specifically how you ah, incapacitated him?"

"I managed to get my arm around his neck and choke him out. Actually, I thought I had killed him because he was clearly unconscious. But the EMT people discovered that he had a pulse."

"How do you feel about his being alive?" she asked.

"One more death would not help anything," he responded coldly, although he was beginning to think homicidal thoughts about her.

"You were in the service, were you not, Mr. Greco, in Iraq I'm told. Did you have occasion, in combat situations to …". Now she seemed to be fishing for something, and Marius was struggling to control his rising anger, some of it at himself. But he was also getting nervous about something else she might know and he preferred to shut this down, all of it.

"I can't see where that experience has any relevance at all to what transpired the other day. In fact, I don't understand why you are so interested in why Mr. Aziz is still alive, if only barely."

The counter question didn't bother her. "It may be that usually these perpetrators end up killing themselves, or are killed by law-enforcement. It is a rarity that there are circumstances in which they are apprehended and we might be able to learn of their motivations. Furthermore, this terrorist was captured by someone who actually knew, rather knows, him. That's unusual."

"In fact, I did not know that it was Mr. Aziz's neck that I had my arm around. I had no idea who it was because he was wearing a *balaclava*. It wasn't until after he was completely out cold and the EMT removed it, that I recognized him. He could've been Osama bin Laden for all I knew."

KGK looked a little taken aback because she was not informed that Aziz had been wearing a *balaclava*. "We'll be taking a short commercial break now from our interview with Mr. Marius Greco, the man who put a stop to the terrorist attack at Palatine High yesterday."

The picture now turned to a photograph of Aziz that appeared to have been taking off of a Facebook page. He was not smiling, but clearly a rather benign looking, boyishly handsome, young man. His thick dark hair was brushed directly back, and he affected a thin mustache. His dark eyes held a friendly gaze in them.

Marius just glared at her.

"How are you doing Marius?" she asked in that tone that she had used that morning. The implied familiarity of the "Marius" didn't fit his mood.

What Marius wanted to say, the words actually forming up and his mind, was that he was feeling like he was in the middle of another terrorist attack. "I'm not certain where you are going with this interview, Karen," he said, countering the familiarity, "but you must realize that if I tear off this mic and storm off this set on live television, you might be stuck doing a demonstration on how news anchors apply lip gloss."

"I do indeed, Mr. Greco. You also might at the same time make more celebrity for yourself than you want. I am sorry to have set your teeth on edge. Let me move off the subject we were on. I think our audience would like to know a little bit more about you, rather than just you in the context of yesterday's events."

Marius wasn't quite sure what she meant by that, but he was resolved to stand and fight if she continued with her apparent ambush tactics.

KGK stiffened to attention from the message in her ear piece. "We are back live with Mr. Marius Greco, the teacher at Palatine High who put a stop to the terrorist attack that has killed four persons and injured several others. I want to go back to the beginning of our interview where I introduced Mr. Greco as someone who insisted on not being referred to as a hero for his intervention in the attack and his subsequent, shall I say, neutralizing of the perpetrator, whom we now know to be Khalid Aziz, a seventeen-year-old student at Palatine

High. I do want to return for one more time, if you will permit me Mr. Greco, too your resistance to being called a hero, when many people in this community, and beyond, consider confronting someone armed as was Mr. Aziz, an act of high courage on your part."

"First of all, let me say that I think the term hero has almost become cliché these days. Anybody in a camo uniform is called hero, and now it is extended to people engaged in almost any kind of activity, even teaching. I don't see anything heroic in what I did. It was mere self-preservation in a situation that I would have preferred to resolve without one more person being killed, including Mr. Aziz. I would prefer that people leave me alone and stop measuring me for some statue in the town square. I don't want to be your local hero. It's almost impossible to avoid being corrupted by this stuff. Do You realize that a local car dealer wanted to give me a new car as a reward for my heroic deed, but he also wanted me to do a half dozen commercials. He is just one of the local businessmen that sees some commercial advantage in my so-called heroism. Already, local politicians want to drag me out at every opportunity, despite the fact that I'm a registered Democrat and they all seem to be Republicans. This sort of celebrity is unnerving, the positioning, and orchestrating, the right phraseology and photo ops."

"I suppose you must regard me as part of that same process," KGK responded in a tone that seemed almost designed to elicit a denial.

Marius sensed it. "I will have to let you answer that for me. Frankly, I think the media are more dangerous than the public, with your power to shape public perceptions. I do know a little bit about the influence of media; it's a dimension of my field of study."

"That sounds like an excellent segue. What brings a young man from the nation's second-largest city, and clearly a world city almost in motion pictures and other media, to a small town in upstate New York without even an exit on the New York State Thruway, or an airport of its own?" The lack of a Thruway exit was a sore point that had long angered locals. The Erie Canal went right through town and the railroad was nearby, but the lack of the Thruway exit was like an insult that they had not made it into the 20th Century.

"Well, first of all let me say I am not on the run from some terrible crime, the mafia, or from Russian hitmen."

"A relationship gone sour then?" She asked, with a smile.

"Not really," Marius replied, wondering if she might know something.

"You might regret asking since the answer is not likely to be very interesting to your viewing audience. But the main reason that I am here in Palatine is related to research I am doing in preparation for my doctoral dissertation in urban anthropology at UCLA. The subject of that research deals with the transition of America from a country of farms and small towns to one of big cities and metropolitan areas. Coming from LA, where I was born and grew up, small towns, other than Andy Hardy movies and some classic small-town films are not part of my experience. I am interested in how this transition has been portrayed in American cinema. So, I thought my dissertation research would be enhanced if I actually spent some time living and working in an American small town. My doctoral committee agreed, as this type of research methodology is not uncommon in my field, and fortunately, a teaching position became available at Palatine High and here I am. So, you can understand why I am more interested in just blending in then being regarded as some sort of local celebrity."

Marius paused. There was no audience, no class of students, to gauge whether or not he was having a soporific effect, except for KGK. She seemed interested, but she might have been listening to something in her ear piece as well. He could talk about this subject for hours, but he knew this was certainly not the place or time.

"You have been here a year and half now," KGK said, "have you made any significant discoveries for your dissertation?"

"I don't think that your viewing audience would be very much interested in hearing some of the elements of my early draft. But one thing I might say is that back in the 1940s, the period of prime comparative interest to me, nobody would have had a computer and an Internet connection to look up what country someone with a name like Aziz might be from, what language he spoke, or the name of the God he worshiped. Yet, as some of your older viewers might remember, Palatine was a place that was clearly run by a White, Protestant power structure. Today's American small town has been hauled, often unwillingly, into the global and metropolitan world that we live in now. Many have disappeared, others swallowed in the wave of suburbanization, some hang on in sort of a nostalgic desperation. I see the American small town as the country's canary in the coal mine, and Mr. Aziz might be a canary."

KGK was now aware that Marius had stolen her show, had given it a narrative, and an arc. The only thing she could do was fall into line and grab part of it. "You put that very interestingly, Mr. Greco. Perhaps, had Mr. Aziz remained in your class, his life might not have taken the tragic direction that it did."

Marius was schooled well enough in the twists and turns of dramatic situations. He knew he had gained the upper hand and he wanted to finish holding it.

"Let me say one more thing, before we are out of time," he began. "You seemed to be interested in the earlier part of this interview as to whether there was some reason why I did not end Mr. Aziz's life. Maybe there was some instinctual impulse, something from the academic side of me that wanted to be able to know what was it that made a young man take up a rifle and kill his fellow classmates and his teachers. If he ended up dead, we might never really know, but if he was alive, and maybe we could learn something. So, maybe it was an instinct, maybe just a moral prohibition against killing, even killing a killer, I don't know. I have been in combat in the Middle East and I can tell you that it is difficult to know what will happen, and what one will do when something happens, in that given moment. But if we can learn something from this offense, I think that's better than remaining in an attitude of darkness and hatred."

"I must thank you not only for your interesting thoughts, Mr. Greco, but also your sense of timing. Since we are just about out of time, I want to remind our viewing audience that they are welcome, indeed urged, to submit their comments to our online website at WPAL.com/feedback. Thank you and good evening."

KGK's producer came on the set and engaged her in conversation, allowing Marius the chance to remove his microphone and make his escape. He did not have any interest in doing a postmortem on the show with her. He did have a very strong interest in a nice cold margarita, some chips and salsa, and maybe a chat with his colleague, Josh. He was out of the station and into his car quick as a thief.

III

Lupita's

As the sole Mexican food establishment in Palatine, Lupita's Tacoria was like a combination of his mother's kitchen and a shrine to Marius. He liked to keep teasing Jesus Castro, Lupita's husband, about what he must have had to do to get a liquor license in New York, especially with a name like Castro. They were probably the only other Californians in Palatine, Jesus was from La Mesa, a city near San Diego, by way of Tijuana. Marius would order a salad sometimes, but always ask the Mexican, "Mmmm, very fresh. Did you pick this yourself?"

Tonight, Marius approached the bar. But Jesus was ready. "Congratulations, sir, you are our one-hundredth customer today! Please enjoy a complimentary beer."

"Hey, thanks! Lucky me, huh?" Marius replies, settling onto a stool.

But Jesus says, as he is serving him the beer and Marius takes a heavy swig, "Of course, and it's only five dollars!"

"What? I thought you said it was complimentary?" Marius complains.

Jesus grins, stretching his thick mustache and flashing his even, white teeth. "It is." He pauses. "You have beautiful eyes, sir."

"And people think we shouldn't build a wall on our Southern border," Marius responds.

But when he reaches for his wallet Jesus says, "Let's just make it our complimentary hero's special today."

"Christ, not you, too. What do you want in return, for me to dress up in a burrito suit and wangle customers through the front door?"

"Nah, seriously, I am proud of my Californian amigo."

"Well let's keep it low profile, okay. It's only two days and I can't take a piss without somebody thanking me for my service."

"I saw you on the TV tonight. You showed that gringa not to mess with the California guy. But I think she has the hots for you."

"You need to cut down on the tequila, amigo," Marius says. "By the way, substitute a nice icy Margarita for that hero beer. Seen Josh?"

"Yeah . . . right behind you."

Marius turns just as Josh Berman grabs both of his shoulders. "Achilles," he says in his low, gruff voice, squeezing a bit harder. "Hey, Zeus," he greets Jesus with a grin.

Marius ignores the heroic reference, as does Jesus. It's their custom. "I thought you might not be able to make it tonight," Marius says.

"Rachel agreed to switch the kids' bath night with me. Anyway, I figured correctly that this is exactly where you were going to turn up after your television debut. For a while there I thought she was going to go full-on Barbara Walters ambush on you. What happened during the commercial?"

"I played my Sicilian father card, and I guess it worked. She kind of folded."

"Or she fell in love with our hero," Jesus interjected.

"Let me know where I can get one of those Sicilian cards," Josh asked. "As you know, I come from the rabbi father tradition; although I think he would have smacked her with the Torah."

"You should know where to get one." Marius was referring to Josh's roots in Brooklyn. Josh was one of the first teachers to welcome Marius when he first arrived. Berman had been at Palatine High for four years. There was an immediate professional connection between them; Josh had worked as a cinematographer on some films in New York and his position at the school was teaching film and video technology. Together, they enjoyed playing in a somewhat alternate universe that consisted of elements and characters of Bedford Falls from *It's a Wonderful Life*.

"Here, I brought you some tomatoes," Josh said, putting down a small bag on the bar. Josh almost always arrived with fresh produce. The very reason that he was here in upstate New York and not teaching at some school in the Hamptons, out on the island, or even the Newhouse School down the road at Syracuse University, was that Rachel had always wanted to farm. "That can happen to girls who are brought up on an Israeli kibbutz." Rachel was from a Russian Jewish background that did not fit squarely with Josh's intellectual, but conservative, family from Austria. But Josh, a burly, awkward guy with a full beard and receding hairline, was totally in love with his Russian beauty and probably would have followed her to Siberia. Rachel was a full-figured woman with bronze red hair, high cheekbones, lips like sofa cushions, and large, green eyes. "She could've been a movie star, and she decides to be a farmer married to a zhlub like me," Josh said more than once. Marius agreed, "Think Greer Garson," he would respond. "No, think someone between Garson and maybe Susan Hayward. How about . . . ?" They had played this at least a dozen times.

Jesus shoved his face in the bag. "Hey, these are fresh and smell good. Believe me, I know tomatoes. How about I take these and do you guys up a nice TJ salsa. I got some avocados, too. Perfect t' go with the margaritas. You want some Josh? I'm out of lox and bagels."

"Anything but one of your burritos. Is the English translation for burrito 'methane bomb'? Rachel exiled me to the barn."

"Chips and salsa coming up," Jesus said, walking off with the vegetables.

"What's up with you, goombah. You're kind of quiet. You don't seem yourself today?" Josh said.

"Really? Do I seem to be anybody else you might recognize?"

"Yeah, George Bailey."

Marius took a swig of his Margarita, screwing up his face at the salt. "Ya know, I think you might've nailed it. I've only been a hero for two days and I'm beginning to feel Bedford Falls closing in on me. This is how George must've felt when the old Savings and Loan was going under."

"I don't think I do a very good Clarence, goombah. Remember, I'm a Jew, even though I haven't been to synagogue since that Nazarine was in short pants."

Marius took another sip of margarita. "I gotta get back in that classroom in a week or two, or whenever this thing calms down sufficiently, if ever, and be in front of those students who are going to be thinking of me differently now. For most of them I will be the hero the media are making me out to be, but there's going to be some kid, maybe a couple, in that room who are going to be looking at me in a different way. They're not going to say anything, but they're going to see me as a guy who did what the establishment—the same establishment that puts up with the racism, the misogyny, the homophobia, the xenophobia, and the rest of it—and that maybe I'm the one that deserves to be in a coma."

"The ole 'price of fame'," Josh said.

"The problem is that I think this whole hero thing is going to fuck up my work on my dissertation. My methodology needed me to be rather anonymous, at least somebody who fit in a little bit but was not regarded as anything special, in order to be able to elicit the kind of conversation that comes without any special admiration or intimidation. My methodology is kind of like those Middletown studies that were done in Muncie. But this really screws things up. I might be stuck here forever trying to get it done, like George Bailey."

"Now let's not go looking for any bridges, George. I don't have my wings yet."

"Fuck you, Clarence," Marius said with a smile.

Jesus arrived back in the table with a nice bowl of avocado salsa and a basket of fresh warm taco chips."You guys are gonna devour this. Lupita says she can do you a nice carne asada if you're still hungry."

"Carne Asada! See, George, you won't have to eat Zu-Zu's petals tonight.

"Fuck you, Clarence."

"Now you are never going to get to heaven with an attitude like that, George."

"Fuck you, Clarence. I'm a hero that kills Muslims."

"Hey, see what you can do with this one. A Jew, a Muslim and the pig walk into a bar . . ."

Marius sometimes believed that if he thought he was going to have a certain dream, he would. So, he did his damnedest not to think of the dream he most dreaded. But he ended up that night with the taste of the chips and salsa still in his throat, sweating, breathing heavily, anxious to the level of panic attack. It was the Jazmeen dream again.

The running in the dream was the worst part; his legs were heavy and unresponsive, but when he awoke his bedsheet was all jumbled at the bottom from his thrusting legs. Running from her brothers, Jazmeen's brothers, with their flashing knives. They were always yelling something in Arabic, which he didn't understand, but nevertheless understood its meaning. They wanted to unman him, castrate him in some dusty unpaved alley that, for reasons only the subconscious knows, was a snippet of an Iraqi village transposed to somewhere in LA.

The first part of the dream was usually the same. He would be with Jazmeen, that burgundy hijab framing that breathtakingly beautiful face above her T-shirt, skinny jeans and Chuck Taylors. He always thought that she had no idea how beautiful she was, a forbidden beauty, a dangerous beauty. That hijab seemed to make it all the more so. Some of the other girls at Westmont High had a malignant envy of her, others wanted to be her, at least as beautiful as her.

In the dream they were always talking someplace, behind a building, beneath the bleachers of the athletic field, sometimes in an empty classroom. Marius was always nervous, always scanning for danger. She obviously had some feelings for him, but they always seemed to be of respect and admiration, not carnal desire, or so he told himself. She needed to talk, she was metaphysically needy, and he felt he owed it to her since she had first started on this path from something he had said in class. But talking to that face was distracting.

The problem was that he knew what was going to happen. He had had this dream before, several times. He was still having it, and worried that he might always have it. Marius also knew that he had fallen in love with her, a combination of desire and terror. "She's only sixteen, he would keep telling himself over and over again, then, "She's Muslim," over and over again, "forbidden fruit." They never touched, just talked.

Then at some point they would show up, the brothers, and Jazmeen would scream "No, no, no!" But Marius would start running, that heavy-legged, struggled running, dream-impeded running, running from those flashing knives, from those Arabic taunts, until he jolted himself out of that dreamscape.

The following morning Marius took a look out the window to see whether the media activity might have calmed down in front of his house. There were fewer vehicles, but he was disappointed to see a group of people who were constructing some sort of shrine made principally of small American flags that they were sticking into the ground. He groaned.

When he went out the front door to confront the decorators, he was greeted with a round of applause. Then media sprung to attention, setting down their coffee and donuts and grabbing their cameras and recording equipment.

Marius did his best to maintain some geniality. "Morning, all," he greeted no one in particular. "I'm going to have to ask you folks if you wouldn't mind removing those from my lawn," he said to a rotund woman whose mammary abundance was stressing the tensile strength of a "God Bless America" T-shirt. Another woman was already approaching him with a gift of the organization's T shirt.

"You deserve this recognition," she responded.

"Well, I don't mean to appear unappreciative, but it brings unwanted attention and infringes on my privacy. I really would appreciate it if you remove them." Marius could see that a couple of reporters moved closer, and a cameraman shouldered his videocam. The lady made no motion to begin removing the flags.

"We did check with Mr. Crandall to see if it would be okay to install our flags," she said. Crandall was Marius's landlord.

"Yes, but this is my residence," Marius protested, "and I am entitled to the privacy that I pay for with my rent of it. I will remind Mr. Crandall of that. At present, I will thank you to remove the flags." He turned and went back into the house, exited from the back door and went out for his run.

But when he returned the flags were still there, although the patriots had left. It wasn't until he had removed all twenty-two flags that were sticking in his lawn and placed them in a grocery bag on his porch, all for the camera of WPAL, that he phoned Mr. Crandall to inform him that his permission was grounds for breaking his lease.

IV

The Alien Hero

In LA, the land of "what have you done lately," Marius knew that his celebrity would last until the next shining new media thing came along. He would be able to drive out of his neighborhood within which there would even be those who would hardly recognized him, into the vast urban sea of anonymity. The celebrity would be confined to the media, as long as the media was interested in him.

Not so in the 22,000 population of Palatine. School was closed for little more than a week and as he made his way around town running various errands there were a lot of waves and thumbs-up of acknowledgement, as well as the spontaneous outburst of applause from three women at the local supermarket.

Ever since he arrived in Palatine, Marius felt like an alien, the proverbial stranger in a strange land. He had done his background reading for his dissertation on the literature of small-town America as well as anyone. He had been through Edgar Lee Masters' *Spoon River Anthology* about how her small town failed to appreciate the dreams of an aspiring young actress, and the fictional small town of Gopher Prairie, Minnesota in Sinclair Lewis' *Main Street*. The longer he had been here, the more he had come to appreciate what Henry Van Dyke wrote in 1895 in *The School of Life* that: "A little country town with its inflexible social conditions, its petty sayings and jealousies, its obstinate mistrust of all that is strange and its crude gossip about all that it cannot comprehend . . . may be as complicated and hard to live in as great Babylon itself."

Places like Palatine had long been the source of jokes and put-downs by sophisticated urbanites. He came across quips by Elbert Hubbard, such as "There isn't much to be seen in a little town, but what you hear makes up for it," and Robert Quillen's definition of a "hick" town as "where there is no place to go where you shouldn't be." Josh liked fellow Brooklynite Joey Adams's references to small town boredom as "a place where there's nothing doing every minute," and reputed church-going habits as "where people go to church to see who didn't."

Actually, he really knew about fitting in from his parents. They were immigrants from small towns. Papa from Bisacquino, Sicily, a small village just south of the Corleone of *Godfather* fame, and birthplace of the director of *It's a Wonderful Life*, Frank Capra; mama, from Cabo San Lucas, down in Baja California. They were immigrants, which is probably the reason, along with their being from small towns in traditional societies, they emphasized so much the idea of fitting in, or at least if you didn't fit in you did not challenge the prevailing cultural milieu, you became something like a decoration.

Small towns like Palatine got their borrowed names from biblical and historical sources. Townships all over upstate New York were named by a surveyor with an affinity for classical Rome. There were townships like Camillus, Pompey, Marcellus, and Cazenovia, even a city named Rome, scattered around Central New York. And just up the Erie Canal from Palatine was the small, but somewhat renowned, Palmyra, New York, birthplace of Mormonism, where its founder, Joseph Smith, reputedly received golden tablets from an angel named Moroni. Local lakes, mountains and forests often retained their indigenous names from the local native peoples, the Mohawk, Iroquois, and Huron, but the Eurocentric settlers of small towns sought their historical connections and adopted renown from their own kind.

In small towns it was also easy to pick out the non-locals, and the non-locals to recognize one another. Marius and Josh recognized that in each other from the first faculty meeting that Marius attended. Now, hardly a week went by when they didn't get together at Lupita's for one of their seminars on their favorite subjects, movies and fitting into small-town life.

"I get it why some of these places are so damned conservative," Marius remarked in one of their first conversations on the subject. "Other than the ones that don't get swallowed up in the suburbs of some metropolitan city, most of these burgs are vestiges of a time when this country was supposed to be composed of mostly farms and villages. America started out as a colony, a place to be exploited by Europe, but the War of Independence changed all that and along came the big cities that grew mostly by the influx of the new wave of immigrants, the Irish, Italians, Jews, Germans, and people who no longer wanted to live and work on farms and in small towns. Cities were where or you could get ahead quick, and one didn't have to own farmland to do it."

"Yeah, what is it that they're now calling farming and small town and country?" Josh asked.

"'Flyover America'," Marius suggested.

"Right, Palatine doesn't even have an airport. Y'gotta fly over it. Did you know that the guy who first laid out this town tried to make it in the form of a cross? He was Cicero Trent, and he had big plans for the place, or maybe he was just in competition with Joseph Smith who was founding Mormonism just up the canal in Palmyra. They say that you can still detect signs of the cruciform layout of the town, although the park lands that were supposed to demarcate the cross apparently fell to real estate pressures. Capitalism appears to supersede Christianity even in flyover America. I guess it was a flyover town for God as well. Places like Palatine somehow got left behind in the progress of the 20th century. Look, it's on the Erie Canal, a transportation route superseded by the rail-road and the Thruway. The state is speckled with these places that got left behind by progress. There's a place to the West called Gloversville—they used to make leather gloves there, but not anymore—they are conservative, stuck in the past, and stagnant or losing population."

"The older cliché, you remember, was calling these places 'one-horse towns'."

"Exactly, they have about one of everything, one TV station, one newspaper, one supermarket dry goods store and drugstore—until they are consolidated into a Walmart—and of course one high school. Oh, and let's not forget, one bank, like the old Bailey's Savings and Loan of Bedford Falls." Josh said, conflating their two favorite subjects.

But Marius corrected him. "No, actually there was Mr. Potter, too. Remember, Lionel Barrymore?"

"Right, how could I forget Mr. Potter. I remember that scene between Barrymore and Jimmy Stewart where George tells the greedy old man off," Josh recalled.

"Yeah, but the old man gets even when George is in financial trouble . . ."

"Oh, yeah, because Uncle Billy lost that $8000," Josh said, his excitement rising at remembering so much of the movie.

Now their conversation had transited from Palatine to Bedford Falls.

"He was a boozer, that Uncle Billy," Marius said. "So, when George goes to Potter for a loan Potter slams him right in the nuts when George offers his insurance policy as collateral: *Look at you. You used to be so cocky. You were going to go out and conquer the world. You once called me "a warped, frustrated, old man"! What are you but a warped, frustrated young man? A miserable little clerk crawling in here on your hands and knees and begging for help. No securities, no stocks, no bonds, nothin' but a miserable little $500 equity in a* *life insurance policy. [Potter chuckles] You're worth more dead than alive!"*

"Yeah, and Potter hates the immigrants who were moving into the new subdivisions of Bedford Falls, people he calls riff-raff."

"That's what I think is the interesting thing about that movie," Marius said. "In 1946, when it came out, people might not have seen, in the immediate postwar, what was about to happen socio-politically in the country. The war had not only set in motion a massive upheaval, especially in the attitudes of women and minorities, but in other elements of society as well. The GIs were fighting for a nostalgic world that would not be there when they returned, right?

"*The Best Years of Our Lives*, right?" Josh interjected without any need to elaborate.

"Right. There was the G.I. Bill and then VA mortgage insurance, then the interstate highway program, and soon enough there were a lot of people who were able to achieve that dream of a car and home ownership in the suburbs. We see the beginnings of that in *It's a Wonderful Life*, and how people like Mr. Potter didn't like that a lot of them came from the immigrant class, the darker complextions. And he didn't like that the Bailey Savings and Loan catered to them. I'm betting that this got in there because Capra, himself an immigrant, was one of the screenwriters."

"There's this myth that American has been very welcoming to immigrants," Josh said. "I call it the Emma Lazarus myth—those lines about 'send us your huddled masses'—what bullshit. My people were not allowed in when that St. Louis ship full of Jews escaping the gas chambers tried to land here and were refused entry. They had to go back to Germany. The only ones they let in were less than a thousand Jews who were on a Navy ship called *The Henry Gibbins* as "guests" of President Franklin D. Roosevelt during the Holocaust in World

War II. They were temporarily housed at Fort Ontario right up the road from here in Oswego, New York from 1944 to 1946. They were expected to go home after the war, when they had no homes to go to. What a country! At least Oswego was one small town that wasn't xenophobic."

"But most small towns somehow managed to remain almost frozen in some Norman Rockwell poster pre-war past, some nostalgic Wonderful Life that most Americans only engage every Christmas when the movie is shown on television," Marius said. "The rest of the time it's flyover country."

"Remember when we were referring to Palatine as flyover country?" Marius asked Josh in their most recent Lupita's seminar, just two days after he had removed those flags from his lawn.

"Until some immigrant kid brings a gun to school and shoots the place up."

"And self-anointed patriotic strangers start sticking American flags all over your lawn. Did you see the news last night?"

"Yup, and you know that some national feeds picked it up."

"Yeah I got emails to document that."

"You would think that I was about to replace them with those black ISIS flags the way those ultra-patriots were whining about not being able to appropriate my property for their little chauvinistic demonstration. And, of course, there was Ms Gagan-Kemp playing it for all it was worth for her ticket to the big time."

"Jesus thinks she has the hots for you."

"Oh, she might want to fuck me alright, but not quite that way. I called her this afternoon to let her know that I thought she and her crew had really delivered a cheap shot. Her crew got the names of those flag freaks before they left so she could follow up with them over that video. You would've thought that I was desecrating graves in Arlington. She didn't deny that I was sort of set up, and in fact, invited me back on her show if I wanted to defend myself. I told her no thanks. But she did say to me that she would like to meet for a chat, and that it could be off the record."

"See, Jesus has probably got it right."

"Bullshit, but I made a date with her."

"Make it someplace where I can set up a nice spy-cam, would'ya?"

"Don't expect a sex scene. A murder, maybe?"

"How about another beer?" Josh asked, and called Jesus over. "Hey Zeus, two border guards and a Mexican with a leaf blower walk into, a bar . . .".

Jesus is ready. "Not that two, gay Jewish border guards joke again."

"Ooooh, he got ya that time, amigo," Marius said to Josh.

V

Easy Street

Marius was certain that he was going to be greeted by a round of applause from his class the first day back since the terrorist attack. Except for Kenny Pratt, who was in his wheelchair, the entire class stood as they applauded. Some whistled and whooped.

Kenny was not in a wheelchair as a result of the attack, but from a childhood injury. The only student in his class from the attack was Melissa Nolan, her left arm in a sling from the bullet that passed through her wrist. She was the only one who did not applaud.

"You get to do this one time, this time," Marius said, dropping his notes on the lectern. Every repetition will bring the class GPA down five points. Understood?"

"We saw you on television, Mr. Greco. You're a star," Jeff Banning shouted out.

"Don't believe everything you see on television, Banning," Marius responded. "I've told you, the only thing you can trust as solid truth is whatever I say in this classroom. And, as Groucho Marx said: I never tell the truth." He loved the conundrum. "Today we're going to concentrate on Charlie Chaplin's truth. This is truth in black-and-white, and silent, and I don't want any groans about that." There were, of course, a few audible groans, and snickers.

"Okay, I don't think this should be necessary by today's standards, but I am required to inform you anyway. Today's film, *Easy Street*, is a 1917 Mutual production by Chaplin, and starring Charlie along with a company of actors that he often used. I have to alert you to the fact that it does contain some sex and violence, although I think you've seen more explicit stuff and worse in theaters and on TV today, not to mention the Internet. But, according to the rules that I needed to agree to for approval of this course, I have now informed you, and anyone who thinks they might be offended or otherwise negatively affected, may remove themselves now or at any time during the screening."

"Is there any nudity, Mr. Greco?" Kenny asked.

"Nope, not even close. And no dirty language either, since it's silent. No blood, no guns, but there is a scene that does involve some drugs. Anyway, it's only about twenty-five minutes long, probably too short to corrupt you. So, let's have a look at Chaplin's *Easy Street*." Marius turned on the video projector.

"Well, what do you think? Marius asked twenty-five minutes later.

"I thought you said it was silent," Bobby Harrison commented, "there was music."

"That was added later on. But, actually there was live music, usually played by a pianist or organist in movie theaters. They tried to do their best to fit the music to the action that was on the screen. But what do you think the movie was about?"

"I think it was about what happens when you cram all of these weird-looking people together in one street. They end up kicking the crap out of each other. They don't have enough food or space to live in—did you see that guy feeding those kids like they were chickens?" Bobby said.

Caitlyn Myers spoke up. "I agree that the living conditions were terrible back then. But what I noticed the most was how women were treated; beaten up, threatened with rape, and forced to steal."

"It's about the cops. They can't seem to control the violence. And anybody can become a cop, like Charlie, and he ends up being a hero because he's just as violent as the rest of them." That sounded strange to Marius, coming from Jerry Lennon, whose father he knew to be a sheriff's deputy.

"I don't think it's much different today," Kenny said. "We've just progressed from batons to guns."

"Was that filmed in a real city slum street, Mr. Greco?" Justin Cummings asked. "No, that was a movie lot in Hollywood, at Chaplin Studios. But in 1917, there were plenty of streets like that in American cities." Marius wanted to get into more of the meat of the film and its broader implications about American society, but his approach was to elicit some lines of discussion from the students and then weave them into the fabric of his lecture. That way they would feel more involved in the process. These were movies, images and narratives, not differential calculus, so it was usually not difficult to get thoughts and opinions.

"These people are always fighting with each other in the streets. A lot of them look like terrorists with their beards and weird clothing, if you ask me." Richard Ferdette, a big, red-faced farm kid volunteered. Richard rarely spoke up in class.

"Yeah, but nobody asked you, Richard," Kenny snapped, craning his head backward to address the big football player directly.

"Easy boys," Marius cautioned. "Do you want to expand on your opinion at all, Richard?"

"No," Richard said at first, then, "they just don't look like Americans to me, that's all." A couple of other guys in the class murmured in apparent agreement.

"Kenny?" Marius said, allowing his interest in having a spirited dialogue to contravene his earlier caution.

"He makes my point for me," Kenny responded. "Of course, these people do not look like Americans. They just got off the boat from a whole bunch of foreign countries. They probably don't speak English either. And it's obvious that they're all competing for a limited amount of space on that street. I think the good thing about this movie is that it shows that we haven't changed all that much. We are still suspicious of immigrants coming into this country, supposedly polluting our so-called American ways, taking our jobs, and threatening our women. It's even worse for them when they are not White." Then he craned his neck back towards Richard again, "And what are Americans supposed to dress like, Richard? You're wearing farmer's coveralls most of the time. Where are all the farmers in this country?" This was a rather low blow, since Kenny knew that family farms were struggling and in decline. But it wasn't irrelevant to his point. Farms were part of the American lore, like small towns, and that dimension of America was in decline, and they laid much of the blame for that on the big cities and the immigrants that were filling them.

Marius sensed an opportunity to introduce something that he had in his notes. "Most of you have heard or read that poem about the Statue of Liberty. I think you have all encountered it in your American history class. I'm referring to the poem by Emma Lazarus where she writes about the statue inviting the 'huddled masses' from 'foreign shores,' the 'wretched refuse' of the earth. Sounds just a bit like that description of the people in *Easy Street*, doesn't it? Well, have a listen to this xenophobic poem, written about the same time by a guy named Thomas Bailey Aldrich. It warned:"

> Wide open and unguarded stand our gates,
> And through them press a wild, a motley throng—
> Men from the Volga and the Tartar steppes,
> Fearless figures of the Hoang-Ho,
> Malayan, Sythian, Teuton, Kelt and Slav,
> Flying the Old World's poverty and scorn;
> These bringing with them unknown gods and rites,
> Those tiger passions here to stretch their claws.

In street and alley what strange tongues are these,
Accents of menace alien to our air.

"Heck, I don't even recognize the names of some of these places or peoples. Bailey titled his poem 'The Unguarded Gates,' which sounds like it might be a good anthem for those people who want to build walls to seal off our borders against illegal immigrants. Ironic, isn't it, since Bailey himself had to be at least a descendent of an immigrant, since the only true Americans are the Native Americans."

Kenny sensed an opening. "Yeah, but he was the right kind of American, or should I say the White kind of American."

"There he goes again, Martin Luther Kenny," Robert Shermerhorn entered the fray.

"Strike up the oom-pah music, the Aryan has arrived," Kenny countered.

"You wouldn't be such a wise ass if you weren't sitting . . ."

Marius needed to shut it down. "Alright, alright, let's try to keep this on the high intellectual plane worthy of Palatine high school." But he had not counted on the vortex of fear, anger, and grief that stirred the emotions of the student body. The subject was too close to its tipping point. There was an almost palpable surge of emotion taking over the class.

"This is all fine and theoretical," Geoff Banning broke in, tension in his voice, "but the reality is that it was a fucking immigrant who came into our school a little over a week ago and killed and wounded a lot of good Americans. Now he's going to come out of his coma one of these days and, who knows, some slick lawyer from New York City will get him off on some legal technicality. It would've been better if you killed'im, Mr. Greco. That motherfucker should be dead." Banning was almost losing control, and Marius understood, since he knew that Andrew Borden, one of the dead, was a close of friend Banning. Still, he couldn't help think that forty-five minutes earlier Banning was calling him a hero. It was also clear that the class was now agitated and was feeling more than thinking. "You know that Khalid guy has an older brother and a sister, and who knows how many other relatives around. Their religion encourages them all to be martyrs, so maybe we haven't seen the end of this. You yourself should be taking care, Mr. Greco, because they might be wanting to get some revenge." Sheriff Cavanaugh had actually mentioned the same thing to Marius, which is probably the reason that the deputy's patrol car had been parked in Marius's street since all that press activity went away.

"I don't want to get into the whole thing about who has the best or worst religion," Marius began. But I would agree that religion is probably the main problem we have in relations between peoples and the assimilation of immigrants into American society. In fact, I am surprised that some of you did not pick up on that in the film I just showed you."

Marius was going to call an end to the class at this point if they remained agitated. But they seem to come calm down a little, so he decided to press on further, since this was one of the main teaching points he wanted to get out of the Chaplin film.

He continued. "Remember, the film begins with Chaplin, apparently a homeless person, waking up from sleeping outside of a crude building that is a mission or a church. He enters not for religious reasons but because he is broke and hungry, and in fact tries to steal the collection box. That set-up is pure Chaplin 101. In many of his movies he is the illiterate little tramp who stumbles into situations that he has little awareness of, but by luck or persistence he ends up solving some kind of a problem. In that sense he is a stand-in for the immigrant struggling to fit into a new society.

"There is always a girl, too, and this one is the organist at the church who is so happy that Charlie decided not to steal the collection box and to become a policeman, even though his motives are not of the highest sort. Then, after all the running around and finally subduing that big brute of a guy and beating up all of those bearded foreign-looking guys, at the end of the movie we see that the bar is turned into a religious establishment and peace and harmony come to *Easy Street*. And Charlie gets the girl. So, what is the message of *Easy Street*?"

Thomas Beard raised his hand. "I thought this movie was about immigrants, sir. Are you saying that Chaplin is promoting religion?"

"It's about both immigration and religion, but Chaplin is certainly not promoting religion, he is actually satirizing it. Chaplin himself was an immigrant from the poor areas of East London. He knew the immigrant experience of crossing the Atlantic in steerage class. But what he is satirizing is that becoming an American is not simply a matter of obeying laws and learning English, but also of accepting the predominant faith. It is part of the accepted process of assimilation, the mystical notion of the "melting pot." Chaplin satirized a lot of these American practices, in films like *The Immigrant* and *Modern Times*, so much so that he became the enemy, and a target of, J. Edgar Hoover, who was the head of the FBI."

"So, what is wrong with people becoming Christians, learning English, and becoming more American?" Melissa Nolan asked.

"Nothing," Marius responded. "So long as it is voluntary. People should be able to keep their language, or become bilingual, and keep their religion if they want to. We would be a lot less interesting country without pizzerias, Chinese takeout, and different kinds of religious feast days. Assimilation into American society should not mean a complete loss of one's prior identity."

"But America is a Christian country," she countered.

"You will have to show me where that is written, Melissa,"

Marius responded, doing his best to mask the rising frustration in his voice. "Anyway, isn't the important thing that people are allowed to practice any religion they prefer, rather than having a government impose a faith upon them? Or even not practice any religion at all? I think that's what the establishment clause is all about."

"If people practice certain religions, or are atheists, they will have different morals, morals that are different than those of Christianity. It's important that people abide by the same morals," she affirmed. Marius thought the somewhat archaic "abide" rather biblical.

"Well, it seems Chaplin provoked an interesting discussion. But we've run out of time for today. I'm sure the subject will come up again, as I know it to be an element of many motion pictures. See you next time."

***

It took less than three days before word made the rounds from one of his students to his or her parents and finally to Mr. Schmidt, Principal of Palatine High. The note, which was in Marius's faculty mail slot, made no mention of the reason for the summons. When Marius showed the note to Josh, he smiled, and joked: "Smoking in the men's room again? Surfing porn sites on the school computer? Taking up-skirt photos of Miss Crane? Naughty boy?" Home economics teacher, Miss Crane, was so hot that boys signed up to take her class.

"Dunno, I'll find out later this afternoon. I haven't been called to the principal's office since I got caught in the middle of a hallway punch-up between a bunch of rival Chicano gangbangers in 10th grade high school."

Everybody called Mr. Schmidt's office "the aquarium." Marius had been in the fish-decorated office only one other time, when he had first arrived and signed his contract papers. Schmidt had asked him at that time whether Marius was a fisherman. The wood-paneled office was a museum of New York State freshwater fish, their glistening, taxidermized bodies on lacquered wooden plaques affixed to the dark, paneled walls amongst pictures of principal Schmidt in his boat, smiling and holding up his conquests gave one the feeling of being at the bottom of an Adirondack lake. Other than two framed diplomas, there was no indication that this was the office of an academic administrator; no books, no photos of graduating classes, no academic awards. It was just fish: bass, large-mouth and small, pike, muskies, trout, carp, catfish, even the smallish sun fish and perch. There were salmon, too. He liked to point out most people didn't expect salmon would be found in New York. The thing was to not get him talking about fish, which Josh warned one might be "bored to death and end up on his wall."

Mr. Schmidt himself was a large, heavyset man, as bald as Mr. Potter of Bedford Falls. He was supposedly a descendent of Cicero Trent, the founder of Palatine. He had a ruddy complexion, prematurely spotted from all of his time out on the waters. Students called him "The Beluga." Schmidt was chatting with another gentleman when Marius was admitted to the Aquarium.

"Ah, Mr. Greco, this is Mr. Thompson, Chairman of the School Board," Schmidt said, introducing a thin man who immediately reminded Marius of Mr. Gower, the pharmacist in *It's a Wonderful Life*. "I asked Mr. Thompson to join our meeting here today because it was through him that I was informed . . . well, let me have him tell you."

Thompson's voice was raspy. "The principal informs me that you have been teaching here now one year and a half, Mr. Greco. How have you found that experience? Must be quite a contrast for someone from a metropolis like Los Angeles."

Marius thought it a little curious that neither man had mentioned Marius's newly acquired heroic status. It set him on further alert, and it did not take long for him to find out why. "We meet today because I received a communication from the parents of one of your students in your class about American cinema. The parents communicated to me that their child said that you had spoken negatively about religion, or religious beliefs, in your class, such that it made the student feel uncomfortable. They are a religious family, but since they are not untypical of many families in Palatine, we thought we should attend to the matter with some urgency."

Marius thought it a statement of masterful accusatory vagueness. Nothing was specified, not what Marius was supposed to have said that was "negative" to an unnamed student, child of unnamed parents. Even the form of "communication" was not specified. "What is it that you would like from me, Mr. Thompson? You do realize I am sure that what you have stated here is something about what I said in class, that was taken negatively by a student, that was then communicated to his or her parents, that was further communicated to you. So, I can only wonder what it was that I said, as I do say a lot of things in my class. Can you be more specific as to what it was that I was to have said that is alleged to have given offense to the student?" Marius felt like he was fashioning his response like a crafty lawyer in one of those courtroom dramas.

Mr. Thompson stared blankly at Marius for a moment. "The parents did not say anything like a direct quote from their child, only a characterization that what you had said in class was "negative" about religion or religious beliefs."

"Was any particular faith, or religious belief, mentioned in their communication to you?" Marius asked. He noticed out of the corner of his eye that Mr. Schmidt seemed to be flipping through the pages of an issue of *Field & Stream* that was on his desk.

Mr. Thompson had that blank stare again. "No, but I know them to be a Christian family, as most of our families are here in Palatine, so I would assume that the offense taken was something against Christianity or Christian thought." Marius had already figured that, statistically, that was probably the case. But, since Mr. Thompson was playing it cagey with him, or really didn't know anything at all, that he ought to try to retain the upper hand in this mini courtroom drama. He decided to push it another couple iterations, which might be enough to make it all go away.

"I, of course, recall addressing the subject of religion, because it is a subject of the film that we were discussing—that was, by the way, if it was not communicated to you, had to have been Chaplin's 1917 short film, *Easy Street*—but I do not recall either in my lecture, or during the class discussion, even mentioning the word Christianity. Was it alleged that I said something negative about Christianity?"

Mr. Thompson glanced over at Mr. Schmidt, whose attention was pulled away from his magazine. There was now an awkward silence, with Marius's question hanging in the air. He glanced over Mr. Thompson's head at the large bass on the wall. The bulging-eyed fish seemed to be smiling back at him approvingly that he had "Mr. Gower" by the balls. Marius thought the whole ridiculous business might be over.

But it wasn't. On the other side of his desk Mr. Schmidt had a folder, which he now opened. It was Marius's faculty folder. Schmidt didn't really look at it, but he probably had before the meeting. "I see by looking at your faculty data that you filled out that you are a Roman Catholic, Mr. Greco."

"I was baptized Roman Catholic."

"Yes, that's exactly what you wrote in answer to the question 'What is your religious affiliation, if any'?"

Marius tried to keep his hands, which were now bunching into fists, out of sight. It was like Thompson was playing him like a hooked fish on the end of his line. He was pissed this was not going to go away by making Schmidt look like a jerk.

"I almost didn't answer that question at all, if you must know, since I think it is inappropriate, and probably even illegal, at least in LA. But the fact is, I do have a religious association, as I have stated there, and I thought there might be no harm, and less bother, and so stated it."

"Why would you have any concern about being asked such a question?" Schmidt asked.

Marius smiled. "Surely, you are aware that there're places in this country where Roman Catholics, often pejoratively referred to as 'Papists,' are regarded as a sinister organization. I think that by now pretty much everybody has been exposed to that notion by way of *The Da Vinci Code* and other sources. Religious discrimination exists and I did not want to be a victim of it if it existed here. So, let me ask you a question, sir. Does Palatine have a problem with Roman Catholics?" Marius regarded his question as a risk, but he also thought that it obliquely planted the possibility of legal action into the discourse. Moreover, he was beginning to consider that his unwanted celebrity as the hero of Palatine High might come in handy if this whole business goes sour.

Mr. Thompson perked up. "We have no prejudice against Roman Catholics in Palatine, Mr. Greco. I think the congregation over at St. Agatha's on the corner of 4th and Ash Street would confirm that."

"Have you joined the congregation at St. Agatha's, Mr. Greco?" Schmidt asked. He pretty much expected what the answer would be.

"No, I haven't," Marius answered curtly. Schmidt almost looked like he had hooked another trophy for his wall.

"You would not call yourself a practicing Catholic then?" Schmidt continued.

"No, I wouldn't."

"Are you really a Roman Catholic, then, Mr. Greco?" he yanked further to set his hook.

"Technically, yes. Once you're baptized, that's it, there's no resignation form. Nor was there any deception in the answer I put to the question on the faculty form. Once Catholic, forever Catholic, like it or not." Marius smiled, then, without giving it a second thought, he affectedly made this sign of the cross, saying "in Nomine Patris, et Filius, et Spiritu Sancti," just in case they thought he might be faking everything.

Schmidt and Thompson looked at each other, momentarily confused.

"You seem to have a disdainful attitude toward religion, Mr. Greco, even the faith in which you claim to have been baptized." Schmidt seemed to be taking over now. It was the fisherman in him; he had one on his hook and he was going to play Marius until he could boat him.

"That's not an adjective I would use, sir. I'm much more like what the Roman Catholic Church calls a 'fallen away' Catholic—non-practicing."

"Are you not a Christian, then, Mr. Greco?"

"Perhaps not in the sense some might define it, sir." Marius could feel Schmidt tightening the line. But he was also feeling his own internal conflict. On the one hand, this meeting was beginning to feel like a scene out of the Spanish Inquisition. On the other, it was also shaping up into the sort of intellectual brawl that Marius enjoyed.

"So, how would you define yourself, then?"

"You will have to define what you mean by a Christian first, sir."

Mr. Thompson sprung back to life. "A Christian is anyone who has accepted Jesus Christ as the son of God and as their Lord and Savior. Do you accept that, Mr. Greco?"

"As your definition, sir, not mine."

"Yours, then," Schmidt commanded, yanking the line a little tighter."

"As far as I can tell, the first century Jewish rabbi, Yeshua ben Yusef, better known by his Greek name, Jesus Christ, preached one, consummate, principle. That was 'to love your neighbor as you love yourself.' A version, as I see it, of what is called 'the golden rule.' If you conduct your life by that principle—and I try to do that, although not always successfully—you are a *de facto* Christian. All the rest is narrative embroidery and commentary." Marius felt that this should function as a 'the defense rests' statement. He intentionally put in the first century information and Christ's ethnicity to muddy the waters he was being dragged through. He might have thrown off the hook.

But Schmidt was a determined angler, like his Lord and Savior, "a fisher of men." "So, I take it that you do not regard Jesus Christ as the son of God."

"I do not think that the fundamental principle of Christianity is of divine authorship."

"You are an atheist then, Mr. Greco, aren't you?"

"Depends on what you mean by atheist."

"That you hate God," Mr. Thompson said.

"That's ridiculous. How can someone hate something they do not even believe exists? Can you explain that to me? Atheism is just nonbelief. That's what the word means; it has nothing to do with loving or hating. But what I do hate is being rhetorically maneuvered into the position that there might be something wrong with me because I do not fit into your definition of a Christian, or of a believer. It makes me suspicious that I am being set up for something on the basis of an allegation about something I am supposed to have said in one of my classes that offended the religious sensibilities of one of my students. Am I correct in that?"

Schmidt and Thompson were silent.

Marius began to rise from his chair. "Is there more to be discussed on the subject, gentlemen? If not, I have some classes to prepare for. Some of us teach around here."

"We will be getting back to you after we have discussed this amongst ourselves, Mr. Greco," Thompson said. Schmidt looked like one had gotten away.

"I feel compelled to caution you that I am still a person of interest to the local media and even beyond, but not for my religious beliefs or the lack of them, but for the so-called heroic role I played in shutting down the terrorist attack on this high school. If you want the public to know that I have been put through what amounts to a religious inquisition on the basis of hearsay, I can make that more widely known, with my own commentary on it. That is, if you want your quiet little community on a bend in the Erie Canal to be yanked into a media spotlight on the subject of religious bigotry, I can probably do that for you. I probably do not have to inform you that once one of these things becomes an item for the national media, neither of us will be able to retain any kind of influence upon its trajectory or the shit-storm that might ensue."

Marius clicked off his smart phone's audio recorder after he exited the principal's office.

VI

Jazmeen

The blood swirled with the shower water into the drain. Marius leaned against the shower wall with his fourhead, letting the cool water flow down his neck and back to relieve the humidity, watching the red disappear with an idle fascination. The blood was mainly from his elbow and not the gash on his right hand, where some skin was scraped off by the rough tarmac at the edge of the road.

It could've been worse. He took a blind dive to save himself, and a few feet beyond where he landed was a power line pole that could have snapped his neck. It was ironic, considering where he had just been.

Earlier, Marius left his house by the back door around 10 PM. There was no longer any need for a rear exit; the press vehicles were gone, the Sheriff had removed the bodyguards two days before. The night was still thick with humidity, and Marius was coated with sweat after 50 yards of jogging. As he got out of the developed area, the only illumination was from fireflies conducting their flashing mating rituals over the darkened road. Marius reviewed his afternoon session with Schmidt and Thompson, "the Beluga," and "Mr. Gower", he intoned, smiling. He sensed a certain occupational danger from the encounter, but it was satisfying to him that he had fended off these two rubes, and that Schmidt had failed to "boat" him.

"I know who you are," the nurse said unthreateningly. "I saw your picture in the paper."

"I know I shouldn't be here, at this hour especially. But I happen to be passing the hospital on my run and ... well, I ...".

"Yes, I understand. But you happened to arrive just when the sheriff's deputy has gone to the cafeteria to get a coffee. He might be back anytime soon."

"I just wanted a quick look, to see ... well."

"You should know, too, that sometimes his brother comes at odd hours," she said. "Take just a minute, then you really should go."

Marius nodded, and slipped quietly down the hallway and into the lowlight of the ICU room. The plinking sounds of monitors, humming machines and screens with lines, colored graphs and data struck him like a scene in the service pod from *2001, A Space Odyssey*. Khalid lay motionless, slightly elevated, a strange creature with protruding tubes and lines. Marius imagined, as he had seen in a number of science fiction motion pictures, that Aziz was like a space traveler placed in suspended animation for a journey of perhaps hundreds or thousands of years. But then the thought shifted to being what death might be like. He wasn't sure why he was here now, or what might have brought him here, just that it felt strange that he wasn't the agent of this young man's death, only something like death, maybe something worse than death. Was Aziz dreaming the Islamist's *shahidi* dream of a paradise of virgins and rivers of wine, he wondered, when his thoughts were interrupted by the nurse. "Sir," she said, with no further indication it was time for him to leave.

Now, as he watched his blood swirling down the drain he tried to reconstruct what had happened after he exited the hospital and headed back for home down that fireflies-lit road. It was the sound of that engine, the sound of its increasing revolutions, that triggered his sense of imminent danger. He estimated that he had a few seconds to move over to the shoulder when he would see the vehicle's headlights streaming past him. But then the acceleration, and his instinctive dive into the gravel of the shoulder. It wasn't a moment too soon, as some part of the bumper or fender of the vehicle knocked off his right running shoe. There was no chance to identify the vehicle, much less get sight of its license plate. He postulated that he might have just avoided a dark country road accident. But the sound of acceleration, that was the sound of lethal intent.

"Jazmeen," he whispered her name with the same sense of foreboding. When his father had asked whether she might be the reason, or more specifically, her brothers the reason, that Marius was leaving LA for upstate New York, he gave him his standard reply: it was all about his doctoral dissertation, and not her, or her brothers. But he wasn't even certain himself. He had that sense of foreboding back then, and now it returned because of that incident on the road. He had even had a crazy thought that her cousins found out where he was living now, and maybe they decided to settle things out here. But no, how could they? It was a crazy thought, but now it aligned with the fact that Aziz had an older brother.

Marius sat on the edge of his bed, naked and un-toweled, letting the lazy, squeaking ceiling fan cool his body as these thoughts returned to him, a memory that haunted him for nearly two years now. Her aroma, the memory also of that kiss, his last kiss between then and now. He could almost still feel it on his lips, soft, warm, moist, and hungry. Once again, he knew his mind was going to reel back and try to figure out how it got to that, how Jazmeen just walked into his life one day and it wasn't the same since.

Would he have taken the time with her if she were not so stunningly beautiful, Marius wondered once more? "Lolo-brigida in a head scarf," he said to himself the first time he saw her. There were other Middle Eastern girls at Westmont High school, several, like her, with heads covered in their hijabs.

One could not help linger a look into their framed faces of large dark eyes, full lips, and milky complexions. In fact, it was Chamsi, an Iranian friend of Jazmeen, who introduced them. Chamsi was taking Marius's film class, and had shown Jazmeen a short story Marius had published in an on-line journal that dealt with the subject of the Iraq war. Jazmeen aspired to be a writer, and was intrigued by the unusual style of the story.

Now, here in upstate New York, Marius took out the print copy of his story, essay, confessional, whatever it was, from the file in his drawer. He had probably looked at it a couple dozen times since he left LA, trying to discern if there was some clue in the damn thing, some, some explanation, some meaning in it. He looked again, with some satisfaction, at the graphic the website had created for the piece, a flip cell phone floating in the dark universe amongst planets. And the title, that had suggested itself from the way the term had come into popular usage. And, again, he began reading, like a priest might reflexively read from his breviary, hardly able to remember how he was feeling, what inspired him, when he wrote it:

IN THE MOMENT, a short story of war and existence by Marius Greco

Is that the last face I am ever to see; that Iraqi kid? He must be no more that twelve, and wearing some knock-off Michael Jordon No. 23 jersey, cheapo flip-flops, and a half grin. He flipped that cell phone into the debris and donkey shit at the curb like I used to toss the television remote to my brother. Bobby is twelve, too, but probably playing a video game right about now, probably close to the violent "video game" that is my existence.

Oh, wow! What a concept. My brother is playing some war game back in Rochester blowing up pixilated bad guys, thumbing his controller with determination and termination. And, in some crisscross of dimensions he is blowing me up. He is No. 23, the roadside-kid in this godforsaken outskirt of Baghdad where I am riding shotgun in this godforsaken tin-can Humvee, dressed and armed like a freakin' Robocop and with the sinking sense that my existence is completely out of my control. Christ, what a thought—Bobby controlling my life with a video game controller. Man, I had better hydrate; I'm hallucinating in this 105-degree cauldron.

Just what I was doing when I glimpsed that Iraqi kid, all distorted at first through the plastic of the water bottle I keep shoving in my face. I knew immediately when I saw that cell phone is not at his ear. He wasn't calling anybody but that detonator, waiting for its number— and for this Humvee to be just where he wants it to be. In some invisible cyber-dimension, those numbers are on their way, flashing right by me to where I can't see, but only imagine—to that cart just ahead, or that pile of rubbish by the curb, or maybe in that pothole we're about to drive over. My fate is written in the most mundane detritus of this Allah-besotted neighborhood. In a moment those numbers will get there.

Now I am in that moment. I am so into this existentially-compressed nano-second, because now, in this moment, the blinding flash takes over, and I cannot discern whether time is exploding or imploding, to or from this nano-compressed instant of time. It's just the flash, that dying super-nova flash. No sound . . . yet. Light is the fastest thing in the universe, nothing faster. I remember those documentaries about the dropping of the atomic bomb on Hiroshima. From the B-29, the guys saw the flash first, before the sound, before the shock wave. The speed of light; 186,282.397 miles per second; now how the hell did I remember that? But that's why I see the flash first. My brain is fast, too, that's why it connects the flash to what it already knows comes with such flashes.

No sound here . . . yet. No shock wave . . .yet. Still, in the moment.

I thought I'd be confused, terrified—maybe that comes later, if there's a "later"—but why this sort of clarity, these self-conscious thoughts—all in simultaneity, like dozens of windows piled on top of one another on my computer screen, all "open" and sharing the same two-dimensional space. I can see them all—together, at once. I didn't think there would be a moment like this. It seems like everything is compressed, like I am peering into worlds that I was never able to see before—the space that exists in the universe of an atom, the variety of life that lives in a single drop of seawater. I remember hearing about this in high school science class, but this . . . this . . .

What's making my brain do this? It never could think like this before. I could never handle more than one thought at a time. Now it's like some computer, spilling out everything at once. Is this what they mean by "your whole life passing before you . . . ?" No, it's not the same. It's not the record of life, the times with mom and dad, and playing football, feeling up Alice in my car, eating hot dogs, and that stuff; it's about the process of life, about how it happens. I feel like I am looking at my own DNA and understanding how it works.

Hey! Maybe this is what they mean by "heaven?" Nah, I never really believed that bullshit. The sergeant made us form up for a little prayer session before we set out on this patrol. He says God is on our side. Yeah, well Allah might have something to say about that. So, this can't be what heaven is supposed to be like—my brain downloading everything it knows, or rather uploading everything it didn't know. Nah, Sister Ignatius told me in first grade that heaven was "looking into the face of God for eternity." Christ, that really sounds like fun—for eternity?

Eternity. That would be longer than this nano-second, this moment between the flash and . . . what comes after the flash. I feel momentarily locked right in that moment, like a grape hovering in a square of lime Jello. No, make that like an insect suspended in . . . what's that stuff called . . . c'mon, c'mon, c'mon brain . . . amber! Thought I wouldn't get it in time. What is a "moment" anyway? Something tells me it is a sub-part of a nano-second, some basic, irreducible particle of time—the ultra-present. I am in it, in the moment. But, hey, maybe eternity is really no longer than a moment. Right? There you are, "looking into the face of God," but if that's all you are doing, the only thing you are doing, then the unit of time doesn't make any difference, be it a second, or a millennium. Doesn't matter, because you wouldn't know the difference. Something has to change for you to tell the difference.

And I think I am really about to change. This moment won't last an eternity. It's the transition moment; I am going to be someone else, or something else. The "me," or what was me, is going to change. To what? A crippled human, without some limbs, or senses? Do I want to live without my arms, or legs, or eyes, or testicles, picking up "repairs," getting my "stumps at Landstuhl and prostheses at Walter Reed. Or, I'm going to be bits and pieces, like that poor bastard I saw them mopping up in Sadr City. There wasn't much to ID that guy beyond his DNA. So, what happens if I become a blob of DNA? Maybe it's no big deal, because that's what we are, our DNA; essentially, I'm just this tiny strand of stuff you could carry around in a test tube. Freeze me, then take me out some day and grow a shiny new me. Here he is folks, the new Mike Rossi, version Rossi 2.0. Bring on the Army recruiters. Tell Rossi 2.0 he's going to be a "hero" for going out there and getting those terrorists, the Terminator in camos, Bobby's search and destroy pixel "Army of One."

How the hell did I get into this moment? Am I supposed to be wasted like this? How did I get to the point where this is all right and proper, and patriotic, and keeping America's democracy and way of life safe? Safe from what? The kid in the No. 23 jersey, with the flip-flops? Hey! I am an "army of one," and a kid like my brother is going to take me out with a freakin' cell phone! There is something wrong with this picture!

Whoa, soldier, you are almost getting regretful, and angry. You don't have time to think about that stuff. You're starting to sound like your liberal sister. Angie, with her stuff about Iraq never attacking us. Then uncle Frank, still stuck in Vietnam; wants me to "win this one" because he didn't get a parade. Well, here I am, Uncle Frank—here, in Iraq—and some kid is attacking me. I don't want to think about it. They make a new me and I'm going to journalism school, like I intended.

Hold on a moment, Lance Corporal Rossi. That wouldn't really be a new me, would it? Unh, uh. A new physical me it would be; but the real me is me—my consciousness. The "me" of all those twenty-two years of life and experience, is the real me—my personality. No DNA generated facsimile could be a real me. I would be a biological "replicant." If the new me had no consciousness of the old me . . . well, it means that what I am is not material, it's my consciousness. Is my consciousness in that strand of DNA? Where does that go after this moment? It has to go somewhere. I don't buy into all this soul and heaven stuff, but my consciousness has to go somewhere.

I know what's happening here. I know I am in the front part of that nano-second before everything will start flying apart. It can blow my body apart, but will it also blow my consciousness—the real me—apart? I have thought about it, dreamed about it, a hundred times, so it is all programmed into my brain. I know the concussive force of blasted superheated air, filled with particles of explosives, rock and steel and cow shit from the street are going to be like a mini-"big bang" that will blast matter into a new order, or just dis-or-der. No, not really. The "order" of things contains the dis-order. The dis-order is just the temporary state of things that did not seem orderly to our fragmentary comprehension of things. So, if I become part of what seems dis-order, it's not really so, because I would just be part of a process that is so much bigger and longer and more complex than me and this stupid war, and that kid with the cell phone, and Iraq and Bush and the oil, and . . . it's only a temporary arrangement of some carbon atoms in some cosmic scheme I am only getting a fleeting glimpse of . . . I can't see the forest because I am one of the trees . . . no, one of the leaves . . . This is just a momentary glimpse between the flash of light and the shock wave. But I am not supposed to have this moment; I'm supposed to experience the classic refrain: "he never knew what hit him."

Improvised Explosive Device, I.E.D.; you put a D in front of it and it spells D.I.E.D.

Hey! Am I lucky? Or not? You tell me. Gotta go some-time. This is early; but it's quick. No lingering with Alzheimer's, or cancer. People will say "he never knew what hit him," not knowing that's a pretty good epi-taph for a soldier. An I.E.D., or a round right through the head, is quicker than a stroke or heart attack. Maybe too quick even for pain. Problem is that I have been thinking about this for a long time, and every time you think about it you die a little bit. But I didn't expect this moment, did I? Why bother me with all these thoughts if it's check-out time?

Hell, I never had thoughts like these, never thought I could think thoughts like these. I thought that there were thoughts like these, or that there were people who could even think thoughts like this. See! Is this what happens in the last nano-second; everything starts to become clearer to you? Isn't that a screwed-up way of life: you go through it not knowing a damn thing about what it is, what it's for, or anything, and then you get a flash of clarity for a going-away present.

Hey, maybe No. 23 was just making a phone call and the phone was broken and he's just throwing away a broken phone. Maybe the flash was something else, some reflection of a shiny surface, some bright sun coming through the space between the buildings. Nah. You were given this moment for a reason . . . or no reason at all.

I really wanted to be a journalist. Why all this revelation now, in this instance, this moment? What use is it to me now? By the end of this moment there might be no me, just what can be collected, bagged, flown in the dead of night to some cold warehouse in Delaware, welcomed home like some cargo of plastic crap for the shelves of Wal Mart. I wish I had time to write this down. It feels insightful. Why now? Some philosopher said that "the unexamined life is not worth living," some Greek guy. So why shove it all into a final moment? Just a moment of self-examination before extermination. I can't believe I thought all these things in just a mo . . . .

Marius set the paper down, awaiting some apercu, some

illumination. But again, nothing more than some existential black hole.

He was back to the same question he had at the beginning. Why would an Iraqi girl be interested in atheism? Jazmeen had been brought up in Al Qurnah, near the confluence of the Tigris and Euphrates rivers, which local folklore said was the site of the garden of Eden. Growing up in a strict Muslim middleclass family, the sister of two older and one younger brothers, she went to the mosque with her mother, ate in the kitchen with her, and wore her hijab whenever and wherever it was customary. Now, just one year in Los Angeles where her military officer father was consulting on a secret project. Her father was skeptical about allowing her to attend the local public high school, but he consented because it would improve her English. Now she wanted to improve the way she could write creatively in English.

But there must have been another reason, something deeper and more dangerous, something that she detected in the febrile musings of Marius's story that would allow her to obliquely consider questions and propositions by indirection, through a narrative, the way one might glimpse the Hydra in a mirror, or an eclipse through a pin-hole box.

Their first substantive meeting was in the school cafeteria and could have been regarded as a commonplace teacher-student conference by anyone bothering to take much notice. Jazmeen asked the usual questions an aspiring writer might ask, questions about the inspiration for the piece, and its title, of course.

Jazmeen finally admitted that her fascination with the piece came from a moment of her own experience, a moment of epiphany, a moment, as she was finally able to express it— whisper it actually—that a voice in her confessed that for all her religious practice, her praying, her reflexive utterances of "inshallah," her deference to all things Islam, "My mind would just not let me believe in the existence of God, of Allah. Try as

I might to imagine, to conjure, to love, to fear, what I thought was faith failed me, belief would not come, Allah would not inhabit my heart." Marius could see her large eyes begin to well up, but they did not come to tears. She was apparently beyond that point.

"I know that the word *jihad* actually means "struggle" and can referred to these kinds of metaphysical struggles as well," Marius said, attempting to convey understanding and concern. He was curious, if also a little alarmed to be venturing into what was forbidden territory to an infidel.

Jazmeen's primary emotion was fear as well. She felt as though she was carrying a forbidden, blasphemous secret, that she might accidentally divulge or that others might read in her face. She had heard the references that such weaknesses of faith were the work of Satan, but her doubts extended to the existence of demons as well. Finally, came the outright full disclosure. "It seems to me that you are essentially wondering—in the moment of your essay—whether there is a God, and you only have a moment to consider it," she said, her expression more declarative than interrogative. Her eyes had such liquid depth he felt he could plunge into them. She had let her hijab slip back to expose the matching blackness of the hair at her brow, a few, thin, curled hairs at the edge, like the accents on Arabic script.

"I must tell you, young lady," Marius cautioned, "that I am an atheist, and it is a perilous matter—on several levels—that I should be having this discussion, even under the guise of the subject of literature, with a Muslim woman. I have spent time in the Middle East and I have fewer illusions about what would happen to me were I to be discovered in this situation, and I think that it would not bode well for you, either. He wanted to get up and get out of this situation and yet at the same time he wanted to take her in his arms.

"I need to understand," she said "is it possible to be happy and to live a good life without faith, as an atheist? Chamsi heard you speak and told me that she believes that you are comfortable and at peace with life, but do not believe God exists."

"You were writing about fighting in a war in my country, where people believe so differently than you and even little boys want to kill you. Yet, when you are in the face of possibly your last moment, it is not about God that you think, not about being a *shihadi* that concerns you, but curiosity about what gives the universe that you live in and are a part of meaning to you. You spend your last moment with the question of existence. Your moment lasts 2,196 words."

Marius chuckled, "You did a word count on it?"

"I was curious how many words could fit into a last moment."

"Time is relative, a nano-second can be an eternity, or the opposite," Marius said. But he understood that she understood what the piece was about. She had vicariously put herself in such a moment and it unsettled and frightened her. She must have been thinking about such things before she read the piece, but somehow it struck a nerve. But he didn't want her to elevate it into some sort of manifesto. "I think mostly I was trying to deal with the irony over a guy about to be blown to pieces by a boy the same age as his kid brother who is back home blowing villains into pixels on a video game, and how that irony existentially defines his last moment of consciousness. That's why it's written like a stream of consciousness. You should be careful not to make too much of it."

But Jazmeen seemed to be hanging on every word. "I have prayed for enlightenment, trying to be a good Muslim woman, but I am left only with doubts, and those doubts, especially that there is no god that exists, seem to become stronger. I am afraid that there will be nothing left to take the place of faith if atheism overtakes me. That there will be a void, and nothing to guide my life. I think that is what I fear more than what could happen to me if my family knew."

Marius remembered her words as if they were spoken yesterday. The phone broke Marius's reverie. He let it go to voicemail, then listened to it. "You're still the hero of Palatine, Mr. Greco. Celebrity lasts longer in a small town than it does out there in *LA-LA* land. Let me help you deal with it; I'd like to have you on my show again. Can we talk about it? Your favorite journo. Call. OK?"

Marius was actually glad for the interruption of the phone call because he knew where the dream would lead. Sore and exhausted, he applied some antibiotic ointment, bandaged his elbow and went to bed.

VII

Cauldwell Frye

On the drive down to Syracuse, Marius replayed his dialogue with Hisham Aziz. What the hell possessed him in the first place to go over to the Basra Market he still couldn't quite explain to himself. Maybe it was the dream again, this time the Falluja dream, probably precipitated by his thinking about the "in the moment" essay again and, as always, Jazmeen. No, he debated with himself, it was probably that impromptu visit to the ICU. He was a marked man; probably could have been shot on sight, but he went to the market anyway. There was something he was trying to figure out. He couldn't quite discern what it was, and who or what it was about, he would just throw himself into the situation and some answers might emerge.

The Aziz family had been in Palatine longer than him and it hadn't been easy for them to get established in the small town in upstate New York in the post-9/11 years. They were a family from a small town in southern Iraq and Ibrahim Aziz had been able to cash in his translator services for the American forces just after Gulf War I and when George H.W. Bush sold out on the Iraqi dissident forces that ended up being slaughtered by Saddam Hussein. He got out before he could be tortured to death by Saddam or his sons the way other translators had been. Still, living in New York had not been easy. There was that stew of multicultural ethnicity to deal with, the Jews, Russians, Blacks and Puerto Ricans, and others, and the endless suspicion of Muslims as terrorists living close to "ground zero." At least Palatine was small, and Ibrahim thought he might be able to use his service to the American troops as a wedge of acceptance in a place where there would be less complexity.

Marius didn't know any of this, only that they were Iraqi, and that the family consisted of Ibrahim, an aunt, his wife, Khalid and his older sister, Almaaz, and an older brother. They were all known to everyone in the community because they operated the only 24-hour convenience-liquor store. Ibrahim had purchased the store from an old local family that could no longer operate it at a profit owing to the competition from a big box enterprise fifteen minutes up the road. Although they were foreigners, most of the community was pleased to have a functioning convenience store. It could only be kept open around the clock and make a reasonable profit by employing the entire family, the same demographic advantage that accounted for the ownership and operation of convenience stores by Koreans, and other extended family ethnic groups in large cities like LA. Ibrahim had further ingratiated himself by his willingness to put some purchases on the cuff.

Now the family was a wreck because Khalid had managed to get a hold of an AK-47 in the parking lot of a gun show in Rochester and, fueled with anger and resentments the family had not detected, had done as much damage to them, maybe more, than he had done at his school. They had been grilled by local law-enforcement, visited by the FBI, had their computer hard drives copied, seen a drop in their business, and a decline in their health, particularly that of Ibrahim and the aunt, from the shame.

Hisham was behind the counter when Marius walked into the market. The Iraqi froze and set down the carton of cigarettes he had been opening. Marius wondered whether he might have a firearm under the counter like many convenient stores in LA.

"Ah-lan," Marius said.

Hisham hesitated. Marius thought he could easily be dead in a couple of seconds. There was no way of telling from the blank expression on Hisham's face. But then he noticed a slight relaxation of the tenseness in the young Iraqi man. *"Ah-lan was ah-lan,"* Hisham replied. Marius could see that he was handsome, with deep eyes, like Omar Sharif, and well-muscled. Marius had seen his picture in the school's trophy cabinet. Hisham had been a star player on the soccer team a few years back.

"I . . . ah, I probably should not have come here, but . . . ," Marius hesitated. Hisham said nothing. "I would like to know if the doctors have told you anything about the condition of your brother, if they expect he might come out of the coma?"

"Why do you want to know? Why do you care?"

"Ma rafsh," Marius replied, because he really did not know.

"You want to speak Arabic? Why? Do you think it'll make anything different? How did you learn your Arabic? Killing Iraqis? Somalis? Yeminis?"

"Bat kal-im a ra-bee shway ya." Marius admitted his Arabic was not conversational.

"Then let's stick with the *in-gi-lee-see.*"

"I meant only respect. I'm just here to say there was nothing I could do. Nothing. I had to protect those students. Yes, and myself, too. I know what it is like to be in a fight for your life. You will do anything to stay alive." Marius wanted only to explain, but was surprised that his words had a tone of apology in them.

Hisham just seemed to sag. "I saw you there at the hospital. But you did not see me. Why were you there?" he asked.

"I don't know. I wish I knew. I'm not sure why I am here."

Hisham paused. He seemed to relax a little more. "I go each night after my father takes over the store. He does not want to go, but also feels guilty about it, I know. My sister commutes to teach engineering part-time up at Oswego State, so she has little time to visit. The nurses at the hospital are not unkind. I think they have a way of knowing." Hisham related this as he opened the pack of cigarettes and took one out. He held up the pack toward Marius. Marius declined, but took the gesture almost as the equivalent of a middle easterner's offer of tea.

There was a long silence, and since there were no customers Hisham stepped around the counter, took a quick glance at the security camera covering the store from a corner, and stepped outside the door. Marius followed and they stood side-by-side. Marius wondered if this might be a signal that their conversation was over. Hisham took a deep drag on the cigarette and exhaled almost with a sigh.

Hisham spoke in a low, plaintive tone. "It would have been better if you'd killed Khalid, Mr. Greco. Don't you see? My brother wanted to be a martyr, a *shihadi*, and now he is a half-dead body with tubes and needles." He hesitated. "He is cursed. And we are cursed. What will happen if he does become conscious again? There will be a trial, there will be attention from the newspapers and television, and Internet. Our family will have no peace. And then what will happen to him? People will want him to die. They will want to stick needles and tubes in him and watch through a window as he dies. They already have needles and tubes in him. Why do they not just finish your work?"

Marius flinched, as much at the "your work" reference, as to the unintended existential torment it had caused.

Hisham continued, as though Marius was the only person to whom he could say this. "Do you know I have gone to the hospital each day, mostly at night when no one is there, just a couple of nurses, and the shame is not so great. And I sit with my brother. And you know what, Mr. Greco? You know what? I think of how easy it would be, maybe how better it would be, if I just turned off the oxygen or cut one of his lines, and he would be on his way to Paradise, and maybe my family, could—*inshallah*—find a little peace." He stepped out the cigarette.

Marius thought that he might have led him outside to say these words out of reach and recording of the store's security camera.

"I am truly sorry for your family," Marius said, "and sorry that I am an instrument of fate—he purposely avoided reference to God or Allah—in its pain and sorrow."

Hisham said nothing and turned to enter the store.

"Can I ask one thing?" Marius said.

Hisham stopped, holding the door open.

"Was it you?" Marius said.

"Me?"

"You . . . on the road?"

"On the road, the truck?"

"Yes. Someone tried to run me down. It would've killed me. After I left the hospital."

"It wasn't me."

"*Sa-heeh?*" Marius answered, slightly surprised.

"Yes, really. Not me. If Allah wanted you killed, he would've done it in Iraq," Hisham said in a solemn tone.

It was that fatalistic certainty in Hisham's voice that returned to Marius as he crossed the New York State Thruway into North Syracuse. He smiled at the notion that, as an atheist, apparently there was at least one deity looking out for him. It was like gods were always trying to get into the game of existence, to insinuate their narrative into the processes of nature. His image was always of the Olympian pantheon, hovering above and messing about in people's lives with all of the vices and virtues of their subjects, who were hardly worthy of their deified status.

The area north of Syracuse originally belonged to the indigenous peoples, particularly the Onondaga Indians, after whom the county and a nearby lake were named. But like so much of upstate New York this was a vestigial demographic residue. White men had long ago acquired and put their stamp upon this territory. The University area to which he was headed occupied a knoll called Piety Hill where Methodists had founded their university in 1820. Since the insurgence of the Jesuits in the 17th century, followed by various Protestant denominations, to the founding of new faiths, like that of the so-called Latter Day Saints up in Palmyra, the White man's God ruled here, established as it had been most everywhere with the sword and the cross.

The amphitheater lecture hall at Syracuse's renowned Maxwell School of Citizenship and Public Affairs hardly seemed an appropriate venue for a lecture on atheism. But the subject of the evening was the issue of the separation of church and state, a legitimate enough fusion of metaphysics and civics to occupy the rising semi-circle of seats that faced the large global mural behind the podium. Moreover, the speaker was Cauldwell Frye, founder of the Institute for Reasoned Discourse, an auspice whose title might apply as aptly to statecraft as to faith-craft. A stack of Frye's bestseller *Much Adieu About Nothing: A Testament to Atheism*, waited on a table off to the side for purchase and signing.

Frye began with reference to the proximity of Hendricks Chapel, the Roman Pantheon-like inter-denominational church at the top of the "quad." "What a better locus for supplicative prayer for whatever deity oversees the fate of your disciplinary major than at the very center of campus," he rasped in his Mancunian accent. "The Methodists who founded this place back in the 1820s are to be commended for their ecumenism. Which brings me perhaps a bit clumsily to my theme for this evening: Thoughts and Prayers." This was the principal reason Marius had made the journey down to Syracuse, the phrase of condolence that has become the vocal reflex of the American self-inflicted mass killing.

There were snickers among the audience, which Marius anticipated would be composed mostly of students, but was actually evenly split between students and rather elderly people from the community. The students had notebooks and laptops out, so many might have been there on class assignment. Many of the elderly had copies of Frye's book, which they were probably intending to get signed. Frye was witty and clever, notoriously acerbic in debates with believers, constantly pushing his mane of grey hair away from his ruddy complexion. He had been a professor of ancient history at Durham University for many years, but liked to answer when he was asked his profession, "football hooligan." He was a rabid Durham City AFC fan, wore his team scarf everywhere and, in deference to the red cross on the team escutcheon averred that "if God existed, his team would be Durham City Association Football Club."

"Thoughts and prayers," he began, "the wonder is that they could coexist in the same sentence. Thoughts, or prayers, works better. Perhaps I should redo my title. But we hear the former conjunction far too much these days, the knee-jerk response of politicians and others to acts of terrorism and mass violence. The victims are said to be in our prayers; the survivors, and the bereaved families, are all offered this customary box of verbal chocolates to assuage their pain and sorrow as though, with the proper reflex, they had been written up in some snobbish book of manners.

"Praying is not thinking; praying is wishing. It is wishing for things as we would want them to be, or to become so through the supplication to some deity or saint. It is not thinking to understand things as they are. Praying is the lazy person's mental calisthenics. It is a mystery to me what can be accomplished by praying on the behalf of someone who is already dead, presumably already serving an eternal sentence in heaven or hell. Some religious leaders also pray that the dead will pray for us. I concede that there is a bit more sense to that, but why bother with the strange turnabout, we should just pray for ourselves. Better yet, think."

"Prayer is a waste of time. Want to let your god know that you respect him—get up off your knees and go do something nice for somebody. Do some good. I can think of about a zillion things you could do. But quit being a lazy ass that is trying to get into heaven by kissing deity derriere so that later the Lord will pass you those winning lottery numbers. By the way, the only short way of winning the lottery is to die and be reborn as a Filipino postal worker. And when you do win, do some good. Donate to a charity, or buy my books; it's the same thing.

"As atheists, who dispense with all this bowing, scraping, and begging all day and night, in the church, mosque, synagogue, and clogging up the streets in saffron robes carrying rice bowls, spinning prayer wheels, we have more time than all these pious lay-abouts. The credulous believe in the efficacy of prayer, but we believe in the efficacy of effort.

"Need an example of that? I always loved the story about the boy who prayed to God for a bicycle:

"When I was a young boy I prayed for a new bike.

I prayed and prayed, but it never came.

Eventually, I realized Christianity doesn't have to work that way.

So, I stole a bike . . . and prayed for forgiveness."

The applauding audience loved the joke; it was pure Cauldwell Frye. Marius scribbled it down.

"But seriously, now, let us take up the most famous prayer in history: when Jesus prayed in Gethsemane that his Father might 'lift this cup'—the crucifixion—from him. But if it is his Father's will that Jesus die on the cross, then his Father's will be done. So what Jesus was praying for is that—if his Father had already made his mind up—his "Father" might change his (the Father's) mind. You see here we have the problem dealing with the dogma that Jesus—as the Son of God—was one of the three persons of the Trinity, three persons in one God. So why didn't Jesus, the Son, *already know* the answer to his prayer to his Father (or Himself), which would have made his prayer superfluous? And by the way, will someone please explain to me how some gospel writer forty years after the night in Gethsemane knew what Jesus was praying (and weren't, as the gospel says, the disciples all asleep even if Jesus was praying aloud?) You know, if those apostles had not been goofing off by sleeping they could have gotten together a prayer circle and maybe got Jesus a reprieve.

"Because prayer circles are a new wrinkle. Apparently, you can get yourself or your wish as the subject of one of these crowd-sourcing-the-Lord supplications. A variation of the chain-letter idea, whereby the power of the prayer is enhanced by overloading God's email account. But it seems a little scary to me, I must say. It could get out of control. Somebody might get a prayer circle going on you—"Oh Lord, please make so-and-so's bald husband start growing hair again"—and he wakes up some morning looking like a werewolf. Remember, prayers are wishes—so be careful what you wish for."

It was good intellectual standup comedy, but Marius was feeling himself a little dissatisfied with Frye's humorous approach just when the British atheist became more relevant. First, he had to hear Frye tell his joke about praying and knee-replacement surgery. It was good material, and Frye was so good at it that Marius worried that atheism might become a religious cult of its own sort, with the dogma that consisted mostly of put-downs of ten millennia of the way humans have dealt with their fear of death in the unknown.

"Enough with prayer, then," Frye continued, "I don't want anyone to start praying that the lecture be over. Thoughts are more interesting."

Frye was a speaker with masterful timing, and in a debate, he was absolutely devastating. He himself was out of Campion Hall at Oxford University, run by the Society of Jesus, and named after the martyred St. Edmund Campion. There, he had learned to be "Jesuitical" in his style of debate, deconstructing terms and arguments of his opponents in systematic rhetorical autopsy such that his opponents often felt that they had been drawn and quartered. He took no prisoners.

"Everything happens for a reason," Frye intoned, pushing his hair back and his glasses further up his nose. "We've all heard that one before. There are people who actually believe it, even though when you ask them for the reason something happened, they are unable to explicate the matter beyond some vague and fallacious *post hoc, ergo propter hoc*. Karma. This of course is closely connected to the idea that God, or maybe Fate, has some sort of plan for everything and that within that plan, therefore, everything actually happens for a reason. But the reason is that something happened before it and therefore must be its cause. One has to wonder, of course, whether there are things that "don't happen for a reason" as well—so-and-so did not fall off that bridge for a reason. So how do we go about explaining the presumed causes behind everything that happens. It is a vision of existence in which "all the dots" are necessarily, logically connected, not empirically but by sequential juxtaposition, in which all effects are causes and all causes effects—that logically leads back to the very first dot.

"To believe that all things happen for a reason is, ultimately, to believe that everything is fore-ordained. And of course, in the believer's apologetics, there is necessarily an author to all of this. No reason to have proof since God acts out his reasons in mysterious ways."

Frye paused, scanning the semi-circle of seats in search of any of the credulous attackers who often filtered their way into his public addresses. He prodded: "Isn't there anybody here to offer me a reason that God created Hitler to kill six million Jews? After all, everything happens for a reason, does it not?" There were no takers. "Isn't somebody going to tell me that their beautiful child died of influenza because God must've had a reason to bring it home to heaven?"

Still there were no takers. Then somebody in the first row stood, a man who looked like he might be holding a Bible in his hands, pushed himself up from his seat.

"If nothing happens for a reason, Prof. Frye, then why are we here?" He seemed a nice old man, and there was no aggression in his voice. In fact, he reminded Marius—as his mind always seems to conjure these associations—of Clarence, the angel in *It's a Wonderful Life.*

"Beats me," Frye responded. "All I know is that we are here. We are a bunch of self-aware temporary arrangements of carbon atoms. But, unaccountably, self-conscious temporary arrangements of carbon atoms. *Cogitamus, ergo summus.* Me, personally? Well, I'm here to sell a few books. That seems good enough reason to me."

"Look, seriously. Atheists might wonder about such questions, but we don't approach them in the same manner as believers. Believers are looking for something that they want, need, or for escape from something they fear, and there are plenty of places for them to find it. Non-believers are looking for the answer to show itself to us. We are not scriptural; we are empirical. Everything I know with some confidence, I know in some sort of sensate manner. So far that does not include God. I cannot see, hear, taste, smell or feel in any sensual way the presence, therefore the existence, of a god. There's no evidence that he, she, it, exists, especially as some white-haired old guy that Michelangelo conjured up that looks just like us and is that author of a book of contradictory nonsense called the Bible. Anyone who claims to know what they cannot see, hear, taste, smell or feel in any sensual way is possibly mentally ill. See that homeless guy off his meds and babbling to some imaginary friend, and see that lady kneeling and praying to a statue of the Virgin—now tell me the difference."

By now the elderly questioner had slumped back into his seat, perhaps regretting his curiosity.

"I would like that fairytale to be true," Frye forged on. "I try to be a good person, and wouldn't it be nice if there was a benevolent deity that would reward me for that, rather than afflict me with a mortal disease? Wouldn't it be nice if evil got punished, not just here and now, but for eternity? Wouldn't that all be comforting, to believe in all that, to take up the 'grand delusion'? Most people think that atheists stand for nothing, that they are amoral nihilists who find no meaning in life. We are sorely judged, so negatively that surveys show that Americans would sooner vote for a Muslim as president then they would for an atheist. But I contend that those people are wrong on every count. Moral behavior is rooted in our humanism, not religiosity; atheists are not nihilists, but celebrate that this life is the only life they are likely to get. And for them the meaning of life is self-defined, not fore-ordained. We are concerned about the fate of mankind here and now, which is why we are sometimes called "secular humanists," another appellation that is scorned from the pulpits.

"And let me tell you why I feel we are important in the fate of mankind. The believers in the afterworld feel that they are here on earth in preparation for some eternity in heaven or hell. Earth, and their time upon it, is merely a preamble to that narrative, merely an anteroom to paradise. So how much should such people care about that earth? The Bible even says that there will be some final Armageddon in which pretty much everything will be destroyed and in the second coming of Jesus only the believers, the faithful, will be ascended with him to the clouds. The earth, the solar system, the galaxy, the entire universe, presumably it was all put here as some grand cosmic stage props for this one final scene written up in the Book of Revelations. So, should religious believers care very much about global warming, widespread famine and disease, nuclear proliferation, or bothering with world peace or even the cure for cancer, when surveys tell us, many of them expect that this final scene will come in their own lifetime. Presumably, only their concern about avoiding sinfulness deters them from having one hell of a final party. While the believers are waiting for Jesus to forgive their sins and cart them off, we atheists feel there is plenty of work to do. Belief is easy; atheism takes hard work. Thank you. Signed copies anyone?"

Marius kept repeating Frye's last sentence as he drove up Interstate 81 in the night, fighting off drowsiness from the heavy Italian meal and half bottle of wine he relished at the Italian restaurant on the edge of campus. "Belief is easy; atheism takes hard work," he kept saying aloud, adding "and it never ends, it never ends."

Marius had already admitted to himself that it must be his obsession with motion pictures that always seemed to raise a quibble with Cauldwell Frye's contra-position on "everything happens for a reason." Now he lay in bed the morning after returning from Syracuse, Frye's confident remarks having simmered overnight in the stew of his subconscious, ruminating once more on the question of whether "destiny" threatened the foundations of his atheism. After all, what was a motion picture narrative but an example of an art form in which everything happens, indeed must unavoidably, happens for a reason. Motion pictures were nothing if not narratives in which characters are destined to play out their "scripted" destinies.

As usual, his mind turned for confirmation to George Bailey's so-called "Wonderful Life." There, right in the opening scenes, was the perfect illustration of destiny as two angels observe from the heavens as George rescues his drowning brother from a frozen pond only to lose his hearing in one ear. His brother goes on to be a pilot in WWII and George, despite his hankering for adventure beyond Bedford Falls, ends up stuck in his home town bourgeois existence running the family savings and loan bank. Movies were scripts, with characters motivated and moved by the whims of screenwriters, or the novelists they drew from. The George Baileys, Mr. Tibbs and Jim Starks of the movies he screened were all, in a manner of speaking, "destined" to carry out their roles.

Marius lay there, his lecture notes flashing before him, what he called "showing the gun." "If the director shows you a gun in some scene," he would say in class, "it's not just for the hell of it. You can be sure he will 'pay it off' later on and that gun will figure in the movie's plot." He had often reflected on how cinematic art—what he liked to call 'reel life'—was different in this respect from real life. In the movie, like George's deaf ear that gets 'paid off' later, everything does happen for a reason, because the screenwriter knows we need reasons to connect the dots of the narrative. Life does not work that way—unless we believe that God, or a couple of angels in a Capra movie, has our destiny all scripted out for us.

Marius had heard Frye elaborate on this at a lecture at UCLA. "Is race destiny? Is gender destiny? Nationality? "Yes, life is full of circumstances that are the results of lineage, DNA, geography and such. These are circumstances that are delivered upon us unbidden, and do indeed have consequences. But I would not call those consequences "destiny." Einstein once famously said, in what could be regarded as a rebuttal to the randomness of quantum mechanics, that 'God does not play dice with the universe,' suggesting that the deity might have more of a hand in matters than some of us would agree. But keeping with the gambling metaphor, it might be true that we are all dealt a poker hand to play by circumstances, but the consequences of how we play are the result of how others at the table play their hands. Either all is fore-ordained, or all is chance; I'll take my chances with chance," Marius remembered Frye nailing down his position with a customary memorable phrase.

And yet a thin wedge of doubt continued to plague him, somewhere in the edge between "does art imitate life, or does life imitate art? In some sense. this is the behavioral psychologist's insistence that we have no truly "free will," and the belief that we are only acting out some god's will. Art had closure, he reflected; the edge of the painting, the last line of poetry, the end of the movie. But the end of the movie was a false ending, was it not? He always wondered what happened to the couple who walk off into a "happily-ever-after" sunset. Every ending is just another beginning, a "sequel" as Hollywood might put it, or an "afterlife" as a believer would put it. In the "chaos theory" of physics, every cause is an effect, every effect a cause; every flutter of a butterfly wing in the Amazon, an influence on the rainfall in the Punjab. His mind reeled at the ineluctable fact that Frye was certainly right about one thing—atheism is damned hard work.

So why did he find himself standing there in that ICU wondering why the hell he was there, what had impelled him to go there. Was it his "choice," his "chance"? Was it "destiny"—was everything, his Iraq experience, Jazmeen, this job in a town he never knew existed, and Khalid, the killer kid in a coma—pointing to some outcome? Had fate cast him in the role of the "hero" for a reason, if any of this was really happening for a reason?

VIII

In the Heat of the Night

"Hey Zeus," Josh greeted Jesus as he set down the cervezas and nachos on the table. Marius cracked a smile in anticipation of their custom of kidding around with the proprietor "Descartes walks into a bar. The bartender asks him, 'would you like a beer?' Descartes replies, 'I think not,' then disappears."

Marius guffaws.

"You know a lot of dumb shit, teacher Josh," Jesus says.

"Good one," Marius says, mentally recalling that he had heard Cauldwell Frye use the third person plural *cogito* a few nights earlier. But, tonight he wanted some perspective from his teacher colleague at Palatine High.

"So, what's going on with the local hero these days? You said you didn't want to talk to me about this in the faculty room. Sounds very John le Carré," Josh says, lifting a taco chip to his mouth.

"Well, remember I told you about that business with our principal and that school board guy broached after my class on *Easy Street*. Did you ever have the feeling that you are in one of those science fiction movies where you come into a town that you think you know, but something isn't right about it? This is just a rhetorical question, but I think you know what I mean. Charlie, the gas station attendant who played on the high school basketball team with you, doesn't even acknowledge you when you pull in his station to fill up. Your old aunt Maude seems to look right through you and says things completely out of character. Even your first girlfriend treats you like a perfect stranger. Something funny is going on, like in *Invasion of the Body Snatchers*, but you can't quite put your finger on it."

"Not me. I'm from Brooklyn, don't forget. But you grew up near Hollywood. You shouldn't expect normalcy either."

"Seriously. I've been in this town nearly two years, and it's beginning to feel a bit weird."

"Well, it's not like this has been a normal beginning to the term, has it, with you becoming a local hero and all that?"

"That's what I mean. I'm not sure that everybody likes the idea that I have become their local hero. You get put up on a pedestal, and suddenly the pigeons are shitting on you. You're too exposed, and immobilized, too. Suddenly, what you say is parsed, sliced and diced."

"No good deed goes unpunished. Who said that, anyway?" Marius says. "Some guy who makes fortune cookies in Chinatown, I think."

"I screened *In the Heat of the Night* in class the other day. It's one of the films in my sequence on the dark side of the small town in America. I've already shown them *It's a Wonderful Life* for the bright side.

"'They call me Mr. Tibbs'," Josh said with Poitier's inflection. "But didn't Steiger win the Oscar?"

"Yeah, it won Best Picture, too. How could it not? Jewison directing, Silliphant's script, shot by Wexler, then a great cast. It beat out *Bonnie and Clyde* and *The Graduate*. Great year for American cinema."

"So that didn't impress your kids?"

"Not that part, but I think it touched some nerves that might have a different sensitivity than they did in the '60s. A lot of water has gone over the dam in American race relations since then."

"Yeah, but you were living in a big multicultural city during most of those years. A lot of that water gets recycled in small towns like Palatine. Holding on to a lot of their old stuff has become the raison d'être for places like this. So what kind of an approach do you take with this film?"

"How much do you want to know?"

"Let's find out. Jesus has plenty of cervezas and nachos."

"You already know that it is perhaps an archetype of the dark small town film, of sinister themes that often are rooted in bigotry, small-mindedness, ignorance, intolerance and violence. The central issue in Southern small towns is always about either race or class."

"It's not so different up here. Small towns everywhere seem to be some sort of throwback to the manorial system of the Middle Ages," Josh commented. "Sorry, you were saying?"

"I agree. *In the Heat of the Night* seems to have all the ingredients: a dramatis personae consisting of a sheriff who is hooked into all of the 'good ole boy' relationships, a town 'Mr. Moneybags' in the character of Mr. Endicott, who likes to control everything and is the leftover plantation 'massa.' There are petit bourgeois businessmen, an array of bigots, black-bashing youth, an over-sexed vixen who likes to run around in the buff, all stewing in a soup of distrust of anything new or alien to it, even if accepting it has economic advantages. It's America's 'original sin,' and it's so bred in the bone that it seems like it would take the fires of Hell to burn it out."

"I like the allusion. Well, the Civil War was pretty hellish and that didn't do the job."

"As with many such films, the plot catalyst is the outsider who, as is often the case, finds himself in the snare of a place and circumstances that become his worst nightmare. Tibbs is a cop from Philadelphia—that's Pennsylvania, not Mississippi, "city of brotherly love"—who happens to be waiting for a train out of Sparta, Mississippi, on the night that a wealthy Chicago businessman who is building a plant in the town turns up bludgeoned to death and dumped in the middle of a street in town in the middle of the night. Being Black, he is by pigment, as well as circumstance, hauled in as a suspect by a dopey local deputy. He receives the expected accusations and rude treatment until, when asked what he does for a living up there in Philadelphia, Pennsylvania, he identifies himself a homicide detective. In getting this confirmed by phone, Sheriff Gillespie, played by Rod Steiger, is offered Tibbs' services by his supervisor in Philly. At first Gillespie declines, but does ask Tibbs to have a look at the body of the murdered man."

"That's the scene of the famous 'they call me Mr. Tibbs' isn't it?"

"Yes, but no matter what the putdown, it doesn't seem to daunt Gillespie much. I suppose that's because he feels secure of his racial superiority inside his white skin."

Josh raised a questioning finger. "Unless . . . unless, like a lot of White supremacy or, for that matter, attitudes of racial supremacy of any kind, it is merely a mask for an abiding insecurity."

Marius smiled. "Spoken like a person from a truly oppressed people."

"You don't agree?"

"No, I do," Marius answered. "I think that what bigots hate in the people they hate is what they actually admire but find lacking in themselves. The Nazis must have hated Jewish intelligence and commercial acumen and at the same time coveted them."

"You left out our nicely trimmed schlongs."

"I think there's a bar on the edge of town where they appreciate that aesthetic."

"Maybe that was what Gillespie also envied about Tibbs," Josh offered.

"Maybe. But I think Tibbs represents several aspects of big city values and behavior. He is the rationalist, concerned with forensic evidence, and not allowing prejudice to rush him to judgment, although he succumbs to that in a later scene. He makes a salary and holds a title that would be unheard of—especially for a Black man—in a small Southern town in those times and circumstances. He is 'professional' and technical. He represents position earned on "merit" and competence, rather than birthright, and certainly not skin color. This is especially made clear in the scene in which he examines the deceased, requesting chemicals and measurement instruments and establishing the time of death with logic and a knowledge of anatomy. It ensnares him in the plot as assuredly as Brer Rabbit punching the tar baby."

"That was a nice Uncle Remus Southern folklore reference," Josh interjects to let Marius know he is still paying attention."

"Gillespie, on the other hand, displays a number of the negative small town behavioral characteristics: quick to judge, a disdain for outsiders, narrow-mindedness, and a willingness to bend to the demands of local power wielders. With his Stetson, aviator glasses, and boots, Gillespie is almost a parody of the stereotype created by Sheriff Bull Connor, the real sheriff who unleashed police dogs on freedom marchers and young black children trying to integrate schools in Mississippi in the 1950s. What saves the performance from simple parody is Steiger's ability to infuse his role with humor, incipient compassion, and moral conflict, all for which he received an Academy Award.

"This film's most interesting dramatic motion is the juxtaposition of these traits and the uneasy detente of two men who find some basis for mutual respect. Gillespie saves Virgil's hide from a beating or worse by young punks, and Tibbs, in turn, solves the crime by apprehending the murderer, using not only his detective skills and turning his race to advantage. One scene, when Gillespie, against his wishes, drives Tibbs to interview local plantation-master, Endicott, adds depth to Poitier's character as well. When Endicott realizes that Tibbs regards him as a suspect, he slaps him across the face as though he were any Black man in his employ. Tibbs immediately returns the blow and both Endicott and Gillespie (as well as an old, Black servant in the room) are too astonished to do anything. Once outside, Tibbs, still pumping adrenaline from the experience, claims that he is going to get Endicott, whereupon Gillespie brings the detective up short by telling him his desire for vengeance means that he is "no better than the rest of us."

"Tell me if I'm wrong, but that was the scene that stirred things up in class," Josh said.

"Yeah. You must know Isiah Evers. He's one of the only two Black kids in the school, and he's only half-Black."

"I know of him, the football star. I've had the girl in my class, Amanda Robinson."

"So, in discussion I suggest that the "no better than the rest of us" scene is the central issue of the movie. Right off the bat, Mike Hudson goes all Sheriff Gillespie and is spouting off about non-White people taking over and that Tibbs making a big thing out of being called "Mister" and then slapping the plantation owner, Endicott, and it is all about Hollywood sucking up to what are going to become the dominant audience."

"You know that Mike is the nephew of our dear Sheriff Cavanaugh, do you not?"

"Now I do."

"Kinda took me by surprise because he hadn't said much before that. Also, there didn't seem to be much objection to what he was saying until Isiah spoke up. That surprised me, too. He says, as much to the whole class as to Mike, "So what's the brother supposed to do, just let that cracker whip his black ass? We don't take that White shit anymore. And don't tell us we just like you, just because we're respectin' ourselves and fightin' back. We ain't you,'" That didn't sound like the diffident bag boy at the market, or the modest football star. More like a Crip or a Blood. Somebody uttered a ventriloquistic 'You sure ain't,' from the back of class, but I couldn't locate the source and let it go.

Josh set down his drained beer glass. "A movie, even a scene, or an image or line of dialog in a movie can be like a hand grenade. Art suggests possibility, because it is made of a choice from possibilities. People brought up in this 'neck of the woods,' as they would say, find such liberal notions of possibility a little threatening. Curiously, some of these towns in the Mohawk Valley had houses that participated in the 'underground railroad' for fugitive slaves, and Christian preachers who were abolitionists. And then there were people here—the Mormons over in Palmyra, for example—who regarded African-Americans as lesser beings not worthy of the same status as Whites. Now, this area is a hotbed of conservatism that's a helluva lot closer to Sparta, Mississippi, than where you and I come from."

"Mind if I add that to my dissertation?" Marius said. "Maybe what got to Mike is that final scene with Gillespie carrying Tibbs's suitcase for him to the train. I mean, it's sort of a defeat for Sparta, Mississippi. Their racism, stupidity and violence all work against them and they end up losing a chance to advance economically with the new industry, even though it's a threat to parts of the old power structure like Endicott. Tibbs is more intelligent than them, and pretty much retains his self-possession. Gillespie has lost respect, has been called an N-lover, and could lose his job. He is the dilemma of the small Southern town all wrapped up in one character, a character ultimately more complex and interesting than Tibbs, which is why Steiger ended up with the Oscar. I thought that Gillespie must be the reason Mike Hudson spoke the way he did; he didn't like that kind of sheriff. But Isiah said something interesting to me when I ran in to him in the hall later on. He said: 'Hudson don't like it because everybody that Aziz shot was White.' I hadn't thought about that factor until then."

Josh says, "That is interesting. We White guys tend not to reference things that way. Let's test this." Josh calls Jesus over, orders a couple more beers, and then says, "Jesus, a white guy, a black guy, and a brown guy walk into a bar . . .".

"Yeah?" Jesus responds, expecting a punch line. He waits, then repeats, "Yeah?'

"Whaddya think?" Josh says.

Jesus smiles. "What do I think? What do I think? . . . Must not be a bar in Palatine."

"See," Josh says to Marius. "See?"

IX

Pillow Talk

Photos, signs and messages fluttered in the autumn breeze and several aluminized plastic balloons had lost enough of their helium to cause them to dance drunkenly against their tethers. Candles had melted into wax blobs, a few incongruous posters, one of the pop star Prince, another of Donald Trump, had sagged in the rain, and the ubiquitous teddy bears and a stuffed Hello Kitty looked almost as ready for the trash bin as the bouquets of dead flowers. There had been talk already of replacing this shrine of ephemera with some plaque or cenotaph as a more durable remembrance, but the inevitable debate about its form and content, as well as its location, promised to outlive memory.

Marius looked down at the variety of dying connections to the departed, wondering vaguely at their meaning and significance and what compulsion toward neatness and symmetry caused him to reach down and re-posture one of the four white crosses that had fallen over just as he heard the voice behind him.

"Doing a little memorial upkeep, teacher?" KGK said.

Marius turned to see the stylishly dressed news anchor taking a sip from her Starbuck's latte grande.

"Just the obsessiveness of a high school teacher, like re-aligning the students' desks after class. What brings you to school today, a remedial broadcasting class, or some other journalistic errand?"

She ignored the snide remark. "Yes, actually, I had to meet with principal Schmidt about the roundtable show that the network is pressing me to produce. You would know about that if you would return my calls and texts. The network wants to do a show with a national feed." KGK refrained from showing any excitement in her voice, since such a show might provide the big break—and the escape from Palatine—that she had been yearning for.

"Sorry about that. There's just been a lot of, well . . . well, pick an excuse. I'm sure you've heard them all. I know from your messages that you want me on the show. I would really like to get past all this stuff and back to some semblance of normalcy."

"You might get your wish soon enough. To be honest with you, these sorts of things are only newsworthy until the next whack job that can get a hold of an assault rifle or the makings of a bomb," she said, taking another sip.

"Yeah, I suppose. Except for that guy connected to all that life-support apparatus at the hospital. He is the one you really need on that show. Haven't we burned my fifteen minutes of fame?"

"Look, how about we let my expense account buy you dinner this evening and let me tell you a little bit more about the show. You won't be obliged, so long as you don't order the most expensive thing on the menu." She grinned. "Just kidding," she added in that little sing-song manner he found cute.

Marius snorted. "I have to buy CDs of the movies we are using in class out of my own pocket, and you have an expense account? Okay, I am enough of a feminist to let a woman who makes quadruple my salary take me to dinner, especially as she wants to drain me of my last few minutes of fame."

KGK smiled. "Don't be so presumptuous. I might have other motives as well, Mr. Greco. And, since you are such a feminist, your masculinity should not be threatened if I pick you up in my BMW. Around seven, say?"

"Time enough for me to have my tux cleaned and pressed. Now I must go enlighten and entertain the next generation of Palatine." Marius turned to pass through the gate.

"Your little cross fell over again," she said with a smirk.

Marius kept walking. "Have a Roman centurion set it back up." He realized as he was entering the building that he was already looking forward to the evening.

Lying beside her in the post coital body heat and its musky aromas, Marius wondered whether what had just happened would have occurred had he declined her invitation to be on the show. Would she have given herself to him at all or with similar enthusiasm and abandonment as before as a method of persuasion, or as reward? Or had this been, as it seemed, nothing so transactional, but just pure emotion, maybe the overture to deeper possibilities? He certainly was not going to bring the subject up and perhaps spoil what had been, whatever its etiology, rollicking good sex.

KGK had fallen asleep, her slightly heaving breasts a little rosy, and a skein of her blond hair stuck with sweat to her forehead. It would have made a nice Ingres "Odalisque," he mused.

Marius stared up at the ceiling fan, his mind reviewing the previous few hours. The dinner had been a frank exchange of personal information, more like a combination of a first meeting from an on-line dating site and a job interview. Family background: He, working class Italian-American from California; She, from East Coast (Connecticut) professional parents of English and Irish descent. Education: He, Catholic schools until UCLA; She, private girls' schools, Bryn Mawr BA, Communications. Ambition: He, "I'm a anthropologist, an academic hoping to become a university professor teaching

American urbanism, hopefully abroad."; She, to be a "respected" broadcast journalist.

In the extra flattering candlelit corner table, KGK looked as good enough to devour as the filet mignon. She had that "good breeding" look about her and the soft light accented every fine bone structure under the unblemished skin. Such symmetry and aesthetic proportions always had struck Marius as what he called the "Alfred Hitchcock beauties," the Grace Kelly, Tippi Hedren, Kim Novak types that seemed out of reach as much as the debutantes and homecoming queens, not for the swarthy sorts like Marius Greco. But he also realized that his actress references were not always an accurate indication of the girl underneath. KGK had contorted and writhed with savage ferocity underneath him that she took control, ordering him when she detected his climax close to "Wait! not yet!" It was a willfulness and mode of command that seemed to come with a certain breeding, and Marius felt that, in a way, he was crossing class lines, like the gardener cuckholding the seigneur of the manor, taking something to which he was not entitled. He liked that feeling, it made the sex illicit, forbidden, *sinful*.

Earlier, at dinner, she applied some of her interviewing skills. "Marius, you were very reluctant to get much into your experience as, if you will allow me to use the term, a hero. But we're not on camera now. Are you more willing to go there— off the record."

"I'm an academic, and so, inclined to look for the motivations behind social behavior. The local authorities, the businessmen, and the media, which is just another business actually, are interested in what happened to this kid for different reasons. He falls into a stereotype, or is in need, or an easy explanation like too many violent video games, or some aspect of Islamic fundamentalism. I just don't tend to look at the world the way these people do, and I am suspicious that they're just looking for something that I might say that they can employ to confirm and validate their predispositions."

"Wow, you said that just like an academic."

"See what I mean? Have some more wine, my dear." Marius continued. "I want to know why that kid picked up that gun and came to his school where there are more people interested in his well-being than probably any other place, and started shooting people in cold blood? What turned him into a killing machine? Is there any way in which we are responsible? Does anybody really want to know anything about young Mr. Aziz? The two FBI guys who interviewed me seemed so bored they were putting me to sleep. They've seen so many of these incidents now because they have become a staple of the news, like the weather—'today will be warm and sunny and it is expected that somewhere between five and twenty school kids will be murdered by the Second Amendment'. Actually, what happened here could've happened in dozens of other locales over the past couple of weeks. It's circadian, now built into the very rhythm of American life. Circumstances just dictated that it would involve me, here in Palatine."

"Which must raise the question in some people's minds," she said , "what' s a good-looking California dude doing here in the middle of American flyover country? Fate? Or did your plane run out of gas?"

"Actually, I have what I regard as a pretty good reason for being here."

"Really! I thought people were either born here in Palatine or exiled to here, like me. Maybe you can give me a clue as to how I can get the fuck out of here. Tell me."

"C'mon, a Bryn Mawr girl, the next Diane Sawyer or Barbara Walters, should be able to figure that one out."

"You really want to know? It's not a juicy news story."

"Try me. It depends on how it is told. Anyway, there's always a backstory."

That last remark gave Marius pause, but he had just enough wine to go with his natural loquaciousness to say 'Fuck it, what can go wrong in talking about your dissertation research.'

"Every time a bell rings, an angel gets his wings," he said.

"Every time a bell rings, an angel gets his wings? From that Christmas movie?"

"That might be enough for a start. But there's more to the movie than that. Most people your age might recognize that Ernie and Burt, the cab driver and the cop, were the models for Ernie and Burt on Sesame Street."

"Really! See? I've already learned something from your research."

"So, why, you probably are wondering, am I so interested in this movie that they show on pretty much every television station every Christmas. Well, if all goes well, I hope to get my doctorate at UCLA in urban anthropology. I am particularly interested in the social changes that took place as America transitioned from a country of farms and small towns to a metropolitan society. I like to look at social life as it is portrayed in the arts, particularly motion pictures, and *It's a Wonderful Life* is a classic American small town film that has lodged itself in the American consciousness, thanks to its replay every Christmas. Although it was filmed in California its setting was supposed to be a small town named Bedford, Falls in upstate New York, a town perhaps not too different from Palatine and others in this area. So, my research for my dissertation involves a comparison of what I regarded as the myth of the American small town and its reality. I convinced my doctoral committee that an interesting way to research this subject might be to actually take up residence for a period of time in a small town and to collect data much in the way that was done in some classical sociological studies back in the 1930s.

Since I was already a high school teacher in LA, I looked for openings in upstate New York and, *voilà* here I am. Having become a local hero, as you like to put it, kind of destroyed the anonymity required for this type of research, which is why I would like things to get back to normal—whatever that is—as soon as possible. There, now you know everything."

"Every time a bell rings, an angel gets *his* wings." she said, stressing the gender.

"Yup, just angel stuff. Not enough of the story to get you out of Palatine, I'm afraid, reporter lady."

"You never know. Does Khalid Aziz have an angel looking out for him?" she said, returning to the subject.

"Who knows? I don't know if Muslims get guardian angels, like Clarence, the one in the movie."

"Unless it's you, Marius. Hear any tinkling?"

KGK awakened from her cat nap, stretching like a feline. She began to trace his abdominal creases with her finger.

Marius watched her body change shape from one fetching form to another, then spoke first. "There was supposed to be an after-sex cigarette moment, don't you watch any movies?" he said. "You don't happen to have a pack, do you? I don't smoke, but I would like one."

"Yes. I thought you'd never ask. But you didn't even have a pre-sex pack of condoms," she said, slapping him on the chest.

"Trust is everything in any relationship," he said, watching her tear open the pack of Marlboro Lights.

"Has that replaced 'was it good for you, too'?" she responded, handing him a cigarette and a lighter. She giggled when Marius coughed on his first inhale.

"I wasn't lying when I said I only smoke after sex," he said, his face scrunched to stifle another cough.

"Well, maybe you need to get laid more often."

"Really? I'm beginning to see a paradox here: more sex equals more cigarettes, a tug-of-war between love and early death."

"Your cat seemed to enjoy the drama," she teased.

Marius snorted. "That's Woolley. He's not mine; he came with the place and thinks he owns it."

"Woolley?" she said.

He glanced up at the cat, now on its usual perch on the window sill, looking out.

"Yeah, Woolley. I think he also surfs porn sites on my computer when I'm out. I named him after Monty Woolley, the actor in *The Man Who Came to Dinner*, the 1942 movie with Bette Davis. Woolley played an academic guest who slips and brakes leg and they can't get rid of him."

"Another cinematic reference. I know you grew up near Hollywood. Is life a movie for you? Do you have a movie name for me?"

"It's pending. Norma Desmond? Scarlett O'Hara? Mme. Bovary? What's her name in *The Devil Wears Prada*? But Diana Christensen keeps popping up."

KGK knew the reference. "Diana Christensen is the racist lackey of the imperialist ruling circles in *Network*?" she said with mock umbrage.

She got up from the bed and began dressing. "There is something that I did not get to ask you last night that I am curious about," she said, her back to him,

"What could that possibly be? I thought I told you everything. Probably more than I should have. Too much 'in vino veritas'."

"Why did you stop and look at that student shrine for so long yesterday morning?" She said as she slung her purse over her shoulder and adjusted her collar.

"I think all of those fading notes and pictures, the melted down candles, and the deflating balloons just hit me with the ephemerality of everything. Eventually the emotions abate, memories dim, people become unable to remember the victims' names. Time maybe does not heal all wounds but our instincts are to get back to normal, even if it's a new normal."

"Okay, then. One more question."

Marius was going to object, but she got it out.

"Who is she?"

"Just put the money on the dresser and get out," he said, rolling over and covering his bare ass with the sheet.

She left with a self-satisfied smile on her face.

———

"What is that scent you are wearing this morning? Not very masculine, if you ask me." Josh said to Marius, who was standing there jogging in place in the school parking lot. Marius happened to run in to his colleague on his run just after KGK had left his place.

"I think it's called Shalimar. That's what she said it was. Jesus, can you actually smell it on me? Was just kidding when I told her to just leave the money on the dresser and get out. Now I actually smell like a *putana*."

"Listen, *amigo*, you know I'm not the prying sort, but —"

"KGK."

"Really? I had you down for Miss Crane."

"Miss Crane?"

"Yeah, you know, the pretty school district nurse. She's here once a week. That short, bobbed hair, an ass that looks like a ripe peach even in a nurse's uniform, perky tits . . ."

"Yeah, I know who you mean. Didn't know her name."

"Some of the boys like to come up with an excuse to go see her because they have a hard-on for the rest of the day. The jerk-off rate jumps about three hundred percent."

"Really? Sounds like you know."

"Yeah, I had to see her one day to bandage a thumb I cut with an Exacto knife and mine lasted until I got home. It's a sin to waste a hard on." Josh was looking down at Marius's crotch when he said it. "I think she wears that same perfume. My schlong remembers."

Marius was still jogging in place. "Where, may I ask, is this conversation going?"

"KGK, you said. Was it good? She strikes me as one of those types who looks better than she *shtups*."

"Sorry, sir, I don't understand Yiddish. C'mon, I'm not going into those details. I might smell like a whore, but I do have a shred of integrity left."

"Oh, sure, you'll be lordin' it over th' rest of us drunken, porn-loving scum, won'tcha now," Josh replied in his best Thomas Mitchell 'Uncle Billy' Irish lilt.

"And stop looking at my crotch, ya perv. There are CCTV cameras all over this place that can have us down for Oscar Wilde and Bosie in the school gossip mill." Marius stopped jogging in place and turned to stretching his hamstrings. "Okay, just between us Victorian fancy boys, she was as good as she looks."

"Your secret's safe with me, if you don't mind my adding it to my private sexual fantasy catalog," Josh said with a mischievous smirk. "But why do I detect a note of reservation in that admission, may I ask?" He dropped the smirk.

"You noticed, huh?" Marius hesitated. "I had a lot of wine at dinner last night, and the grape makes me garrulous. I didn't trust this woman from the get-go, and there I am, blathering on about myself, even though I know she's a journalist who probably sees me as a stepping-stone in her career and doesn't mind giving me a good roll in the hay to serve her ends. On the other hand, we hit it off at other levels, and she is not just one of your stereotypical blow-dried, bouffant airhead news-readers. We had some real fun together and I felt a connection. Then, in the next moment, a wave of sobriety sends my thoughts to Faye Dunaway in *Network*. Anyway, I consented to be on this show that she's going to do about what would be the appropriate measures that could be taken to prevent these kinds of terrorist attacks. I've been running since 5:30 this morning wafting the scent of Shalimar around town while having second thoughts about it all."

"Well, amigo, I can only supply you with what I am told is an old cautionary Yiddish proverb probably learn the hard way in some god-awful East European *shtetl*." Josh affected his best Jackie Mason accent. "Zumtimes ze fucking you get ain't virth ze *fucking* you get."

Marius ceased stretching and headed off jogging back towards his house. "Reassuring wisdom from a people who once thought it was a good idea to settle in Germany," he shouted back over his shoulder.

X

Khalid

Twenty-four days before the school attack

Khalid had put up a pretty good fight for his size. He was a good soccer player and had a powerful kick. But there were too many of them, four who jumped him, and another who was mostly a bystander. He couldn't tell who any of them were. It was dark, and three wore balaclavas, while two others wore rubber masks, one of an almond-eyed extraterrestrial, and the other of Ronald Reagan. The balaclavas and masks also made it difficult for him to recognize any of their muffled voices, although they didn't say much beyond calling him a "fucking sand monkey" and a "rag head" while they beat him into submission and secured his hands behind his back with what he took to be authentic zip-tie handcuffs before pulling a sack over his head. They then yanked him to his feet, shoved him into the back of the pickup and held his head down to the metal floor that smelled of some kind of animal shit.

Khalid had been spending Tuesday evenings at Helene Lagarde's house being tutored in French. His abductors knew right about where he would be on the road as he biked back home. All they had to do was cut him off in the dark spot, and it all went according to plan except that one of the guys would be pissing blood from one of Khalid's kicks to his kidneys, and another would have a very sore pair of testicles. Khalid half expected that he might end up hanging from a tree, or lying in a field with a crushed skull. Then again, they just might beat him up and dump him.

But they had other plans for him. He wondered what those plans were when they arrived at what his nose told him was clearly a barnyard of some sort. They yanked him out of the truck and threw him inside a barn that by its smells and animal sounds seemed to contain sheep and pigs. He laid there for a couple of minutes listening to their mumbled deliberations, but not able to comprehend anything that was said.

"Get his pants off," one of the guys said, as two others hauled him to his feet and shoved him over some kind of a box or crate, face down. He could feel the heat coming off some kind of an animal not far from his face.

"Hey, what is this? What the hell are you guys doing? Knock it off! *Yu'af*, stop!" Khalid shouted. It was the first words he said, he realized.

"You'll find out, you fucking sand monkey," one of them said.

Khalid's pants were now down around one of his ankles and he struggled to get free, but with his hands cuffed, and no ability to right himself, he was helpless.

Two of the guys hooked their feet inside his and pulled his legs wide. They held his arms pinned to the crate. Khalid squirmed, but to no effect. "Hey, stop this shit you guys," he yelled.

Another guy reached down and grabbed Khalid's testicles. "Wouldn't take much of a slice to take these little fuckers off," he chuckled, and yanked them, causing Khalid to moan. "Yeah, then it's no 72 virgins for you, motherfucker. Hey, should we check his dick? Maybe he needs to be circumcised."

"Jesus Christ, are you guys crazy?" Khalid screamed. "I never did anything to you guys. If this is a joke, it has gone far enough! C'mon, lemme outta here. I won't say anything about this."

"Don't be using the name of Our Lord, sand monkey. Where's your *Allahu Ackbar* now, motherfucker?" one of his restrainers said.

Then the one with the Reagan mask said, "Anybody wanna go first?"

"Hey, first what? You guys faggots? You guys are gonna pay for this!"

"No way, sand monkey, this is free."

Khalid was about to protest further when he felt a finger inserting something greasy into his anus followed instantly by a surge of pain as he was penetrated by a penis.

"This is what it feels like when you Muslim bastards rape Christian girls," the violator rasped, thrusting with painful force. Khalid tried to restrain his groans to retain what was left of his manhood.

Khalid strained against those holding him down, unable to free his legs. In a moment the first rapist finished his business and a second took his place, thrusting and laughing. "You filthy faggot bastards," he screamed, "filthy faggot bastards!" But his voice was close to breaking into sobs. He turned his head to the side to see the guy wearing the ET mask masturbating as he watched the proceedings.

Khalid thought he was about to be raped by a third guy, but only heard him cursing because he was unable to get himself erect enough to accomplish the task. But the humiliation was not over.

"Alright, porky video time, then," Khalid heard ET say when he finished his masturbation. He was still being tightly held down and had almost completely run out of energy trying to gain release when he heard the squeal of the pig. The animal was not very large, but was a mature male. It struggled to get away as the boys attempted to get it mounted over the back of Khalid.

"Let's see how you like this one, sand monkey," one of the guys said.

The pig was squealing. Khalid wanted to scream, but his throat was dry. They were trying to pull the pig's trotters over his shoulders, but were having a difficult time of it. "Hold the fucking pig still," ET commanded, "or all I'm going to get is blurry pictures with this phone."

"I don't think this pig wants to fuck this sand monkey," another of the guys said.

"That's okay, but it's going to look like it did. Just hold him a little bit longer."

Khalid was doing everything in his power to keep from crying. That was all that was left of his dignity, of his manhood.

"Okay, I've got enough. Let the pig go, and put the sand monkey back in the truck," ET ordered.

On the way back through the dark country road, Khalid lay against the cold steel of the truck bed, tears running down his cheeks while his abductors laughed and joked, especially about the pig. Khalid's pants were still down around his ankles, and in the cool breeze of the night, he felt he might be bleeding from his anus onto his thighs.

"I don't know why that pig didn't want you, sand monkey. I thought you were a pretty good fuck. We know you Arabs like it that way." They laughed.

When the truck arrived back to where he had been abducted, one of the boys took a knife and sliced through the zip-tie handcuffs. They immediately shoved him off the tailgate of the truck with their feet and he landed in the gravel of the roadside. As the truck sped away, spraying gravel against his face, Khalid heard them laughing, one of them saying, "We did it, Mick. We did it!"

"Shut up, asshole," another replied. "What did I tell you about names. Somebody might hear you."

XI

Melanzane

Josh was already at their favorite table and well into a pitcher of beer when Marius arrived. "Hey, Marius, did you hear about the dyslexic guy who walked into a rab?"

"Let me guess: they threw him out because he got knurd?"

"Clever, very clever. I didn't know you spoke dyslexic."

"I might have to speak it tomorrow night. I'm on KGK's show, again. But this time with Sheriff Cavanaugh, Rev. Thorne, and Mayor Vreeland."

"August company." He poured Marius a beer.

"Yeah, the Caesar, Pompey and Crassus of Palatine."

"And you, Marc Antony, the hero. I saw the teaser on TV yesterday. The topic will be 'What's to be done,' presumably to prevent the next tragic event. I guess that makes Ms Gagan-Kemp Ms KGCleopatra. Any preliminary ideas?"

"Yeah. Why me? One occurrence of me jumping on and subduing a terrorist kid doesn't make me an expert on terrorist prevention, does it?'

"Everything's relative, my friend. You're the only one who has done that. Plus, you have served in the military—and thank you for your service, sir."

Marius winced. "Alright, then, tell me what the hell the Rev. Thorne and Mayor Vreeland are doing on the program. At least the Sheriff should know a little about confronting dangerous persons. But Thorne? What's he gonna contribute, some scriptural quotes and thoughts and prayers?" He turned to Rachel. "So, Rachel, you probably had more experience than anybody in this town dealing with Muslims when you were growing up on a kibbutz. If they're talking about terrorism on this show, I'm sure the whole Muslim thing is going to come up. Any advice you can give me?"

Rachel smiled and swept back her rich auburn hair that she wore in cooling tight curls during the upstate New York humid summers. "You might be asking the wrong Jew, Marius. Things were a bit isolated on the kibbutz and I probably saw more Muslims when I immigrated to Brooklyn as a teenager. In Israel, there are all kinds, some of which, as you probably know, are even Israeli citizens. My aunt in Haifa has Arab neighbors who are Israeli citizens and also Christians. How's that for identity ambiguity? They are lovely neighbors, too."

"I should've warned you that my wife can get a little bit Talmudic, Marius, despite the fact that she shares your metaphysical aversions," Josh said. He gave his wife an admiring smile.

"It's true," Rachel said, "I spent more time reading Marx and Engels than the Torah. I pretty much take my Middle Easterners as they come. And that includes Israelis as well, since I never got on well with ultra-orthodox Jews, and I oppose the Israeli settlements in the West Bank. As long as I'm being confessional, I suppose you should know that I sell my surplus produce to the Aziz family. Hisham and I have never had a quibble about price, or anything else." She then picked up a bag from beside her chair and slid it across the table. "But I saved some of these for you because I know they are one of your favorites."

Marius opened the bag. "Melanzane! These are beauties. Thanks." He held up one of the large, glistening purple eggplants. "I hope Hisham wasn't upset. These would make a great baba ganoush."

"He asked if I had any aubergine. But these are *melanzane*," she said with a wink.

"This is why there will never be any peace in the Middle East," Josh said. "Because my beautiful wife has some kind of a thing for this goombah from California."

Rachel was grinning. "Naw, he's two-timing me with that *shiksa* newscaster." Turning to Marius. "You might be jeopardizing your relationship with your *melanzane* dealer, Marius," she kidded.

Marius returned to the more serious subject. "Regarding Hisham, I'm beginning to get a little worried about him. Did you see that picture in the paper that some photographer managed to get of Khalid lying there in the ICU? Well, Hisham called me about it the other day, upset as hell, because he regarded it as a great insult to his brother, and also to his family."

"Why? I saw that photo. That could've been George Bush or a chimpanzee lying there with all of that medical equipment obscuring the image," Josh said.

"That doesn't matter," Rachel countered, "the name below it said Khalid Aziz, and that's enough to give offense to a Muslim."

"The article didn't help either," Marius said. "Conspiracy theories have been making the rounds and the paper seems to think it's good for boosting circulation to repeat them. The other day they ran a photo of the funeral ceremony for three of the victims beside an article suggesting that there might be an Al Qaeda cell in Palatine. Apparently, some members of our few Muslim families in Palatine have been pulled in for questioning and there have been some ugly things said to them on the streets. Some, like Mr. Tawfiq, the guy with the brake and tire business, are supposedly looking to sell out and leave town."

Josh surveyed right and left over his shoulder and leaned in closer to Marius. "You might want to lower your voice a little, amigo. There are some people in this town murmuring that the liberal, California guy might not be as patriotic as they want in one of their heroes. Remember, this is 'Bedford Falls' and the insularity of these gossipy small towns accelerates the flow of information. This place could turn into 'Pottersville' pretty quickly and you could be looking to move out with the Tawfiqs."

"Thanks, Clarence. I don't know what I would do without your celestial wisdom," Marius responded.

"Zu-Zu's petals," they said, simultaneously fist-bumping.

XII

What Is To Be Done?

The program opened with the rapid montage of launching missiles and aircraft from aircraft carriers, explosions of various sorts from bombs and IED's, crumpled buildings, mangled dead bodies, flag-covered caskets, American soldiers in full battle kit, and turban-headed, AK47-carrying indefinable sandal-shod insurgents, prisoners, beheadings, shots of Saddam Hussein, Osama bin Laden, Bishar al-Assad, and others—ending with the station logo and call letters and a title of the program: "Countering Domestic Terrorism: What Is To Be Done." It cuts to a live shot of KGK over the subscript: WPAL Host & Moderator Karen Gagan-Kemp.

This was KGK's big chance. The network had strongly considered pushing her aside in favor of one of its national correspondents to host the show. But the producers decided that it might be best to keep the show local in focus and development as a slice of Americana in the turbulent early stages of the 21st-century. But then again, Marius knew that the local news-anchor, who was looking quite fetching, in a blue- green frock that was halfway between figure-revealing and demurely professional, could be persuasive in other ways.

"Good evening, ladies and gentlemen. We are live here from our WPAL studios in Palatine New York with the second of our programs dealing with the school shooting fatalities that tragically shook our community several weeks ago, adding our community to a growing list that includes Columbine, Newton, and others. If you missed our first program, an interview with a courageous teacher at Palatine high school who risked his life to end that shooting before the lives of others might have been taken, that interview is available on podcast at WPAL.org. That gentleman is again with us tonight, as one of our panelists on this show about countering terrorism. He should be familiar to us all by now. Thank you again for coming, Mr. Marius Greco, teacher of Anthropology at Palatine high school."

Appearing on screen was a shot of Marius, who was smiling, almost imperceptibly before returning to a straight face. "Tonight, he will be joined by Rev. Ezra Thorne, Pastor of Risen Savior Baptist Church, County Sheriff Jerry Cavanaugh, and Mayor Ard Vreeland." The camera panned from one to the other with Thorne and Vreeland looking composed and confident, Cavanaugh slightly ill at ease. "Thank you also for coming, gentlemen, to help us in addressing perhaps the most difficult question that has faced this community since it was founded in the early 19th-century—what is to be done about domestic terrorism? We have a small studio audience that we hope is a reasonable representation of the community and we will be taking questions from them later on in the program." There was scattered applause as a camera swung around for a shot of a small studio audience. "Mayor Vreeland, if I may begin with you, how do you think we should address the question of what is to be done about terrorism in the community?"

Vreeland took a swig from his water bottle, fiddled with his name plate in front of his microphone, then adjusted the angle of the microphone, stealing a few moments to compose his thoughts. It also gave time for everyone else to wonder how sober Vreeland might be. His gaunt alcoholic's ashen complexion reminded Marius of some ghostly character from a Bergman film. In fact, the Mayor's great-grandparents immigrated from Uppsala, the town in which the director was born, and established a Saab dealership that was now the only outlet for every make and model of car, truck and tractor in the county. The Vreeland successful vehicle monopoly also financed three generations of Palatine mayoral campaigns. Vreeland Enterprises also owned a couple of dry-cleaning establishments, a septic tank company and the local Farmers Insurance franchise. Ard Vreeland was also the County Republican Party chairman. How he managed to run his business as well as the city with so much vodka pumping through his veins undermined the hypothesis that it was because of the vodka.

Vreeland, often called "Vod" behind his back, took his cue from European concerns. "I think that the fundamental problem facing America is immigration." Given that Vreeland pronounced the word think as "tink," and Scandinavian– accented other vocabulary that made him sound recently off the boat, he seemed to have no problem with his views on immigration sounding like hypocrisy. "We are allowing people into our country who do not share our values and do not respect our institutions. Dey come from a different culture dan American culture, and it seems to me they are not interested in fitting in. They stay mostly to themselves and the ways of their old countries. American culture is being polluted. We need more restrictive immigration and I agree that the Supreme Court upheld the President's ban on people coming from terrorist countries." Vreeland had acquired a decent American vocabulary that lacked the word hypocrisy.

Marius could feel his toes curling in his shoes. KGK asked if anyone wanted to comment on the mayor's remarks, but Thorne and Cavanaugh chose to lay low for the moment. But she sensed from Marius's facial expression that he was struggling to hold back. "Mr. Greco, you hail from a state that borders with Mexico. What are your thoughts on immigration as a contributor to the terrorist problem?"

"That is an interesting point the Mayor makes about culture. I can see where immigrants from very different countries can contrast in some ways with cultures such as those in, let's say, France or Germany, or even Sweden. Those cultures have well recognized features that are derived from their language, cuisine, and of course their ethnography. But if we are to apply the same question to America should we not ask the question of what is the culture of America? I would maintain that it is much harder to define and, in fact, the culture of America is much more an amalgam—what sociologists in the past used to refer to as the "melting pot"—of many different immigrant groups, including native populations. Ironically, then, American culture is in many respects, immigrant culture." Suck on that, you fucking hypocrite, Marius thought.

The mayor doubled down. "But immigrants today have to assimilate into the general society. Dese people prefer to keep to demselves. It's obvious. Look at the way da women dress; dey walk around covered up and scarves, and some of them you can't even see their faces. That's not American.

"But people of color—and it is usually people of color who we are talking about in the immigration debate— are not always allowed to assimilate," Marius rebutted. Consider the long record of school segregation, Native Americans stuck on reservations, the Chinese Exclusion Act, etc. Doesn't sound to me like a lot of interest in promoting assimilation. And we can be quick to revoke their rights as citizens as we did with Nisei internment camps in WWII. We seem to have a problem with people's skin color in this country."

Vreeland was not going to let go of it. "I do not deny that these things have happened in American history. But in towns like Palatine, where my family has lived for three generations, we have had neighborliness and a sense of community. People did not feel that they were among strangers. We looked out for each other. Now I don't know who that person is next to me in line at the market, or even if we speak the same language. How do I know they are not planning some act of terrorism? I don't understand how some of these cities are now calling themselves 'sanctuary cities' where even the local police will not cooperate with federal authorities to arrest illegal immigrants. That is not civic responsibility, it is liberal insanity."

Marius was smiling to himself. Questions of ethnic diversity and assimilation were smack in the middle of his academic discipline. Thorne and Cavanaugh were still silent, perhaps out of deference to the mayor, or perhaps waiting for when the subject turned more favorably in their direction. "I think it is part of American mythology," Marius said, "that its cities and towns have been melting pots that turned immigrants into some form of homogenized citizens. The ideologies seem to be that immigrants needed to cast off their old European or Asian ways—and clothes— and blend in as some undefined notion of 'homo-Americanus'. In fact, that never really happened. Immigrant groups tended to cluster geographically in Little Italys, Germantowns and Chinatowns, Black Belts, and re-settlements of East European Jewish shtetls. In many respects, this was socially necessary in order for these peoples to exploit their own cultures and talents and support one another to get an economic foothold in their new country. And it should be needless to say that these, what we urban anthropologists refer to as 'ethnic enclaves', were also enforced by the suspicion, prejudice, and discrimination that has always attended waves of immigration. Those words of Emma Lazarus's poem about the Statue of Liberty . . .". Marius stopped himself abruptly. "I'm sorry, I seem to have lapsed into a lecture. Forgive me, it's an occupational predisposition."

"Homo-Americanus, that's a new one for me, Mr. Greco. Just in case that comes up in my ministry, now that you have said it on the television," Thorne began.

"It's a reference to species, not sexuality, Reverend," Marius responded curtly. Marius saw the pastor as an African-American version of Orson Welles, same jowly face, same girth, but almost the opposite of the thespian's *profundo* voice.

Thorne grinned widely enough to expose a gold-crowned incisor. Many in the community already knew his views on homosexuality from his scathing letters to the editor of the paper and his appearances on local Christian radio shows. He loved to use the word 'buggery' and, as far as he was concerned, homosexuality was a "lifestyle choice" that the Bible said guaranteed an eternity in hell.

Thorne's pedigree was what he called "underground railroad." His great-grandparents were runaway slaves from Georgia and Thorne took pride in the fact that he had found his great grandmother's carving on a basement beam in a farmhouse outside of Rochester, New York. She had scratched in the original slave name, taken from the owner, McCants, through which she incised a slash, and wrote "a thorn in his side." The Reverend often talked with great pride about his great-grandmother's setting of the McCants' fields and barns on fire to distract and occupy his overseers and to cover their escape. Their freedom name became Thorne, although, paradoxically, the Reverend took up the same religious denomination as his family's former slave master—Southern Baptist. Rev. Thorne himself had never married, had no siblings, so he would be the end of the McCants/Thorne chapter of American race relations.

Thorne was unaware that he almost was not the religious invitee of choice, since there had been a spirited debate amongst the production staff as to whether "Pearly" Gaites should have represented the religious side, especially since there had been quite a competition between the two pastors in filling their pews and collection baskets. At one point there had been the suggestion that Fr. Kearney from St. Benedict Catholic parish might serve as a compromise between the Protestants, except for the fact that a news item about priests' sexual abuses in

Louisiana broke and Kearney didn't want to be anywhere near a journalist with a microphone. The best choice might have been Imam Ahmadi, from the local mosque, but the one staff member, a Black intern and also a Muslim, who suggested him was laughed out of the room. "Palatine is not a big metropolis like those places you are talking about, Mr. Greco. Maybe people don't have to fit in New York and Los Angeles the way they should and they can be illegal without big city people minding. But we Palatine folk do. We don't want our taxes paying for illegals freeloading off of us, taking welfare and committing crimes." Thorne droned on with chapter and verse of contemporary xenophobia, while Marius loaded up a response that countered every exaggeration and falsehood, beginning with everything the Reverend was saying was anti-Christian. But he caught an admonitory glance from KGK and limited his response."

"I think it might be a little unfair to always place the adjective 'illegal' in front of the word immigrant these days, Reverend. And studies have shown that even 'undocumented' immigrants pay taxes, unlike churches, which are, as I am sure you know, exempted from paying taxes in America. By that calculus, it is churches that are freeloading off of the labor of immigrants."

There was audible mumbling and a few hands of applause from the studio audience. In the audience, some found Marius's remarks uncomfortable and offensive, but there were others who did not. KGK sensed that the program was turning out to be the local establishment versus the local hero, so she tried shifting the subject. If she was going to demonstrate that she could handle this type of on-air encounter, she needed to keep it from going off the rails. She turned to Sheriff Cavanaugh, who thus far had been silent. "Sheriff, the subject of criminality among immigrants has been mentioned, but I have read news reporting that immigrants, even so-called illegal or undocumented immigrants, actually have lower crime rates than the general population. Is that so?"

"Yes, I have heard the same argument," the Sheriff responded, pulling himself out of the slight slouch he had fallen into. Not many people knew, and for his own reasons, Cavanaugh decided not to challenge that number, that the Cavanaugh family were descended from among the five thousand or so Irish immigrants who labored constructing the Erie Canal that passed through Palatine just a couple of blocks North of where they were assembled. Seamus Cavanaugh, who had immigrated in 1819 and found work on the Utica to Rome segment that opened the same year, chose to settle near Palatine before the rest of his family came over in 1822. Over their long history in the local area, the Cavanaughs, first starting with a livestock farm that was still in the family, expanded into other areas of the community, particularly in local government and, as was typical among the Irish, into law enforcement and fire protection. Jerry Cavanaugh was not the first Sheriff of Palatine. "Those statistics are confirmed by our experience here in the Palatine area. Some of the immigrant labor, particularly the seasonal labor, who work on local harvests, would sometimes get into some drunk and disorderly behavior when they get some money in the pockets, but I don't find this exceptional as far as our local crime statistics are concerned. We are dealing with something quite different tonight. I think we have to be concerned about criminal types who are part of international organizations that are bent upon acts of terror equivalent to acts of war. We as yet do not know if the school terrorist attack that is the basis for this program tonight was just a random event that was influenced by some young man who had access to an Al Qaeda, or ISIS website, or whether there is some deeper and more pervasive operation, similar to that which produced 9-11, that is in place. We are dealing with new elements here that we cannot be complacent about.

I know there is all this talk about sanctuary cities and whether or not local law-enforcement should be involved in rounding up undocumented immigrants. But they may not be the real problem here. Most of them are law-abiding and are just looking for a better place to live and work. In a strange way, it is a smaller and more sinister cohort of immigrants that are out to destroy American life, not join it. I think we need to concentrate on them. Palatine is no longer an isolated community in the Mohawk Valley; mass communications and the Internet have pulled us into the global world, at least as far as ideas and political ideologies are concerned."

Before KGK could ask a follow-up question, Thorne asked the Sheriff what he thought about the proposals to arm teachers. "Maybe if our teachers and administrators were licensed to carry firearms . . .".

Cavanaugh cut him off. "I don't see that solving the problem, and perhaps even making it worse. You can train a teacher how to use a firearm, but there is no way to train them adequately as to how to use it in an active shooter situation. In a fire fight and in a civilian context, it becomes very difficult to sort out the bad guys from the good guys. In some towns in Texas. they even allow students to carry firearms onto campus. Once the shooting starts, it can easily turn into mayhem with many innocent victims. And, as far as I have been able to tell, most teachers are not interested in being armed."

"I might ask teacher Greco if, based on his experience, he would like to be armed in the classroom," KGK said.

"I'm in agreement with the Sheriff on this," Marius responded. "One of the things I learned in the military is that the perpetrator has the advantage of initiative. We keep hearing gun enthusiasts saying that 'what you need to stop a bad guy with a gun is a good guy with a gun.' Well, it rarely, if ever, happens, despite the many people who are openly carrying firearms these days. Would you, Reverend, support the idea of arming preachers, or gospel singers? After all, there have been at least two so-called terrorist attacks that killed parishioners in churches in South Carolina and Texas, not to mention the infamous Birmingham bombing during the Civil Rights Movement. Had those people been armed, they still would not have had a chance. By the time the perpetrator pulls the trigger, it's already too late. If this problem is to be solved, it has to be well before that."

"Then maybe we have to keep these kinds of people out of the country to begin with," Thorne answered. "Maybe the problem does lie with our immigration."

"Except that the three Church killings I mentioned were perpetrated by white American, Christian citizens, not immigrants" Marius countered. Marius was feeling rather good about how things were going. This time, although he was in the middle of the discourse, he was not its prime focus as he had been in the previous program. Moreover, he enjoyed this kind of give-and-take. It reminded him of those spirited graduate seminars back at UCLA, especially the Film Theory seminar with Professor Trevor St. George. St. George was a mind-crushing academic who felt that Ph.D. students needed to be able to back up their opinions with facts and logic. "If you think you can get away with just 'I like it,' or 'I don't like it' in my class, you are going to feel like your brain has been pulled out, stomped and pissed on," the crusty Brit would forewarn. St. George had influenced Marius to come to regard intellection as a form of combat between truth and ignorance. In this form of discourse, there was no point in taking any prisoners. The trip was to not come off as an intellectual smart-ass.

Thorne, unused to such challenges to his preaching and prophesizing from a pulpit, looked a little bewildered by the insubordination of a high school teacher. People didn't usually disrespect his clerical collar and his silky maroon shirt.

To Thorne's relief, Mayor Vreeland decided to elaborate upon his earlier remarks. "I feel that when these attacks take place in small towns like Palatine, it is like an enemy is trying to strike at the soul of America," Vreeland opined. "Small towns are where the real America lives, where people can know each other and care about each other. Not like those big cities where everybody is a stranger."

It seemed that the mayor was going to say more, but just stopped there. The dead air of the broadcast caught KGK unawares and Marius could see that she was struggling to come up with some sort of segue.

"If I may, madam moderator," Marius said.

She looked up from her notes and just nodded affirmatively, so Marius continued. "As an anthropologist, I was quite interested to hear the mayor's remarks with respect to strangers. Strangers have long been a subject of interest to anthropologists, particularly to those working in primitive societies. Some of what we have learned aligns with what the mayor has been saying about local suspicion and fear of strangers in the community. Some primitive societies are innocently open and welcoming but, more often than not, many of these remote peoples understand that strangers coming into their community can be very threatening, not only bringing with them diseases to which aboriginal people have no immunity, but also ideas and behaviors that can be disruptive to the local culture, not to mention the threats that new metaphysical ideas can pose for witch doctors and shamans. Many of these societies decided that the best thing to do with strangers was to kill them. In fact, we know from other sources, such as the whalers who were often the first White men to encounter some of these peoples, that they were not only killed, but cannibalized. One account I read said that the locals referred to the unlucky whalers as 'long pig'."

"Surely you are not suggesting that as a solution to our immigration problem are you, Mr. Greco?" Vreeland said with uncharacteristic irony.

"No sir," Marius responded. "Even in crazy La-La Land where I come from, we stopped dining on East Coast long pig a long time ago—although it must have been a delicacy."

There was some giggling in the audience.

"So, I presume that you are a stranger we can trust, then, Mr. Greco," the mayor responded.

Marius smiled. "Well, I'm not exactly what you would call a vegetarian, sir."

Marius heard a loud guffaw from the studio audience that he distinctly recognized as that of Jesus Castro.

KGK saw the levity as an opportunity and announced that they would be going to commercial break and would be taking questions from the studio audience when they resumed. Mayor Vreeland immediately jumped up saying something about "the facilities," but probably just wanted to get out of sight to take a pull on his flask.

During the break, while KGK conferred with her producer, Marius scribbled a few notes of thoughts intended for his dissertation; Cavanaugh took a call from his cell phone, and Rev. Thorne seemd to be in silent communication with his celestial boss.

KGK: "Welcome back to WPAL's special program Countering Terrorism: What Is To Be Done. I am your host and moderator, Karen Gagan-Kemp, along with our panelists . . . If you are just joining us, in our first session some interesting questions and opinions were provided by our panelists. Now we would like to initiate some interchange between them and our studio audience. Audience members just raise your hand if you have a question or a comment and one of our staff will bring the microphone to you."

The first question came from a pudgy, but cute, young lady in the front of the studio audience. Marius recognized her as a checkout girl at the local market. "Why do these Al Qaeda [she pronounced it like cicada] people always seem to want to shoot school children?" she asked with a direct innocence.

No one on the panel spoke up. "Anyone?" KGK inquired.

"I don't think that we should assume the attacker was a member of Al Qaeda," Sheriff Cavanaugh responded. "Thus far, we have been unable to find any indication in the Internet traffic we have been examining on his computer that he has accessed any of the websites that are known to be Al Qaeda, ISIS, or any of the other known terrorist organizations. Nor have these organizations as yet claimed any credit for the attack."

"I don't think we should lump all of the groups together. They don't even agree with one another. The Sunni-Shia division can be especially vicious, even more so at times than towards Westerners," Marius added.

"You seem to be quite well informed on the subject, Mr. Greco," Vreeland commented. "I found it to be as valuable information as how to clean my rifle, Mr. Mayor."

KGK jumped in. "Correct me if I'm wrong gentlemen, but I believe Mr. Greco is the only one in this forum who has ever served in the Middle East." She already knew that Sheriff Cavanaugh had been in the Marine Corps, but had never been deployed, that Rev. Thorne would never have been able to pass a military physical because of his weight, and that Mayor Vreeland apparently had ironically avoided military service during the Vietnam years by serving on the local Draft Board. "Therefore, he's probably been closer to any member of Al Qaeda than anyone else on the stage."

"You were an officer in Iraq, then, Mr. Greco?" The mayor asked.

"No sir, I was just a corporal."

Marius caught an exchange of smiles between the mayor and Rev. Thorne.

"But you shouldn't underestimate corporals. Mussolini, Franco, and Hitler all started out as corporals," he said with a grin.

"Were you engaged in combat situations with enemy forces?" the mayor asked.

"I regarded it that they engaged me. Yes. But I don't know why we are pursuing the subject of my brief and undistinguished military career. Being over there doesn't necessarily give one a better understanding. Sometimes it's difficult to see the forest when you're one of the trees. Perhaps we could move on." He looked over at KGK.

"Is there another question from the audience?" KGK asked.

Marius smiled when his friend Jesus stood up. But he wondered what kind of a question he had.

"I would like to return to the question of immigration," Jesus began. "I am not a Spaniard. I speak Spanish because that's the language spoken by people who conquered my ancestors. I like it. It's the only language I have never known, although there are a few indigenous words, like from Nahuatl, that have made their way into it. But I am of native descent, Indian. My people came to North America, they say, originally 10 or 12,000 years ago when the ice retreated and we came from Asia. Now some are saying that it was even 30,000 years ago. But the white people who conquered the native peoples and exterminated many of them regard us now as newcomers, as immigrants, to the land that was our land tens of thousands of years ago. My native land is Southern California, but they want to build a wall to keep my people out. I am somewhat a foreigner again, as I now live in the land of the Iroquois nation, who are closer to me than my White neighbors. When you call me an immigrant you are wrong; this was our land first.

When you call us undocumented, you are twice wrong; we don't need documents to live in our own land. And third, when you associate people you call 'undocumented aliens' with terrorism, you were three times wrong. Gracias." Jesus sat down.

"Did you have a question, sir?" KGK asked.

Jesus stood up again. "Yes, do any of you like good Mexican food?" Josh, who was standing at the back of the studio audience, started a round of applause.

When the applause died down, KGK recognized the waving hand of Gloria Sexton, reporter for the local newspaper, *The Sentinel.* "First, I want to congratulate KGK on the excellent job she is doing on this program in bringing to the fore the important safety issues confronting not just Palatine, but other communities like it." A perfunctory scattered applause followed what a bristling KGK knew to be insincere praise. The two women disliked each other. "I do have a question for Mr. Greco. You said, sir, that you had served as a soldier in Iraq in the infantry. As you have also said, you are probably the only one on the panel who has fought in Iraq. I do not wish to pry into your memory of that time, but only to ask you if there is anything in that experience or other experiences you might've had with Arab peoples that might have influenced or inclined, even subconsciously, your encounter with Khalid Aziz? And let me thank you for your service, sir."

Marius really did not want to go back into the subject, and hated the almost cliché "thank you for your service." "Since I am beginning to feel like this is a court-martial, let me tell you that I can produce honorable discharge papers. But let me say this. No one goes to war and is not changed by it in some way. Some people are wounded, either physically, mentally or both, but others are changed in more subtle ways, ways in which they relate to people who are very different from them. I fought in a war in which the enemy look just like the people we were supposedly liberating. We fought right among the women and children and old people, and oftentimes we could not tell who was friend or enemy, or whether the person passing you in the street, maybe even a child, was not a walking bomb." Marius briefly considered, but rejected, mentioning that he had written an essay about such moments. "When you are that close, it is not just the dismembered body parts you see, but also how much destruction you are doing to the social infrastructure of a society . . . , I really have no more to say on the subject."

"I think we have time for a couple more questions," KGK said. Slightly apprehensive, she recognized the Rev. Carson "Pearly" Gaites, who had been patiently coiled like a local rattler in the front row. Pearly raised himself up to his full five foot, four inches of Jeremiah posture, clutching his trusty New Testament. "No one seems to want to address the most important subject of this colloquium, including my colleague from Redeemer Baptist Church, so I will take up the cross. I don't know about you, but I was horrified and disgusted that nowhere in these two hours moderated by our local news anchor has there been a single mention of our Lord and Savior, Jesus Christ, not even by someone on the panel who is supposedly ordained to carry the word of the gospel to the people." That made two jabs at Thorne, who now pulled himself out of a semi-somnolent state. "We heard many explanations and suggestions from the so-called experts and the studio audience, ending only in debate and speculation, and confusion about how to respond to these acts of terrorism. We Christians have endured terrorism from the very beginning of our faith, from persecutions by the Romans, to the sinister kidnappings and murders of Christian children by Jews in the Middle Ages, to inquisitions by the Roman Catholic Church, and slaughter at the hands of the armies of the Vatican in the counter-reformation and, of course, the usurpation of the holy lands of the Bible by Islam. Our beloved Savior, who died on the cross for our sins, did not leave us an easy path to salvation. We have been tested. Satan moves among us, and we must recognize and take up arms against his works. And Satan, the great deceiver, is working through the assistance of these terrorists. And we are complicit in their heinous deeds because we have allowed them into our communities believing the Satanic deceptions of the communist-liberal-atheists that they deserve to live and worship their false gods right here in our community." Gaites had shifted right into his preachy cadence.

"If I may, Reverend, did you have a question?" KGK interrupted.

Before Gaites could respond, Josh spoke up from the back of the room. Marius smiled to himself, already mentally composing a bar joke that begins with "a Jew, an atheist, and an undocumented alien walk into a bar ..."

The strain in Josh's voice was evident. "Why are you evangelists always trying to blame Islam for this, rather than blame religion in general—you believe that something is ordained by your god and that justifies any action you take in its fulfilment. Your means justifies your god's end's—not the other guy's. It's always that other religion that is the evil—the other. Christians went from being a briefly persecuted faith to the official faith of the Roman Empire and soon enough were acting just like the Romans. They became drunk with power. And when they needed an enemy, there was always some other faith. The Jews were always handy and could be rounded up for a jolly good time as eaters of Christian babies, or the always reliable Christ-killers. Now it's the Muslims' turn to be the supposed force of evil. But the real purpose of religion is to keep people like you, and Rev. Thorne in business, selling fear and the promise of salvation. I don't know whether this boy who attacked his fellow classmates and teachers was moved by some sense of religious *jihad*, or something we may never get to know about. But it is hard to sit here and listen to people who do not know exploit this tragic event to grind their own hypocritical rhetorical axes. . . . And yes, I do have a question. It is when are some of the people of this town going to wake up to the fact that in real life you don't get to select your own reality. Well, I guess that really isn't a question.

"Perhaps that is good then, since we seem to be out of time," KGK said. "I want to thank our panelists, and also those in our studio audience, especially those whose questions and comments helped to make this an interesting discussion. Thank you all and good night."

———————

When KGK encountered Marius in the parking lot after the show, she seemed in a good mood. "I'd like a little company winding down from tonight. I think we were so good together the last time we should ... well, it would be a shame to let it be just one time."

"Yeah, but you didn't leave the money on the dresser the last time," he joked.

"Come on Marius, I think any objective observer would say, if there's a whore in this relationship, it's me."

"You know I'm joking, don't you? It's just a line I saw in some movie I can't even remember."

"Well, I think what I'm suggesting, and that bottle of excellent Chianti that I have in my car, would have to be regarded as quite a different opinion about what could be, ah ... what's that piece of dialogue in that movie *Casablanca*? I think it's Bogart who says to the guy who plays the policeman . . .".

"He says it to Rene, Claude Rains, 'I think this could be the beginning of a beautiful friendship'."

"See, there was a tension between those two in the movie, but they became friends. So why couldn't . . ."

Marius interrupted. "Yeah, I get it. Now you want to be friends? Frankly, I think that's a lot harder. Actually, I've read some sociology that says sometimes it's more difficult and painful to break up from a friendship than it is from an amorous relationship."

"Really?

"Yeah, really. Friendships are actually more complicated. I'm dealing with an interesting one in my next class—in *Rebel Without a Cause*."

"Maybe you read too much sociology?"

"Or watch too much film."

"Okay, I don't want to argue and spoil the beginning of what could be a beautiful… something?"

"Fuck it, let's go. I'm only interested in your Chianti anyway," he joked.

"Well, let's see if we can get some *in vino veritas*, then."

"What? You journos speak some Latin now? Maybe after that wine we can try some *mulier equitans*, then."

"Sounds kinky," she said, pressing the remote unlock on her car keys. The car beeped and the lights flashed on the expensive BMW, like some creature recognizing its mistress.

"Don't worry. You'll like it," Marius said, looking at the conventional keys to his old model Ford, "I'm pretty sure it was a woman who thought it up."

———

The dawn light was just making its way to the seam in the curtains of Marius's bedroom. Woolley the cat could be seen silhouetted on the other side. Marius was dozing, but KGK had been awake for a while, thinking. She rolled towards him and draped around over his shoulder. He mumbled something that was incoherent. "So, what did you think?" KGK asked. "Was it good?"

Marius groaned.

"Was it good?" she repeated.

"Yeah, good, but I've had better Chianti. There's one from a vintner up in Novato that's the best I have ever had."

"That Molière thing, position, whatever, you bastard. Not the wine."

He laughed. "*Mulier, mulier equitans*, although Molière probably tried it, too, being French."

"So?"

"Yeah, that was good, too. You might even be ready for the Olympic dressage team.

"Next time I'll wear spurs."

"Then you better bring more Chianti. Get the Novato stuff."

"Well I really liked it," she said.

"Now you know how much work it is being on top. Makes women appreciate us men more."

"You were pretty happy with how that program went, weren't you? Whose job are you shooting for? Diane Sawyer? Christianne Amanpour? Oprah?"

"You make it sound like I am Diana Christensen again, a schemer."

"I just want you to remember who helped you make it on your way up. If your guests suck, you're not going to look so good."

"Well I have to admit, you were the star of the show—again."

"Well I can't say that those other guys were much competition. A good teacher should know how to shape the discourse and how to connect with an audience. Those other guys are not teachers. They're representatives of a certain constituency, looking at things that represent a certain set of interests. They all have public postures, but they only work well when they are in control of situations. Take them out of their element and it's easier to see through them."

"We seem to work really well together," she said. "do you think we really have something going here, if you know what I mean? Or are you just getting me ready for the Olympics?"

"When I first came here, I thought I knew what I was doing. I had a purpose and a plan that fit its execution, or so I thought. But that's not the way things always work out. I was going to be the participant-observer anthropologist, but the participant part was really subordinate to and supposed to be complementary to the observer. I got dragged out of that by a crazy kid with an automatic rifle. The strange thing is that I had always been interested in what could happen in a single moment and how it could affect the trajectory of a life. I even wrote an essay about it based on my experience in Iraq. And then, ironically, that essay itself altered the trajectory of my life. Weird, huh? So, do we really have something going? You, a Bryn Mawr girl with aspirations that might not be Diana Christensen, but you're the wrong coast. Fuck, maybe you're the wrong color."

She gave him a hard look, but said nothing.

"Sorry, that's what you get from an anthropologist. We are obsessed with cultural distinctions. I am in no position to go beyond a good Chianti and some *mulier equitans*."

"Should I leave the money on the dresser?"

"Naw, this could be the beginning of a beautiful friendship."

"Who is she, Marius?"

XIII

The Dark Side

Marius forced down his piece of breakfast toast before answering the phone. He knew what it would be about.

"Have you seen the newspaper this morning, Marius?" KGK asked without even saying hello.

"Yeah, I saw it," he said with a resigned voice. "The hero of Palatine turns out to be the Antichrist."

"Jesus, Marius, I know you don't owe me anything, but I thought after what has passed between the two of us since all this began, that at least you would give me an edge over that bitch Gloria Sexton at *The Sentinel*."

He took a gulp of coffee, spilling some of it on his shirt. "I didn't give her anything. I don't even know her. I preferred all along that this information would not get exposed and become conflated with this whole goddamn terrorist attack business that is frankly fucking up my life. So, don't get all up my ass about it, because however much you are pissed off, it's nothing compared to how pissed off I am."

"But she made it sound like she had got some of this information directly from you."

"She set me up for that with her question on your program," Marius said through gritting teeth.

"If you don't mind, I have to call my landlord to come and repair the picture window in my living room through which a lovely message tied to a brick was my wake-up call this morning."

"Really?"

"Yeah, really. You should be aware that you have been speaking with, and I quote, 'a Satan-serving bastard that cannot burn in hell too soon'."

"Oh, Christ, no."

"Oh, Christ, yes. They could have at least left the message in my mailbox." Marius had not yet seen the spray-painted "Going To Hell" across his garage door. "You've been in this town a lot longer than me. Perhaps you can tell me if I have any hero chips leftover, or I can expect a mob with pitchforks and torches tonight."

"Marius, I want you to know that if you had confided this information in me, I would've kept it in confidence, on background. I never would've used it like that bitch. I hope you believe me when I say that." KGK knew, even as she said it, that she was being disingenuous. She owed Sexton a debt of gratitude—now she had the answer to the "who is she?".

"Right now, I feel like my belief glands have been ripped out and stomped on. I feel like George Bailey, running around 'Pottersville' in the snow being snubbed by everybody he knows, but who claim they don't know him. There isn't much room to run and duck for cover in a small town."

"I'd like to come over Marius, really I would, but now my news producer is all over me because we have to obviously report on this. It's the story of the day, I have no doubt that national wants to run with it, too. Christ, I wish you would've told me about it, we might've been able to prep some spin on it."

Marius winced. "Fuck spin. I don't owe anybody in this burg an explanation, and there is only one person to whom I owe an apology, and that will never be enough. Let's talk later. You know where to find me; I'll be the guy hanging from a tree with thirty pieces of silver in his pocket."

He hung up the call and picked up the crumbled newspaper from the floor, flattening it out on the dining room table and began reading it again.

Palatine
By Gloria Sexton

"Local Hero: A Shadowy Backstory"

Like a Hollywood movie that nearly faded into obscurity, a story has reached across the country into Palatine, but with a poignant and bizarre relevance. Apparently, the encounter Palatine High Anthropology teacher Marius Greco had with the Iraqi immigrant shooter that killed four and wounded seven before Mr. Greco put a stop to the attack was not his first involvement in a tragic event. The Sentinel has learned that Mr. Greco, the 29-year old teacher who is also working on a doctorate from UCLA, lost his teaching position at Westmont High in Los Angeles following a relationship he had with a female student, Jazmeen Sherazi, a member of an Iraqi immigrant family.

Following what Westmont school officials described as an "informal tutorial" relationship between Greco and Sherazi of a few weeks that dealt with the subject of atheism, Miss Sherazi suffered a brutal assassination attempt by her own brothers. Called an "honor killing" it was to be a mortal punishment for associating with a man her shamed family regarded as an "infidel". Miss Sherazi was forced to drink a poisonous concoction that contained cleaning fluid, but she survived, although with a badly damaged liver that keeps her at death's door from organ failure and can require extended periods of hospitalization.

Notwithstanding a friend's testimony to the contrary during the court trial that placed Miss Shirazi's brothers in prison for attempted second degree murder, Mr. Greco testified that the fault was his for the formation of the association between himself and Miss Sherazi, who was too ill to be present in court. Mr. Greco was subsequently dismissed from his faculty position at Westmont. An injunction issued by the court forbids Mr. Greco from any further association with Miss Sherazi. Both parties denied in statements that there had been any intimate relationship between them, although there was much prevailing gossip at the school, and the brothers had assumed otherwise. Mr. Greco departed Los Angeles shortly thereafter—for Palatine, New York.

Mr. Greco, who teaches American Urban Anthropology using American films has not been open or proselytizing with his atheism, although Palatine school officials interviewed for this article did indicate that there have been a couple of student complaints that Mr. Greco seemed to them "irreligious." An official who asked not to be named revealed that Mr. Greco answered the "religious affiliation" question in his application ambiguously as "baptized Roman Catholic."

It is also known from Mr. Greco's application at Palatine HS that he served in the U.S. Army infantry as a corporal in Iraq. But there was no mention in his application statement of the incident involving a "relationship" with Miss Sherazi. Rather, Mr. Greco wrote that he chose to come to Palatine because his doctoral research was on the subject of American small towns for which he is applying the methodology of "a particpant-observer." Needless to say, Mr. Greco became a significant "participant" with his heroic action to stop the terrorist attack. Most of the people of Palatine thanked God for the courage of Mr. Greco on that day, although, we have since learned, he probably does not see that God had anything to do with it.

Address comments and questions to glorsex@sentinmel.com

Marius crumpled the paper up again, grumbling, "That bitch calls herself a journalist. Nice of her to imply that I was doing God's will while rejecting God. Of course, typical of her sort, she does not pose the question why does their God allow this kid to go on rampage in the first place. Isn't it clever how she made it sound like some angel of death descended on their pious little Palatine? Okay, Cal kid, you wanted to study American small towns . . .".

Marius poked the power-on key of his computer with a rage and immediately began furiously typing in dissertation notes. His mood was as dark as his subject.

Subject: The Dark Side of the American Small Town

The idyllic imagery of the "wonderful life" of small town America also competes with a darker, more sinister dimension of the small town experience. Although small towns still remained with many Americans a representation of the country's essence, identity, and true spirit, for others it began to represent tired old ways of doing things, and some threatening traditions, like bigotry, intolerance, racism, and small town chauvinism.

One of the strongest influences on the representation of the dark side of the small town appears to have been precipitated by the emergence of the Civil Rights Movement. In newsreels and on television screens, many of the first images of the struggle of African-Americans for a fuller participation in society and an end to discrimination were images of resistance by small minds in narrow towns, particularly in the American South. Pictures of police beatings, governors standing in schoolhouse doors, civil rights demonstrators attacked by police dogs or with fire hoses, and the bodies of lynched victims or slain freedom riders were primarily from the small towns and rural areas of the South.

By the 1970s, some television programs were employing negative depictions of small towns as a plot staple. Typical plots involved the encounter of a big city person with a small town, providing the necessary contrast in the values, attitudes, and behaviors of characters. In one episode of the popular television series, *The Rockford Files,* a private detective from Los Angeles, passing through a small town, has a car breakdown that results in his being extorted and eventually set up on a morals charge. His experience, one of becoming prey to an alien world of petty prejudices and vengeance against city people, was a dramatic theme that allegedly has had some basis in real-world experiences.

With the growth of the Interstate Highway System and the number of automobiles, there was more travel from other regions of the country to the South, as well as into other areas of small towns. Experiences of urbanites in these places were sometimes negative, particularly those who were snared in speed traps set up on local roads and forced to pay fines in order to pass through (one notorious small town in Georgia made much of its income in this manner).

Amongst many screenwriters, most of them from New York and Los Angeles, there had already started somewhat of a tradition of taking revenge on small towns through films like *The California Kid* (1974), *Macon County Line* (1974), *Easy Rider* (1969), and *Deliverance* (1972). These films were able to draw upon a mine of novels, some by southerners such as Faulkner and Tennessee Williams, that exposed small towns as places of debauchery, small mindedness, and cruelty. It was as though Andy Hardy had grown up to lead a gang of unemployed, sexually frustrated small-town punks eager to commit atrocities on any alien they could chase down in their gun-racked pickup trucks. Nor did it seem likely that they would be deterred by the stereotypical obese, cigar-munching sheriff who was usually blinded by his mirrored sunglasses to any malfeasance he couldn't snare in his speed trap.

These portrayals were not exclusively of Southern small towns. *Peyton Place* (1957) was first a steamy bestseller of this sort and subsequently a television series. Set in a small New England town, the movie opens with a postcard panorama and the introduction that it is a locale where "time is not measured by the clock or the calendar, but by the seasons." But beneath that thin veneer is a social life that is much like a soap opera, constructed on lies, gossip, illicit sexual entanglements, and dysfunctional families. As the ideal proscenium for human tragedies, the small town was revived and now powered by a stew of dirty secrets, xenophobia, political intrigue, and licentiousness, as in *Our Town* (1940).

In Sparta, Mississippi, as in seemingly all Southern small-town films, the plot-driving themes are always about race or class. It is a social structure—reminiscent of manorialism in feudal societies—of rigidly-ascribed hierarchical levels of class.

The sinister and secretive small town is exemplified in *Bad Day at Black Rock* (1955). Bad things can happen in small, out-of-the-way, towns, like Black Rock, California, a settlement so small it has only a dozen or so inhabitants, and the train that runs by it rarely ever stops. Once again, the catalyst for the plot is the arrival of an outsider, Mr. Macreedy (Spencer Tracy), a mysterious, one-armed war veteran with a mission, who threatens to expose the dark secret of the town of Black Rock.

Black Rock is not much of a town, very much like the set for a western, and in fact, the film has the feel and tension of *High Noon* (1952). When the streamliner train whistle stops to let him off, the conductor says that the train has not had occasion to stop there for years. Macreedy remarks, "Oh, I'll only be here twenty-four hours." To which the conductor replies, "In a place like this, it could be a lifetime." Here again, the dramatic tension is provided by the arrival of the "outsider," the stranger, the "other."

Macreedy is looking for a Mr. Komoko, a Japanese immigrant whose son died saving Macreedy's life when they were soldiers in Italy and was posthumously awarded the Medal of Honor. Macreedy is shunned, stonewalled, and threatened at every turn by the town's residents, but eventually, after nearly being killed himself by Komoko's murderer, he discovers with the help of a couple of guilt-ridden residents that the Japanese man was murdered in an act of "patriotic" post-Pearl Harbor revenge.

Bad Day at Black Rock is not without allegorical references to both the mistreatment of Japanese-Americans during the war, that led to the climate of suspicion and the blacklists created by the McCarthy Communist witch hunts. In contrast to the big city, where social anonymity functions to provide a cloak for murder, the small town requires its opposite, a tight social collusion to keep dark secrets in the dark. Likewise, where rapid social change and social relocation in the big city provide a buffer to resentments based on race and social class, in the small town the lack of these conditions, ignited by the depth of local memory, often form the fundamentals of movie plots.

In Anarene, Texas, the site of director Peter Bogdanovich's *The Last Picture Show* (1971), the threat to the small town is much more subtle and insidious than the appearance of an outsider. This small town is a sad place of dust-blown streets and equally desolate lives in the late 1950s. The closing of the last movie theater in town symbolizes that even the dream world it imported is over. Many small towns in the same time period and in other places were undergoing a similar fate. Emerging shopping centers nearby were killing town commercial districts; old industries were failing or relocated, hope and life were draining out; and the young were eager to join the exodus if they could.

The movie house, pool hall, and café in Anarene are all owned by Sam the Lion (Ben Johnson), who represents the town's better days (and more noble character) and is somewhat of a hero to the two young men upon whom the story centers. If Sam is a symbol of what the self-sufficient, well-adjusted Texan should be, everyone else in town seems to be an emotional mess. There is little more to do in Anarene that conduct motel assignations and adulteries, shoot pool, abuse the local retarded boy, and watch the local football team get clobbered on Friday night (something that, in Texas, is achingly hard to bear).

Duane (Jeff Bridges) and Sonny (Timothy Bottoms) are football teammates and buddies. They also share an admiration for Sam the Lion and women problems. Sonny commences an affair with the much older wife of his football coach (Cloris Leachman), which has a rocky course and is still unresolved by the end of the film. Duane, brash and athletic, has the attention of the prettiest girl in town, Jacy (Cybill Shepherd), but he is too far beneath her economic class and without much future to hold her and overcome her scheming, self-indulgent mother (Ellen Burstyn) whose genes she has clearly inherited. Eventually Jacy ends up with the local rich kids, who amuse themselves with nude swimming parties and heading off to parties in the nearest big city.

By the movie's end, Sam has died, Jacy goes off to college, Duane to the army and Korea, and Sonny languishes in the town. Much of the story is about the death of innocence as it is about the lost better days of small towns and local movie theaters; it ends with the death of the retarded boy, Billy, in a truck accident, in the desolate main street of the town. Anarene, like so many small towns, turned sordid and mean, and seems to have been run over by events in much the same way. An anonymous proverb states: "God made the country, man made the city, but the devil the little town."

The past is always present in small-town stories. Circumstances that would escape notice in the maelstrom of metropolitan life loom larger, and memory always seems longer. At somewhat of an environmental counterpoint from Texas is the portrayal of a small town on an island in Puget Sound in the 1940s and 1950s. *Snow Falling on Cedars* (1999) is a multi-textured story of interracial love and rivalry that is also part mystery and documentary. The young love story between Japanese-American Hatsue Miyamoto (Youki Kudoh) and Ishmael Chambers (Ethan Hawke) provides the core of flashbacks that depict the impact of Pearl Harbor on relations between the Japanese and native residents and culminate in the trial of the Japanese husband that

Hatsue marries during the community's internment at Manzanar. Her husband, a decorated war veteran, is accused of murdering a childhood Caucasian friend who came to own farmland that was appropriated from the Japanese when they were packed up and sent away. Her former amour, Ishmael, an embittered local journalist and maimed war veteran from the Pacific theater, is posed on the horns of a moral dilemma because he is in possession of information that would exonerate the man who is married to the woman he still loves. Not only are these emotions and racism of the small town in this period evoked in this film, but the film also boasts award-winning cinematography of a bleak and chilling landscape with relentlessly tenebrous skies and, of course, forests of cedars frosted with the snows of dark, cold winters. The performances of Sam Shepard, as the town's newspaper owner-editor, and Max Von Sydow, as the defense attorney, force the cast and audience into consideration of moral principles that transcend the times and circumstances of this small town.

Snow Falling on Cedars proves that the small town remains a powerful dramatic template and a mine of movie subject matter, but one that seemingly affords only the occasional nugget in a setting that seems otherwise played out from the richer veins it provided when the small town was not so small a factor in the American urban experience.

It is ironic that *It's a Wonderful Life* was actually released at the end of the small town era in America. The Depression had finished off, economically, many of the small towns that were already weakened by economic changes taking place in the nation. Many young men from small towns went off to war in Europe and the Pacific, passing through New York, San Francisco, and San Diego, seeing the attractions of big cities for the first time and resolving to return to live in them (or the suburbs that would sprout on their peripheries after the war). The new dream was suburbia, and some small towns did survive, economically, if not culturally, by assimilating into the suburban wave where they could.

But by 1960s, Capra's fictionalized, heroic, common man, often associated with small-town values, was passé, rendered irrelevant by the muddled morality of film noir, and the befuddling realities of unanticipated social changes, and anti-heroes that roiled in the wake of World War II. The new common man might be a black activist, a long-haired hippie, a student leader, a feminist, an environmentalist, or a consumer advocate, none of whom had the ideological purity and innocence to fill the heroic role. Rather than an archetype, there emerged an uncommon pluralism. The question was not how to resuscitate the sort of conformity of values and lifestyle associated with the small town, but how to fashion a society out of the increasingly fractious multicultural characteristics of American society.

By 1960, the small town was no longer able to insulate itself from the larger society. Radio, the movies, and television broke through whatever censorious barriers small towns might have erected to repel the intrusion of big city values and behaviors. Suburbs were creeping into their hinterlands, sometimes absorbing them or forcing small towns to share their schools and other institutions with the outlanders. In time, WiFi and the Internet would sap what little insulation these places had as a bastion against influences of the larger society.

Those small town residents who remained were forced to fight a rearguard action through fundamentalist religious sects, anti-big government politics, and even extreme militia groups. These twisted or perverted the original small-town ideals. The one-time elm-lined nostalgic streets of Bedford Falls, or Palatine, became a shaky refuge for those who could not, or would not, accept the emergence of modernism and global urbanism.

Still, the small town makes its way onto movie screens in a metropolitan world, perhaps more often in its dark tones, but sometimes in shades of gray owing to its dramatic containment. In *The Truman Show* (2004) the neo-traditional urban development of Seaside, Florida, is employed as the set for a dark comedy in which Truman Burbank (Jim Carrey) is exploited by an icy-hearted television director (Ed Harris) as the unknowing star of a popular television show in which Truman's life is the subject. Truman does not know that he lives in a false world circumscribed and controlled by the show's producers and the complicity of a cast that includes everyone in his small town. His small town, laid out with retro turn-of-the-century residential architecture and a mall-like downtown, is neat and orderly, and life is an everyday routine of amity and bathos chronicled by five thousand video cameras and enjoyed by a worldwide viewing audience.

Truman is a latter-day George Bailey, who wants to break away and see the world, but when he tries he finds that he is thwarted at every turn, even by his false wife and best friend. Escape only comes when he is able to take a sailboat to what turns out to be the edge of his world, confirming his suspicion that his pleasant small town was in fact a prison that allowed the outside, metro-global world to vicariously retain the myth of the small town.

Nevertheless, there remained a vital current in the American imagination that retained the small town as an ideal preferable to the rising tide of urban discontent. TV series like *The Waltons* helped keep alive the notion that the values that allegedly inhere in small town life could be revived. Ironically, some of the renewed interest in small towns came from the disillusioned political left in America. Young people primarily, disaffected with the Vietnam War, alienated from conventional politics, and seeking freedom to "do their own thing" without the hassles of government or the confining oversight of their parents, sought to establish communes or settle in older small towns. The movement was largely a failure and a disappointment, the emigrant urbanites becoming disillusioned in some cases by the reactionary values and politics of small towns and rural areas that wanted no part of their revolutionary politics and avant-garde attitudes.

Marius pressed the "save" key. Somewhere in the paragraphs analyzing movies of fictional small towns, lay the elements of the reality of Palatine, and the uncertainty of where he fit into the narrative.

XIV

Shihadi

As he had been requested in the phone message left on his phone, Marius flashed his high beams twice when he saw Hisham exit the hospital at 11:45pm. Marius had been waiting in his car for about thirty minutes wondering what the clandestine meeting was about. Hisham tossed the cigarette he hurriedly smoked between the hospital and Marius' car in the parking lot and got in the passenger door.

"Thank you for agreeing to meet me, Mr. Greco, especially like this, at this late hour. But I think it is necessary. This way I will not be seen at your home and, as I will explain, I wish to keep some things from my family at this time. Perhaps I am making a mistake to say these things to you. You are already in a peculiar position as regards my brother and my family, but I am desperate enough to ask if you might be willing to help."

Marius was now relieved that he was probably not going to receive a knife in his ribs, but had already counseled himself that the chosen location, only about thirty yards from the hospital emergency exit, was not the wisest spot for an assassination attempt. His curiosity had now overtaken his caution. "I can't promise anything other than to listen to what you have to say."

"Thank you. I think you already appreciate what my brother's behavior has done to my family. I worry very much for the health of my father. My sister is very depressed and she keeps getting tweets and text messages from those insane Muslim extremists who congratulates her on being the sister of a *shihadi*. These people are only making our lives worse."

Marius nodded. "I'll have to tell all those people who are always bitching that there are no moderate Muslims who speak up against Islamic extremism."

Hisham, made no comment, but just continued. "I did not say very much to you when you came to visit our store, but now things seem to have changed. We still have a mortgage on part of our store and have other dealings with the bank. But last week we received a communication from the bank manager, a man who, like you, seems to understand the complexities of things. He was kind enough to notify me that there had been a communication to the bank from an attorney who is representing the families of the victims of my brother in a lawsuit they will file against my family for what are called wrongful deaths committed by Khalid."

"So, you have not been formally served with any papers regarding this lawsuit as yet?"

"Not yet, but I fear what it will do to my father when it happens, and it might even have an effect upon the teaching position of my sister. I think it would destroy our business. I do not even know where we would find the money for lawyers to defend ourselves. I think you can see that we would be ruined in every way, and I still have not accounted for what the medical costs are going to be for my brother. I am ashamed to say that this evening I seriously considered ending his misery at least and sending him to paradise."

"I appreciate the awful position this will put you in, but I don't know how I could be of any help," Marius responded. "As a matter of fact, I could anticipate that those on the other side of this suit could try to enlist me as a witness of some sort. Why do you think I might help your cause? I am in a rather awkward position."

"I am not certain. But I want to tell you some things you don't know, Mr. Greco." Hisham took a sighing breath, collecting thoughts he had not expressed verbally before. "Khalid was not like his usual self, starting a few weeks before he attacked the school. He came home very late one night in the early hours of the morning. He usually did not come home this late because I knew on this night he wanted for tutoring from one of his classmates. I was worried, but I had already gone to bed when I heard him come in and he went directly into the bathroom. I relaxed a little bit because I knew he was home, and I heard the shower running for some time. I fell asleep while he was still in the bathroom."

Marius wondered where this was going, but said nothing.

"In the morning, he was late coming to breakfast and I only saw him before he left for school. I noticed that he had a—I think you call it an abrasion—on his cheek and a small cut on his forehead. I asked him how he had come by them, and he said he got into a fight with a couple of boys near the soccer field. They called him some racist names. I asked him how he did in the fight and he said he did okay. But I also noticed that he was very stiff in the way he walked when he left for school. At the time I had no idea that he really wasn't going to school."

Marius made a quick calculation that this might've been around the time that Khalid dropped his film class. He tried to remember whether he had noticed any abrasions or bruises on him at that time, but could not recall.

Hisham continued. "Later that day, he was unusually quiet, saying nothing at dinner, or when helping out in the store. Usually, he liked to chat and tell jokes and stories, but that was all gone. From then on he would go to his room and close the door as often as possible. One time I thought I heard him weeping when he was in the shower, but I could not be sure. He was not going to school but spending his time at a spot along the canal where we sometimes used to go swimming when it was very hot. At first, I did not know this because he pretended he was doing homework when he was home and sometimes would mention something about school. My father noticed it too and would ask him if anything was wrong, but he would say that all was fine or that he had some kind of flu or a soccer injury. One weekend he said the team had a friendly match with the team in Rochester and that he had to go there for the weekend and needed one of the cars to drive some teammates. But it was not that. Actually, I think that is when he went to buy those guns.

"I tried to speak with him after I received a phone call from Mrs. Rodriguez, the school secretary, who told me that Khalid had been absent from several of his classes. He gave me some excuse about considering switching to other classes and that he was in between doing that. I know now that he was lying, and I think I know the reason why. I believe that something worse happened to my brother that night that he said he got in a fight with a couple of boys, something that bothered him greatly, that he could not or would not speak about, and also kept him from going to school. I have tried to look for clues of what it might be, but the sheriff's department took his computer, his school notebooks, and I think his phone. One thing that did seem strange to me was that I discovered his belt buckle in the bottom of the metal drum that we use to incinerate some boxes and leaves in the autumn. When I sifted through the ashes in the bottom to see if there was anything else, I found those metal buttons that are typically used on the fly of Levi's pants. There were also a couple of partly melted shirt buttons. He must have burned some clothing."

"That's rather purposeful. Most people just toss or donate old clothes," Marius said.

"There is another thing I should mention, although I don't know if it means anything. I also noticed on a couple of occasions when I have visited my brother in the ICU that he seems to mumble a sound or a word. It was like he was aware that I was there and he was trying to tell me something. He only said it once or twice each time."

"A word?" Marius asked.

"Not one that I know. To me it sounded like 'meek', or 'mick'. But I do not know what that word means."

"Mick could be a name," Marius offered, "an Irish nickname, or slang word."

"For a moment, I think he is coming awake from the coma and I speak to him. But that is all that he says."

"But that is not the reason you wanted to meet with me tonight—to give me a report of the medical and legal problems of your family—is it Hisham?"

"No, sir. I am seeking your assistance. You are regarded as a hero by the people of this community, a man who has respect. You must be the only Christian who would be able to say something in defense of my family because no one else would do that. Otherwise I think that we have no hope, Mr. Greco."

Marius hesitated. As from their first meeting, he again was empathic with the anguish the older brother was suffering, now exacerbated by the prospect of a lawsuit that could destroy what remained of his family. But, again, he felt helpless, as trapped in a web of circumstances as he had felt in Iraq and in LA. Always, it seemed to him, there was this need to assign blame to call some guilty party to account to settle matters, heroes to be honored and villains to be vanquished, good and evil neatly-apportioned. Yet, he knew reality was not like a movie; life was not a narrative that concluded with a walk off into the sunset. It was messy and often inconclusive; it had history. Everything did not happen for a reason, but that did not mean there were not causes. It sure as hell wasn't turning out to be a "wonderful life" in Palatine for the Aziz family, or for the families of Khalid's victims. Finally, the only response he could muster was, "I am not a Christian."

Hisham looked surprised. "Are you a Jew?"

"Even worse as far as helping your family is concerned, I'm afraid. I am an atheist."

Hisham was shocked. "An atheist? I don't understand how you can be against God, Mr. Greco."

"I'm not *against* God, as you say, or Allah, or Yahweh, or any of the thousands of other gods. I cannot be against something I do not even believe exists. For an atheist, there is *nothing* to be against. Do you understand that?"

"I don't know. How can you live without God? It seems impossible."

"Not really, although sometimes think it would be easier to just submit to faith. Isn't that what Islam means—submission?"

"Yes."

"I wouldn't recommend it for someone with your religion. Infidels can be killed for rejecting Islam."

"Atheists are the enemy of Islam, then."

"No. We just do not believe in the existence of a supreme being that is the cause of all existence. But I will admit that atheists think that it might be better if no religions existed because religion seems to have historically caused so much war and human misery. That is why all religions regard us as the enemy—because our disbelief challenges their power. Polls have shown that Americans would elect a Muslim for president over an atheist."

Hisham sat in confused silence. After a while Marius spoke. "I am sorry for what this is all doing to your family, but I don't see any way I can help unless I learn something I can communicate to you. I will just try not to make things worse."

Hisham had a look of resignation on his face. "Well, here is a copy of the letter. It came today. Just in case you can think of something that might help, *Inshallah*." He opened the door to leave. "I have missed my prayers for my brother two times today."

"*Inshallah*," Marius repeated as he watched the Iraqi walk through a cone of parking lot light and into the dark.

_____

XV

Wally & Mary's

The drive through what Marius called the "downtown" of Palatine, but what locals called the "high street," always struck him as reminiscent of a movie set on the back lot of one of the major Hollywood studios. Replace the contemporary vehicles with Ford Model T era substitutes, maybe change a sign here and there or the streetlights, and you could probably shoot a credible scene for *Bonnie and Clyde* in what was left of Palatine's main commercial district. The buildings, rarely more than two stories, or a mixture of 19th-century clapboard siding, or early 20th century brick construction, a number of them now clearly vacant and a few boarded up. Flaking paint, cracked windows, and neon signs with nonfunctioning letters announced that this was a town that has seen its best days some time ago. "Mom and pop" stores and outmoded commercial operations like five and dimes had long been superseded by box stores and malls and now online shopping. There was little traffic on streets riddled with potholes, plenty of parking space, and an overall appearance of dereliction and decline.

The town's halcyon economic days came to an end in the 1950s after a period in which local industries were established to assemble floating bridges and runway materials that were floated down the canal to the coast to be loaded on liberty ships for World War II. When that came to a halt with victory, town leaders made some attempt to refashion the plants into enterprises for peacetime production, but lacked the political clout and connection to the emergent Interstate highway system. The postwar concentration was in the suburbs. This had been the fate of many small towns in the second half of the 20th century. One small town near the Pennsylvania border made combat boots for the US Army. After the war, the boots contract was ironically awarded to a company in Japan. Like many small towns, it was a one-industry town and went into economic and population decline.

Population shrinkage and changes in demographics told the story of many such places. There was some growth from new immigrants due to the depressed real estate prices. It meant new races, languages and religions, setting off a conservative political retrenchment amongst the older locals that burst into open Trumpian xenophobia and White nationalism. Palatine was a setting of sadness, suspicion, and spite that was reflected in the gloomy and foreboding appearance of a bleak and dusty dying town like that of *The Last Picture Show.*

Marius found her right where the receptionist for the *Sentinel* said she would be—at her banquette table of a diner that was so 1950s it might have been a set for a scene in *Rebel Without a Cause.* It might have been considered a perfectly done "retro" style of the postwar urban diner, except for the fact that, on closer inspection, Wally & Mary's Diner was all original 1950s décor.

Marius stood in the doorway for a moment to take it all in. Right underfoot of the original linoleum, a black-and-white checkerboard pattern that had long ago worn through near the entrance and an incongruous square of faux brick had been spliced in. The round seats on the fixed counters stools had been recovered with clear plastic over the cracked original coverings, and the Formica counters, worn bare in spots by countless elbows still had their setups of napkin dispensers, ketchup bottles, salt-and-pepper shakers and sugar bowl. Overhead, lazy fans hung down from a high embossed tin ceiling.

Wally & Mary's Diner was the kind of Americana that thrilled Marius with the same effect that he got when he tracked down some original shooting location for one of his favorite motion pictures. Los Angeles and the San Fernando Valley were full of such sites, but the stumble on a genuine American diner, off the beaten path, evoked a host of noir films. Marius almost forgot his mission.

The only woman was seated at a banquette, hunched over a newspaper, had to be Gloria Sexton. She looked up over the reading glasses that hung at the end of her nose and stared at Marius looking down at her.

"No, I am not the person you are supposed to rendezvous with from your online dating site," she said coldly, returning to her paper.

Marius thought of two or three things that he knew would come out misogynistic, so he did the next best thing.

"I'm Marius Greco."

"I know that," she said, removing her reading glasses and setting them on the table. She gestured for him to sit opposite her. "You've become quite a television celebrity, Mr. Greco. I'm sure that everyone recognizes you now."

"Yeah, as Palatine's resident atheist and Muslim lover, thanks to . . ."

She interrupted. "Peccadilloes, particularly those of out-landers, are part of the stock-in-trade a small-town newspaper reporters, Mr. Greco. But actually, didn't you get a write-up in the LA-Times, inside a few pages, which is where I found the original story?"

"Well, that's kind of the point, isn't it?" Marius responded, "LA isn't exactly a small town and there're bunches of stories like that every day."

"Not quite. These Muslim communities that are settling into American cities are small towns in their own right. A lot of these people come from small towns in the Middle East."

She reached for her pack of Marlboros, took one out, lighted it, and exhaled off to the side with the practiced motions of a veteran smoker. She offered a cigarette to Marius.

"No thanks," he said, looking straight at her. "Look, Ms. Sexton, we could debate the principles of journalism for hours I'm sure, but I am here just to determine whether you intend to build your journalistic career on the rubble of my career."

"Not unless you got some other soiled laundry you'd rather people not know about. I know you think this was a cheap shot, Mr. Greco, but I would not have written the story if it did not appear to have some relationship to the school shooting. As far as I'm concerned right now, I am done with it."

Mary, of Wally & Mary's Diner, appeared at the table with her coffee pot and refilled Gloria's cup reflexively. "You?" She said to Marius.

"Me?

"Coffee?"

"Oh, ah, ya, okay."

Mary produced one of those heavy mug cups from behind her back, placed it on the table, and filled it to the brim. She was as wide as she was tall, but still wore a waitress uniform, and ugly custom-built shoes with Velcro straps. "Let me know if you want something to eat. Meatloaf special today."

"You plan to stay for a while, Mr. Greco?" Gloria said. "If so, I do not recommend the meatloaf. Philly steak sandwich."

"I can go. Enough's been said." He started to get up and reached in his pocket to pay for the coffee.

"Sit." It was almost a command. He retook his seat just as her mobile rang.

"Gotta," she said, answering the call. She immediately began speaking in a language he didn't understand, but sounded like Russian.

Marius wondered why he was sticking around. He did not particularly like this woman. But there was something about her that he found intriguing, something of a character. She was not much to look at, although he felt that with some grooming and makeup she could be more appealing. She wore her dark brown hair and what you call the Cleopatra look of straight bangs just above her eyebrows, hair almost to the shoulder and cleanly clipped. She was stoutly built and her unstylish clothes were in a clerkish grey. When she finished her call he asked, "That language was . . . ?"

"Polish. My sister." She lit in another cigarette.

"She lives here, too?"

"No, Ithaca. Teaches hotel management at the Sheraton down at Cornell."

Marius detected that she said everything with a sort of matter-of-fact sadness. Then, to his surprise, she said, "Don't concern yourself with getting too close to the Palatinos—that's what I call 'em—it usually takes two to three generations to fit in. And then some people will never qualify."

"Like me?" he said, and then ventured, "Like us?"

Gloria removed her reading glasses and tilted her head way back, looking over her own cheeks. She allowed herself a little smile, the first look of being at ease.

Mary now came by with two small plates, each with a sliver of pecan pie. She just dropped them on the table without saying a word.

"I think Mary likes you, Mr. Greco," Gloria said. "She's Italian, you know."

Marius smiled. "Maybe it's the Marius name; it has the same root as hers. But you better not be Sicilian. My mother is, and she warned me about Sicilian women. Too volatile, she says."

"Like us, you say, Mr. Greco."

"Make it Marius," he replied.

"Well, maybe you and I, Marius, do have something in common," she said, jabbing a fork into a piece of pie.

"Being?"

"Good ole Roman Catholicism."

"I resigned a long time ago," Marius said.

"You never really get out," she countered, "It gets burnt into your soul—that is if you really have one."

"So, what's your beef with Holy Mother Church?" Marius asked with a smile.

Gloria took a moment, and another bite of pecan pie, and then motioned to Marius to do the same since he hadn't even picked up his fork. "Holy Mother Church does not hold lesbians in very high regard. Neither does my pious mother Joanna Pomorski. By the way, Sexton is my dad's name."

"It's amazing, isn't it," Marius added, "the Church has its convents and monasteries, cloisters to homosexuality, and schools for molesting children, but you are supposed to burn in hell for 'the love that dare not speak its name'. Hypocrites."

"I did all the proper things to be a good Catholic girl, Catholic elementary in high school in Utica, then on to Le Moyne College, the Jesuit liberal arts school in Syracuse. English lit major, and the required Theology courses. But you are right, there's no place for homosexuals in the Church outside of becoming a priest or a nun. So, I was basically disowned by my mother. I think my father died not knowing I was gay."

By now, Marius was becoming convinced that what he had in common with Sexton was that they were both outsiders in this small town culture, the liberal and the lesbian. Something else about her provoked his interest. She was supposed to be the enemy, someone who poked into aspects of his story that he wanted kept secret, but she exposed for her own advantage. He had tracked her to this throwback diner with a vague purpose somewhere between homicide and a "fuck you," only to become reflexively engaged in a conversation out of a noir movie. He knew that it was his abiding addiction to narrative, the same compulsion that had always drawn him to the movies, that was behind his attraction to anthropology, and eventually led him to the small town in which he was wondering whether there might be a story, or at least elements of a story, perhaps characters of a story, that could be contrasted with an iconic American movie about how wonderful it might be to grow up and live in an American small town. And here was a character that did not quite fit in the story, that might be another contradiction to the mythic side of *It's a Wonderful Life*. Her name suggested that she might fit the role of Violet that was played by Gloria Graham, the coquettish girl who had a thing for George Bailey, but Sexton only fit that role in the perverted and honkytonk Pottersville sequence. Then, there was also that "lapsed Catholic" element to her story that snared his interest, although it turned out she was not quite as "lapsed" as he.

"I must say that I was attracted as much by the atheism in your story as I was by Jazmeen," she said. "I have tried to go there many times myself, but just seem to end up treading water."

"Agnosticism?"

"Yes, I suppose," she said.

"Technically, we are all agnostics, since no one really knows, either way."

"The problem is I still feel a need for spiritual connection. I still need some of that belief. I'm a walking contradiction but, somehow, I feel there might be a way to reconcile my sexuality with my metaphysical addiction. Like these," she said, grabbing the pack of Marlboro's again."

"After your research into my background, you should be able to forgive me if I am rather reluctant to engage in any conversion therapy."

"Still, every time I consider the atheist option, I run into the problem of the void it seems to leave for moral guidance. I see chaos, with all of us left out there selfishly self-judging the morality of our actions. Where did we end up when there is no right and no wrong?"

"People are always asking: how can you be moral without believing in God? As though they are afraid to confront their conscience with their intellect rather than their catechism. Atheists are just as moral as believers are moral, maybe more so, because we have compassion, and a sense of justice. Humans are social animals, and like other social animals, we evolved with some core moral values wired into our brains: caring about fairness, caring about loyalty, caring when others are harmed. Would the 'golden rule' exist if Christ never said we should love our neighbors as we love ourselves? Of course. If you think that atheists are running around murdering and raping people because they don't believe in God, we're going to have a hard time proving that statistically or empirically. The fact is that they are way behind in catching up to believers in these categories. Religion doesn't stop people from making war on each other, it only gives them a false moral justification for doing so. So, ask yourself what you would do differently if you did not believe in God or an afterlife. What would you steal and who would you kill first? Better yet, ask yourself whether people might feel differently about your sexual orientation if they weren't consulting the moral guidance of their faith. Goddamnit, you got me preaching."

She smiled. "Goddammit? See, I told you it was burned into your soul. Don't you have a sense of spirituality of any kind?"

"I think I do, but it does not meet the specifications of what you would call a religious faith. Let me give you an example of what I mean. There are remnants of an indigenous Indian tribe of this region—the Onondaga—who reside in an area near a Finger Lake that bears their name. They were here long before anybody else, and part of a group of Indian nations—the Seneca, Oneida, Mohawk, and Iroquois—that were spread over this area. The religion of the Onondaga, if you could call it that, is based on a spirituality toward the earth, that entails respect for it, which, of course is ultimately a respect for the people who occupy it. I could get with that form of spirituality and, in fact, given the degree of pollution, environmental destruction, and immenent global climate change, it's probably the only appropriate faith I can think of.

"If I needed a god to worship, I know where I would find him, or 'it' would be a better way of putting it. It's right up there in the sky. It's the source of all life on earth. It makes the winds blow, it makes rain, it makes the seasons happen, it gives things light and color. It does everything. If I had to worship, or fear, anything, it would be the rage, or the abandonment of Ra, the sun God. And you know what? He's better than all those other gods that guys who want power through religion have conjured up, the invisible Gods that have to be invisible because then they need priests, gurus, shamans, rabbis, mullahs and the rest to interpret for us what these gods want of us. But their gods are no-show gods; they never show up. Whereas good old Ra, he shows up every day, every fucking day. He's a working-class god. And all he wants us to do is respect the way that he works, because he's working for us. He's not interested in micro-managing your life, or insisting that you give money to your pastor so he can refuel his executive jet, or that you show deference to your priest when he buggers the altar boy, because he's not committing a crime, just a sin. Ah, shit, there I go again. Enough of your journalistic provocation."

"I'm glad I got you to elaborate on your atheistic views," she said. "They answer a lot of questions that came up when I was doing that piece on you, wondering what it is you said to Jazmeen".

"I am assuming that we have been, as you journalists would say, 'off the record' for sometime now in this discussion. Correct?"

"Yes, I hope so. I have been rather forthcoming myself, wouldn't you say?"

Marius readjusted himself on the uncomfortable bank of his seat. "Okay then. Consider the mind and the heart. I cannot make myself believe in God, and angels and saints and heaven, the Trinity and the rest of it, because my mind just refuses to accept that stuff. My mind, whether it's trained in the critical faculties associated with being a social scientist, or whatever, just shuts down and refuses to believe in all of that fantasy."

"What's wrong with a little fantasy? Isn't it a very human thing to create forms of existence that are not real, but entertain and comfort us?"

Marius grimaced. "Have you ever seen the movie *It's a Wonderful Life*? It's shown several times every Christmas. It starts out with a couple of angels in heaven talking about a guy who's having an existential crisis in a small town just like this in upstate New York. So, every kid watching this movie gets the idea that there's an angel up there looking out for everybody down here and whose job is to help us achieve a wonderful life in a small town where everybody loves you. Pretty powerful propaganda for religion. Who the hell would not want to believe in that scenario? Fantasy is not some innocent stuff for children's fairytales. It is not that far from witch-burning, notions of Aryan supremacy, or the idea that homosexuals are the devil's spawn. You see, it's all a part of that indoctrination process that doesn't just come with our churches, but is cleverly enmeshed with what little is left of our secular world. It's in the air we breathe, from our first breath to our last—belief. Belief in that for which we have no evidence of its existence, but makes us compliant little ciphers."

"Belief is really the lazy-minded person's way of dealing with reality. Science, philosophy, history, all that "liberal artsy-fartsy" stuff, are hard to do and require time and diligence. Better to choose your *one*-book, your bible, quran, torah, or book of surahs, whatever, get your story straight, your do's and don'ts all aligned and, of course, your eschatology correct. Better to have a more seamlessly imagined origin of the universe particularly, its *purpose*. Yes, purpose is important, because it serves the narrative functions of belief. Of course, all of this can come more-packaged for the belief-needy—no assembly or batteries needed, no arduous doubt management, or heavy lifting of critical thinking required. You see, there's a reason for all of this reality, and *reason* (and here I am not referring to the process of intellection, but quite the opposite), is the explanation that "everything happens for a reason." Everything moves the plot along—children with leukemia, war, natural disaster, and one presumes murder, genocide, race hatred, etc.—must all occur for a reason, part of the divine plan. The reason might be difficult to understand or accept, but that's okay, too, because God works his wonders "in mysterious ways.""

"So, do you believe in anything, Mr. Greco?"

"Plenty. But that will have to be for another time."

"Then indulge me please, for one more question that has been plaguing me," she said.

"Jazmeen?"

She nodded.

"The heart is another matter. It is whether you believe yourself. So, I will admit that there was nothing I could do to keep myself from falling in love with Jazmeen. Just as there was no way that my heart could really love a God that I did not know in any way, shape or form, there was no way that I could prevent myself from loving her. A Shiite Muslim girl, years younger than me and from a different culture; what guardian angel could've thought that one up?"

"But how does it end? Forgive me; it's journalistic instinct."

"I came here to kill you for prying open my life in your damn newspaper. Then, because I am some garrulous Italian jerk who is the foil for a clever journo, I end up spilling my guts."

"No worries. It's all off the record, unless and until you tell me otherwise."

Marius smiled as he extracted his wallet, but she stopped him. "On me," she said. He extracted a quarter from his pocket and put it in the slot of the ancient jukebox player with flip cards of 1950s hit parade songs, selected one, pressed the buttons, and took his leave. As he walked to the door he could hear the music.

Volare, oh oh
Cantare, oh oh oh oh
Let's fly way up to the clouds
Away from the maddening crowds
We can sing in the glow of a star that I know of
Where lovers enjoy peace of mind
Let us leave the confusion and all disillusion behind
Just like birds of a feather, a rainbow together we'll find

XVI

Small Town

Marius had been humming the melody of Volare all the way home, but running beside it in his mind were flashes of connection between his surprise encounter with Gloria Sexton at the Wally & Mary's Diner and *It's a Wonderful Life*.

"Mr. Gower's pharmacy and soda shop," he announced to himself with satisfaction as some synapses finally made a connection for him as he tossed his keys on the table, "Mr. Gower," he repeated to keep this thought from slipping away. He grabbed a beer from the fridge and made directly for his computer.

Wally & Mary's Diner had brought him to that scene in *It's a Wonderful Life* of the young George Bailey at the soda counter of Mr. Gower's pharmacy, with the young Mary and Violet a few stools down admiring George as he waited to make a pharmacy delivery for Mr. Gower. Marius smiled to himself as he remembered how young, wanderlustful George boasted that his magazine subscription made him a "member" of the National Geographic Society. As a movie scene, it is a masterful piece of Frank Capra, a scene of youthful innocence and ambition that is paid off subsequently in the relationship between George and Mary, but also was seen with the melancholy shadow of Mr. Gower's tragic alcohol-induced error. Wally & Mary's Diner wasn't quite the same setting, but there was some mnemonic trigger in it—those heavy coffee mugs, the Formica counters, the ceiling fans or the juke box—something to do with nostalgia, for a remembrance of things past that really were not quite that way.

He struggled to get these thoughts and connections down in his typo-riddled dissertation notes lest the memories slip away. "Conservatism," that was the connection he was looking for.

Subject: *Notes on Nihil Aeternam Est*

Big-city people are familiar with change—that "*nothing is forever*—is part of the process of urbanism. Small- town people are afraid, or at least skeptical, of change. They seem apprehensive that something is going to come along and upset what they think is an idyllic way of life. That's what makes them conservative. They hold onto some imaginary past, some Norman Rockwell poster version of America that really never was, and now any politician can summon and articulate that myth for them can mold them like putty. They prefer their secular law in the form of Justice Scalia constitutional "originalism," and their moral law in the form of King James "biblical literalism."

They bay at the moon of modernism, the demon of change that seems to make the world and its events so uncertain, so threatening to their comforting certainties and disdainful of their sacred absolutes. So, they strain to hold back the assault on all they regard as good and true—and forever. To most Palatinos, conservative politics and religious faith are the means to preserve the proper values and return to the circumstances of the best expression of their beloved political leaders—the "good ole days." Never mind that there were no "good ole days," only some badly-remembered bad ole days that were less bad than others. But you won't convince people who call themselves Conservatives of that. Their memories are saturated in a gauze-filtered nostalgic dreamscape.

Yet, within the mnemonic orbit of the "Greatest Generation" is Jim Crow: "No Irish, or Italians, Need Apply," castrating gays, segregation and lynching of Blacks, imprisoning and robbing of Japanese Americans, and gender attitudes that idealize keeping women rotating between the kitchen and the maternity ward. They reflexively resist changes to these conditions, still pining for some mythical "Mourning in America" of some misty past. The present has plenty wrong with it, but its parent is the past.

In a political and social context, such attitudes become problematic in that there are large numbers of people in small towns like Palatine and their rural hinterlands who feel that their nostalgic world—a world that is heavily falsified with wishful imagination—has gone down the toilet, or has been sundered by some foreign, godless, unpatriotic plot that is destroying American society as they knew and loved it. They want it back, or protected from any further degradation—they *want not to conserve it, but to re-constitute and perpetuate it,* like one of those Civil War reenactments where the white people retain their supremacy.

Such attitudes have become rooted in a fictional belief that the founding Fathers were bent on creating a Christian nation that would morally install a society where women only worked in kitchens and laundries, and did not have birth control or access to abortions and were subservient to their husbands, when LGBT people stayed out of sight and public life, cannabis was illegal, Black athletes stood respectfully for the national anthem, minorities "knew their place," and prayer was allowed in schools, but not reference to evolution or climate change.

Conservatism and the Small Town

Dickens had it right; usually, when it was the "best of times," it was also "the worst of times," at least for somebody. But politicians, especially conservative politicians are forever invoking a return to something in the past, a "morning in America," a return to some earlier, better, time and place.

So, each Christmas (a conservative myth in its own right) when *It's a Wonderful Life* is reprised for a new generation, the nostalgic myths of the small town— tradition, familism, Christian religious faith—are again displayed to evoke a remembrance and reverence for the way things (supposedly) used to be.

Greek philosopher Heraclitus said: "all things change, nothing remains the same." It is a truth that is the bane of the conservative who basically desires a Reagan's "Morning in America," or Trump's "Make America Great Again," a fictional belief that slave-owning founding Fathers were bent on creating a Christian nation where all were "created equal."

Marius stopped typing to dig into a notebook, flipping

through pages filled with sketches and notations in different inks and pencil, and coffee and food stains. In a few minutes he found the quote he was looking for and returned to typing.

Cardinal John Henry Newman wrote in his "theory of development": "All conservatism is based on the idea that if you leave things alone you leave them as they are. But you do not. If you leave the thing alone, you leave it to a torrent of change. If you leave a white post alone it will soon be a black post. If you particularly want it to be white you must always be painting it again; that is, you must be always having a revolution. Briefly, if you want the old white post you must have a new white post."

Trying to hold back change by denying the progress of science and the conduct of social life is futile. Holding onto the Bible as the prime description and guide to life is to be stuck in a static fairytale of error, falsehood, prejudice and inconsistency written by men in a time when the main form of life was pastoral with no relevance for an age in which billions of humans could destroy their planet several different ways.

Most of these conservatives are Whites who see their self-anointed racial hegemony over American society slipping away in demographic realities that have caused them to haul out their Nazi regalia, erect statues to Confederate generals and barriers to immigration and minority voting, arm themselves against imagined insurgencies, and cozy up to fascism.

Their delusional idyllic world is gone, much of it in a haze of mnemonic filter that leaves out all the negative and keeps the prom photo of when they weighed forty pounds less and had a whole head of hair, juke boxes played their favorite Hit Parade tunes, and is redolent of the first time they had sex in the back seat of that '49 Ford coupe that has long gone to the junkyard. They cling to that sinking existential Titanic that is their youth, that mythic Camelot period of time between the end of World War II and the beginning of those revolutionary 1960s. They would prefer their America in red, white and blue, to the one that is increasingly and demographically black, brown, and yellow.

Conservatives need to heed the words of Heraclitus that "all things change, nothing remains the same." The future cannot be the past.

Marius considered that his doctoral committee might find some of these observations outside the canon of proper research methodology—he could hear his chairman admonishing "It's a dissertation, not an op-ed"—but for the present he would leave it in. It made him feel good.

Marius clicked the "save" key, took a swig of his beer that had warmed and flattened, and let his eyes focus on the white birches in the backyard. He went back and read over his work, and it occurred to him that a relationship with a place could be like a relationship with a person; familiarity could breed an ambivalence as imperfections were allowed time to bleed through, as one became more engaged with the "subject." This was that hazard of his "participant/observer" methodology with its objective-subjective interface. He started a new paragraph.

Americans are historically ambivalent about their urbanism. More and more of them live in big cities and metropolitan areas, but polls consistently show that the majority of people actually yearn to live in small towns and rural areas, despite having no real experience of farming or village life. That has been the bedrock of the myth of the small town in America, and the appeal of *It's a Wonderful Life* as it appears every Christmas, when Americans are most susceptible to nostalgia and myth, when it comes with the spiciness of mulled wine, the aroma of pine, and the bells that make for winged angels. Who would gainsay that?

XVII

Video Night in Palatine

Marius was surprised when he opened the door, his left hand holding the baseball bat that he now kept beside it.

"Hisham," he said, surprised. "What's up?" It was 12:45 a.m., and the Iraqi's face was inscrutable with a mix of emotions. For a few more moments he said nothing and Marius instinctively kept a grip on the bat.

"I apologize for coming like this, Mr. Greco. I waited until this late time because I did not want people to see me come to your home. They might become angry, more angry than they are because of things they read in the newspaper and talking that they make among themselves. They even say things in front of me in my store, I think to make me feel bad. They call you 'Muslim killer'."

"Fuck them. You shouldn't pay any attention to those damn bigots. I'm sorry that my problems are making things worse for you, but there isn't much I can do about it. If I didn't have to finish my research, I would just kiss this place off the way I'm feeling right now. You didn't come here tonight to tell me just that, did you? Do you have some news about your brother? C'mon in," Marius said, leaning the bat against the corner behind the door and pushing the door open.

Marius knew that there were only two options: Khalid had either regained consciousness or was dead, by whatever means.

"But first I must speak of something else. My father does not want me to have anything to do with you. So, you must not say anything in the newspapers or on the television about our acquaintance."

"Why? I have only tried to help your family as best I can." Marius said.

"He read that you are an infidel, and that is like a devil to him. He says you can only bring us more misfortune."

Marius could feel his anger rising. "Jesus, you come here in the middle of the night with this religious superstition bull-shit, Hisham."

"He just believes that you have no morality because you have no god," Hisham replied. "Yeah, well you can just go back to your old man, thank him for me for his service to the US military, and then tell him he can stick his moral judgments up his ass. And ask him who he thinks cares more for his son, Allah, or Mr. Greco? Now, if you don't mind, I have some sleeping to do." Marius moved toward the door and opened it for Hisham to leave. "I thought you might have had some news about your brother."

"Not about my brother. About this," Hisham said, holding out his hand with the cell phone in it. "It's Khalid's phone."

"Really?" Marius said, reaching out for it. "You mean to tell me that the police did not seize this?"

"I remember them looking for it, the FBI, and asking me where it was. I did not know. I guess they never found it. But they took his computer and game player thing. I found the phone yesterday in the storage room. I think Khalid might have left it there when he was putting the bags of Iraqi rice up on the shelf. I don't think he was hiding it, because it was just laying on the shelf next to the rice, but you have to be up on the ladder to see it. They didn't look up there." He stopped for a moment, as if to collect himself for what he was about to say next.

Marius motioned for him to sit down. "Wanna beer or something?"

"*La shukran*," he replied, declining. "I came about what is on that phone."

"A call?"

"No, . . . a video."

"About what?" Marius asked, anticipating something upsetting about Khalid. Maybe one of those confessions that *shihadi* made just before a suicide attack.

"I can only show this to you, Mr. Greco. I could not even show it to my father or my sister. But I need for you to look at it and tell me whether you think it helps to explain why my brother did this horrible thing. It might take away one kind of pain from me, but it gives me another. In some ways it is even worse for our family." He took the phone back, navigated to find a video, and handed it back to Marius.

Marius clicked on the video and did his best to remain dispassionate while viewing it. It was less than two minutes long, and somewhat jerky and unfocused in spots, but there was no doubt about what it showed. The only identifiable face was that of Khalid. When the pig appeared at the end of the clip, Marius muttered, "Aw, those motherfuckers, those goddamn motherfuckers. I am so sorry, Hisham, so sorry, I know what this means."

"My brother could never have a normal life after this. No life with a woman because of this insult to his body, his person, and his faith. They ruined my brother's life, and that of his family also."

"Yes, I know, *Sahib*." It was the first time he used the word friend. "I am so sorry for you . . . for all of you." Marius could feel the tears welling up in his eyes, the same reaction he had when he heard the news about what Jazmeen's brothers had done to her. Again, he felt that horrible wrenching in his gut, a combination of anger, regret, and sorrow. The two men sat together, silent for a few minutes. Then Marius spoke.

"How did this get on his phone? They wouldn't take this with his own phone and then give it back to him. They would want a copy, so they could torment him—and force him to remain silent about it. This is exculpatory, but they know he would never be able to use it."

"I don't know this word, excul . . . that you use," Hisham said.

"It means that this video could be used in a court of law as an argument to excuse what Khalid did at the school."

"No, no, no, *abadan*, never, never." Hisham exclaimed.

"I understand," Marius said, "I, ah . . . [he strained to find the word] . . . *yifham*. I understand." It was all terrible, but the pig was the final, most humiliating, insult of all. "So how did it get on Khalid's phone, is the question."

"I have thought about this. Khalid had his phone synched with his computer so that things like his contacts and calendar and photos would be the same in each. I think that he was sent the video in an email, because it is a mpeg file. When he connected his phone to the computer it put a copy of this video on the phone. Maybe he did not even know it was there."

"Shit," Marius said, "that means if the Sheriff has the computer, then he also has the video. He may already have seen it. So, why has he not indicated that he has this information? Because he also knows that it is exculpatory? Or, perhaps he has told the Mayor, or somebody else with power or influence, and has been told to keep quiet about this."

"I don't understand where you are leading with this, Marius," Hisham asked.

"I am saying that I think the information is safe from becoming public, for now at least. What we need to think about is if there is some way to keep it from ever becoming exposed. I think there might be one sure way of that."

"What is that?" Hisham asked.

"I'm not sure just yet. But right now, I need you to send that video to my phone in a text message."

Hisham gave Marius a worried look.

"Don't worry. I know a way to transfer it to a thumb drive for it will be safe and I will delete it from everything else. I have no doubt you'll keep that phone somewhere safe. I'll be in touch."

Hisham had a worried look on his face.

"You are going to have to trust the infidel on this one, Hisham. We both have our balls in the ringer, and dammit, I am not going to let this town crank it."

"I do not know what you are saying, Mr. Greco."

"Never mind, just trust me." Marius opened the door and Hisham stepped through. "And if it makes you feel any better, you can pray."

"I will," Hisham replied.

Marius smiled. "And while you're at it, thank Allah for the invention of the iPhone, because without it we would really be fucked."

XVIII

Rebel Without a Cause

Marius stopped at Starbucks to get the biggest latte so he could avoid the wretched coffee in the faculty room. It was his first day back on campus since the Gloria Sexton article and he had no idea what kind of reception awaited him in his classroom. He had been telling himself all morning that he didn't owe anybody any explanation or apology for anything, and yet he still felt like the antichrist walking into a papal conclave. The class quieted down immediately as he entered and dropped his notes on the podium.

"Alright, today we're going to change things up a little bit. I have been showing you stuff from another era, about small towns. But today we'll see something that might be easier for you to relate to. It's one of the seminal films in a genre that did not exist in Hollywood before the mid-1950s, what I like to call the coming-of-age youth film. They're commonplace today, especially since the youth niche has probably become the most lucrative segment of the film-viewing market. Young people like to see films about themselves, and the niche has even been divided into subsets that are referred to as 'teen' or twentysomethings or thirtysomethings films.

"For me, *Rebel Without a Cause*, the 1955 film I will screen today, is the benchmark. For some it is *Blackboard Jungle*, which also came out in 1955, the same year that rock and roll music began to gain widespread popularity among American youth. Sidney Poitier played a New York high schooler in *Blackboard*. You might remember him as 'they call me Mr. Tibbs'. But maybe I am prejudiced because *Rebel* was set in LA, my city, and stars another male actor you might have heard about. But more about him later.

"By the mid-fifties, surveys by movie producers had shown that a quarter of movie attendees were between fifteen and twenty-five years of age. So, we got titles like *The Delinquents*, *Dragstrip Girl*, *Hot Rod Rumble*, *High School Confidential*, and even *I was a Teenage Werewolf*. Most of their themes were thinly veiled, and often pathetic, attempts to express sexual frustration, youth's rebellion, against not being understood, even though youth did not quite understand itself.

"Neither child nor adult, neither fish nor fowl, teens were out of synch with their own hormones. Much of that biology centered on their coming of age sexually. Rock 'n roll ballads and teen films bemoaned frustrated teenage love, repressed sexual desires, and pleasures forbidden to their demographic. Adults became puritanical wardens enforcing a morality that seemed cruel and unfair, since nearly all of this lovelorn demographic lived at home.

"The sexuality of teenagers has no defined transition between proscription and permission. If previous generations and societies had their rites of passage, be they tests of courage or ceremonial passages conferred by religious rites, such as bar mitzvah and confirmation, the new generation of youth had none. At age thirteen, a young man of the 1950s was hardly ready to take his place among the warriors, fathers, and landowners of his society. He was more likely to be sweating a passing grade in algebra to get into college. What avenues for expression of manhood remained were left to those who could make varsity sports teams', one of the only remaining equivalents of a warrior class and legitimized opportunities to demonstrate manhood. For the rest of teenaged males, drinking to excess, driving fast, taking drugs, and playing at gangs had to suffice to express primal urges and manhood rites.

"Okay, that should be enough of an introduction. We don't want to spoil the movie. So, let's have a look and see what you think." Marius dimmed the lights, turned on the projection system and settled back to enjoy again a movie he had seen so many times his lips could mimic all of the dialogue. He had also visited nearly every remaining shooting location for the picture in LA.

After the credits rolled, he returned to the rostrum as the students crumpled up their empty bags of snacks.

"Well, there you have it," Marius began, "the beginning of 'parents don't understand their kids' theme that went viral and set things up for those tumultuous 'sixties' you have all heard about. Their kids don't respect them. Some parents are not even there at all. So, youth don't know what to do, what to be guided by, except each other. In this movie two boys are killed, both under stupid conditions. This was right after World War II, after we made the world safe for democracy. We had vanquished the enemies of peace and freedom but, apparently, we didn't know what to do with that peace and freedom and many movies reflected that. Where was the moral guidance to come from? What do you think this film says about American culture, at least at the time your grandparents were your age?"

Isiah Evers opened the discourse with his favorite concern. "I noticed that the only Black person in this movie is that maid who takes care of that Plato guy. And then it made me think that the only Black person in that *Wonderful Life* movie is also a maid for White people. Was there some kind of a rule back then that you could have only one black person in the movie, and she had to be a servant?"

Marius hoped that the discussion would not be deflected by a reference to a minor character in the movie. But he could not ignore its relevance either.

"We have to admit that the Black maid, or the Black butler as well, were pretty much the Hollywood meme for people of color well into the 1950s. Blacks were rarely seen in roles as a professional, and they sure as hell were never allowed to cross over the wall into a romantic relationship with a White person. For a long time, the only Black actor who was able to get close to this was our old friend 'call me Mr. Tibbs,' Sidney Poitier. Even in 1967 when he plays a highly respected medical doctor engaged to marry a White girl who is the daughter of liberal parents in San Francisco in the movie *Guess Who's Coming to Dinner*, that picture almost did not get made because producers thought it would offend American audiences. Poitier was always scrubbed up and well-dressed, and of course well spoken, in order to qualify for even getting close to crossing the racial line. The actor himself began to resent being used in this way. This situation was much the same for Asian actors. Anna May Wong, an early Asian American actress from Los Angeles who made many movies almost always in a stereotypical Asian role, was never allowed to be in a romantic relationship with a White person. If she got even close to that in a role, she was killed off or committed suicide."

Marius decided that he would go no further with the Anna May Wong story, or with the practice of "yellow face" to substitute for Asian actors. After all, there was not a single Asian in his class, or for that matter, as far as he knew, in Palatine.

"Movies up to this time projected the notion that minorities just did not belong other than in the subordinate roles as servants and workers. But what we have in *Rebel Without a Cause* is another dimension of the problem of belonging, of America's youth struggling to find its place between childhood and adulthood, and even confused and conflicted about what they do with that period of social ennui in between. That's the main question I think this movie raises. So, what do you people think about that?"

As usual, Kenny jumped in. "I have a hard time relating to—what is it that you called it, Mr. Greco? And I just Googled it on my phone—social ennui that these kids—and by the way they look too old to be high school kids—were experiencing in Los Angeles in the 1950s. Maybe there wasn't anything to do. You don't see any sports, or interest in arts, or anything else shown in the movie, so the only things, it seems, that are left to do are to pick knife fights and do those chicken car races off the ends of cliffs. I don't think we kids today—with the Internet, you need to have part-time jobs, hopefully to make enough money to be able to afford college—have time to get bored. Anyway, we don't have any cliffs around here to drive over."

"That's it, Kenny," Philip Armitage, Kenny's friend kidded, "you hit on the reason that we are not like those crazy LA teenagers; we don't have any cliffs to drive our cars over."

"Well, I could always roll this chair into the canal. Wanna race, Phil? Wanna see who chickens out?"

Richard spoke up next. "I really thought that was a cool scene, very tense and dramatic. Both of those guys—Jim Stark in his red jacket, and that Buzz guy in his black leather jacket and concerned about whether his greasy hair looks good—and then Jim asking, 'why did we do this?' I mean it's not just a scene about a car race, it's a scene about having to prove something in order to fit in, in order to belong. I like that it happens so fast. In the morning, Jim is an outsider, his tires are slashed , and by the time he is sitting at the edge of the cliff that night, and Buzz is dead, it seems he's accepted by that girl Judy, and he's like a hero to that screwed up Plato guy."

Marius was pleased that one of his favorite movies had caught on with his class, especially when Joanne Gable, who had not spoken up much, seemed anxious to join in. Maybe something about Natalie Wood registered with her. "Yes, but now all three of them are outsiders, and the rest of Buzz's gang are after them. That Judy girl; I don't get her. She starts out like a snobby bitch to Jim, and then as soon as Buzz is dead, she jumps on the next alpha male. And they sort of start like this new family with their kid, Plato."

Caitlyn Meyers picked up on the family theme. "Did you get that relationship she has with her father? Weird. She wants to sit on his lap and give him a kiss like she's a four-year-old. And then he slaps her down for it."

"Yeah, today that would be a #metoo moment," Kenny quipped.

"And did you notice that they're all sitting around the dinner table dressed in suits and ties, and mom's wearing pearls?" Philip put in. "Who eats like that anymore? Today, everybody would be checking their phone, or texting, or in front of the TV."

Still, Marius wanted to pull these various observations into some sort of focus. "So, do you think that these kinds of conditions youth in LA had to deal with in the 1950s are considerably different from what's going on with youth in a small town in upstate New York?" he asked, mining for some contrasts that might pay dividends for his dissertation research. "What else is there to do? The 50s were sort of that way. After all, the country had just gone through the great depression and World War II, and it was kind of difficult to come up with something as significant and momentous as that. America was sort of taking a breather. Even the Korean War, hardly insignificant, and technically still not over, paled in comparison. But what was not appreciated at the time was that the Depression and the War had vastly altered things structurally and socially in the country itself. Minorities would no longer be content in the role of maids and butlers, and women as cookie-baking subservient handmaidens, and young people were going to fashion their own culture, with its own music, ways of dressing, and hair syles. Soon they would be having sex, challenging the prevailing political ideologies, and driving their parents to wondering what the hell went wrong. There was no

Internet with its Google, Wikipedia, and porn; no phones in everybody's pocket, no selfies, no video games. But there was a social revolution."

The class seemed to be taking a moment to digest all of that, then Justin offered an observation. "God! That guy had a really cool car," he said, referring to James Dean's customized 1948 Mercury. "They even made their cars look different from their parent's cars."

Marius especially liked this theme; cars were quintessentially an LA theme. "In 1955, when *Rebel* was released, cars, particularly customized cars and hot rods, were part of the emerging youth culture. But cars were more than just an artistic expression. The car culture displayed in *Rebel* had become part of the solution to the delayed and frustrated sexuality of youth trapped in the newly acknowledged cohort wedged between childhood and adulthood. In *American Graffiti*, cars functioned as the prime means of display and courtship in the nightly paseo on the main streets of the city and socializing in parking lots and drive-ins. Young men had found an ideal expression for the hormonally-induced need to express manhood. They engaged in risky exploits (the chickee runs had their less deadly alternative in late night drag races), and, perhaps most importantly, their hot rods provided a place of relative privacy for sexual escapades that ranged from simple petting to 'going all the way'."

"Could you explain about 'going all the way' in your car, Mr. Greco?" Philip asked.

"Why? Are you having difficulty, Phil?"

The class laughed as Marius turned the joke back on Phil.

"Cars are not only associated with early sex," Marius elaborated, "but also early death. Early death may well be responsible for giving *Rebel* its cult status. If there is 'nothing to do', perhaps death is an option. Buzz wins the chickee run, but only because his leather jacket becomes ensnared in the door handle, and he plunges over the cliff to a fiery end. James Dean, who played Jim Stark, was a twenty-four-year-old 'teenager' at the time he made *Rebel*. He died shortly thereafter in a car crash, becoming the first martyr of the tormented teenager generation. Co-stars Sal Mineo and Natalie Wood also met tragic premature deaths, by murder and drowning, respectively."

Amy Brinke raised her hand. "I didn't see much rebellion against sexual norms of the times in this movie. Jim seems only mildly infatuated with Judy, looking more for a friend than a sexual encounter. Their love scene in the old mansion near the end of the film is quite innocent, not like the almost raw sex we are fed in today's movies. They seem more concerned with family than with sex, especially with Plato's bonding to the young couple as surrogate parents."

"Yeah, but it still doesn't work out for Plato," Kenny broke in. "He doesn't really trust anybody, running out of that planetarium place and getting himself shot by the cops."

"Now we see that shit every day on TV; cops shooting unarmed Black guys," Isiah interrupted.

There were a couple of groans from the back of the room.

Class time was running out and Marius wanted to wrap a few additional points into his lecture. He took the mention of Plato's death as a segue. "Plato's death is again another illustration of the failure of adults to understand the youth. Cops regard them as a criminal element that justifies the use lethal force. Youth are rebellious and resistant and always seem to be getting in some sort of trouble that parents can't abide. Jim Stark complains that his family is always relocating to supposedly 'protect him.' So, he is always trying to fit in, to adjust, needing to make new friends, but he is always awkward at it, provoking tough guys to call him chicken and, putting off girls with his uncool behavior. In some sense, Jim's plight relates to demographic changes in the American urban landscape. The film was made at a time when more parents could move to the suburbs to avoid unsavory inner city influences on their children. But that was attended by a dislocation that required social skills for fitting in and dealing with the forms of prejudice and exclusion that prevail in such situations. *Rebel* accurately reflects a reality of postwar urban America. While Americans have always been movers in a way that Europeans and Asians tend not to be, they were especially migratory post–World War II. The major factor in American internal migration has been the rise of metropolitanism, with its attendant suburbanization, a trend that remains unabated. In a five-year period, a typical metropolitan area will experience geographic moves by nearly half its population, and over a span of five years, a fifth of the population of the region will have changed."

Clare Streeter, who had not participated in class discussion from the beginning of the term, surprised Marius by raising her hand. She was a pretty blond-haired girl, with peaches and cream complexion, always impeccably coiffed and groomed. She was also the star player and captain of the girls' soccer team, and some said was destined for the Division I athletic scholarship. "Our town of Palatine does not seem to fit in with what you are talking about, Mr. Greco. It's small, with mostly the same old families who sort of run the place. It's like a place that has been left behind by all of this progress and growth."

"That's because when they put in the New York State Thruway, they didn't even give us an exit," Philip said. "People don't even know we're here unless they're interested in the history of the Erie Canal. Nobody uses canals anymore. At least the Mormons up the road in Palmyra got to move to Utah, and now they have an entire state to themselves. Maybe we need to start some weird religion."

There were a few ooohs and giggles, some of the students wondering, now that they knew their teacher was an atheist, what he might say. But Marius dodged it. "Maybe small towns like Palatine used to be that way. Some of them have even died completely. But with mass media and the Internet, you're no longer out of the information loop, and information, data, is the new, hot source of wealth that has taken the place of a lot of the older sources like coal, steel and timber. And you people need no longer be anonymous ciphers, some rubes who don't know what's going on in the world. You can have your own Facebook page and your Twitter account. If you want to, and you're clever, you can let the world know that you're here, as somebody with a new scientific invention, or even as a sex star on a webcam. You can read newspapers from all over the world, and access information on just about anything on Wikipedia. You live in a world of globalization. You just have to hope that climate change won't kill us all off before you get a chance to enjoy it."

"Jim Stark and Buzz didn't have computers and smart phones," Kenny said. "Is this film out of date then? I saw that film, *The Graduate*, too, where their father advises—what's his name—Dustin Hoffman, who is the graduate, to get into 'plastics'. But that's not relevant anymore. You should get into computers, data and artificial intelligence, or Bitcoins or rare earths. Isn't that what I should study in college? I guess I'm just as confused as Jim and Buzz were."

"Relevance might be in the eye of the beholder, to steal a metaphor, Kenny," Marius responded. This was right where he most enjoyed teaching, when it took the discourse between him and students to a new level, when they reached the material's existential relevance. "Aren't we all always trying to 'fit in', Kenny? Not just with this or that group or clique in high school, but with the 'system', whatever that is. Some people have the need to fit in with certain religious expectations."

The classroom was quiet, but in a good way. Marius could sense that he had effected that connection that made the classroom a special environment that online courses would probably not achieve. Now he just wanted to 'tie it up and put a bow on it' as a director friend once told him. He loved the feeling.

"There were many Jim Starks in the emerging American suburbs over six decades ago," Marius continued, "struggling to fit into new surroundings and make new friends. *Rebel* made James Dean the first youth film icon. With his mumbling, naturalistic delivery, and his red jacket of rebellion that he is forever giving away, in addition to his early death in real life, which guaranteed his eternal youth, Dean was the forerunner of a hoard of youth entertainment media stars for his generation. By the 1960s, youth had found a cause or causes: racism, feminism, and protest against the Vietnam War. The rebellion turned political. It also provided a basis for another revolution that had been brewing—the so-called sexual revolution. If young people, even ensconced in their university dormitories, could take on weighty issues of society, then they were entitled, they seemed to reason, to act in other ways like adults. In fact, by engaging in political and social issues, they had found a means to give social leverage to their age cohort. Accordingly, music, dress, and film began to reflect these changes. With events, such as Woodstock, youth culture began to create its own private history."

Marius stopped there; 'stretch it, but don't tear it' was another adage of his director friend. He was happy. So good after the disappointment of that article in the newspaper. Not only was the class the best class so far this term, but it also provided some good material from the students for his dissertation. "Think about it. See ya next time."

As the students were filing out of class, Marius asked Mike Hudson if he would wait for a moment to speak with him. Mike was a big kid, probably 225 pounds of farm work muscle that made him a star linebacker for the Palatine Praetorians. Marius could detect some of Sheriff Cavanaugh's DNA in the boy, the broad, square-jawed face, the blue eyes. Mike waited a little nervously as Marius collected the DVD from the player for the projection system and then approached him.

"I know I don't speak much in class, sir," Mike said.

"That's not what I wanted to see you about, Mike. Got something I want to show you."

XIX

Clincher

The Sheriff's office looked exactly like a small-town sheriff's office ought to look, Marius thought as he was ushered in. But it was better than Sheriff Gillespie's office in *In the Heat of the Night*. Bigger, and with a large New York State flag and a U.S. flag flanking the desk chair, and a variety of civic recognition plaques and photos on the paneled walls.

Cavanaugh was looking at a file on his desk, greeted Marius with a half-smile, but did not extend his hand except to motion for him to sit down. "I have already received a notification from one of your neighbors who apparently feels that the swastikas on your garage door are not good for her property values," the Sheriff said by way of a greeting.

"Yeah, she will probably really be pissed off when a crowd of local neo-Nazis shows up for the Nürnberg-style rally I'm holding for them," Marius replied, stone-faced. Marius really wasn't there to discuss the harassment he had received since the newspaper article, but he would play along for a while. "My stereo speakers will be blaring the Horst Wessel song to give the neighborhood that Third Reich ambiance."

"Well, you seem to be taking it all with a little bit of humor," Cavanaugh replied with a grin.

"Yeah, Nazi's are always good for a laugh."

Marius wondered how pissed off the Sheriff would really be if Marius asked him what he had done to earn those four shiny stars he had pinned to his collar, and what battles he had endured to acquire those dubious campaign ribbons affixed to his chest. He wanted to ask the Sheriff if the green and blue ribbon was awarded for bravery in getting a frightened cat out of a tree. Or, if the red and white ribbon was for pulling over African American drivers for having a "broken taillight." He hated pompous displays of authority. But he stifled vocalizing his contempt and just returned the smile.

"Seriously, are you here to request that I post a cruiser at your curb? I think the attitudes of my deputies might be a little different than last time."

"Really? And why might that be, Sheriff Cavanaugh?"

"I think you have to admit that a case of circumstantial evidence about you has been developing, Mr. Greco. We don't know what your experience in the military in Iraq might've done to you. Then there's that business with your Iraqi girl-friend that has a lot of suspicious elements about it. Further-more, even though your actions during the attack at the high school can be regarded as admirable, there are some people now— and I think this is wild conspiracy theory thinking, but it's there—who speculate about your not totally finishing off Khalid Aziz. Now there is word that you might testify on be-half of his family in a lawsuit matter. Put simply, this is not the way someone who initially earned a substantial amount of local goodwill and praise, would squander it the way you seem to have done. And you might be surprised to know that we have CCTV footage of at least two occasions on which you paid surreptitious visits to the ICU where Khalid Aziz is currently a resident." Cavanaugh put his hands behind his head, and leaned back in his leather chair with a self-satisfied smile.

"It's a small town," was Marius's only reply, but he was having flashes of George Bailey rushing around "Pottersville" trying to find somebody who truly believed that he was the good guy who had sacrificed his dreams for his community.

"So, is there something I can help you with, Mr. Greco?"

"Perhaps. There just might be," Marius replied. He smiled to himself, recalling his meeting with Josh three days before.

Three days earlier, the day before he screened and gave his lecture on *Rebel Without a Cause*, Marius rushed into the equipment room where Josh maintained his video equipment. It was only a day after he had shown Josh the video from Khalid's cell phone. Josh had transferred the video to an editing application that allowed him to scrutinize it in detail.

"What's up, amigo? Has this turned out to be something like the Zapruder film, with the guy on the grassy knoll?"

Josh immediately went over and began clicking some keys on the computer. "Better. You're going to be happy you are friends with a video-genius, Marius. Take a look at this."

On the video screen, Marius could see that Josh had been able to focus in on the right side-view mirror of the pickup truck.

"I think they made a mistake bringing this truck into the barn or the building, because this mirror picked up some reflection that is actually pretty clear when you zoom in on it. Now these guys were wearing masks, but we can see here, as I pull in a little closer, one of these guys slips his Ronald Reagan mask up on top of his head briefly to blow his nose. The one with the camera is apparently behind and off to the side of him, so "Mr. Reagan" figures he's not in the shot. But the mirror picks up his reflection. It's just a couple of seconds that he is exposed, but even with the distortion from the angle because it's only picked up by that little round mirror that's attached to the 'things appear smaller' mirror, he's pretty identifiable. I think I can actually take this shot and mess with it in another editing application that will take out the distortion."

"Holy shit! I can identify this guy already. He's in my film class!" Marius exclaimed.

"Yeah, I've seen him around, too. Isn't he the football player?"

"Yes, he is. But more than that, I think he is related to Sheriff Cavanaugh," Marius said.

"Yeah, and also, he is one of the guys who had his dick up Khalid's ass. Only ET guy, who must be the videographer, might not have done that, but then he would have had to hand off or shut down the phone," Josh surmised.

"Christ, this is fucking explosive!" Marius exclaimed. "Can you send a copy to my phone, and also put one on a flash drive for me. But keep this under wraps. I don't want anybody to know about it. Remember, Hisham gave this to me in strictest confidence, and he hasn't seen any faces."

"Gotcha. But I need an address to send my invoice," Josh joked.

"Payment will be accepted in liquid form at Lupita's."

***

Marius allowed Cavanaugh his moment of triumph before he reached into his pocket and took out his phone. He turned on the phone's voice recorder and then switched to the screen that had the video.

"There's something I think you ought to see, Sheriff," he said as he handed the phone across the desk. "Just click the video play button."

Marius watched as the Sheriff's face took on a rosy complexion. As his jaw muscles tightened, he rubbed his hand over his brush cut hair. Marius could detect a flicker of surprise in his eyes.

"That's right," Marius said, "the version that is on Khalid's computer, and which I assume you might have already seen, although perhaps nobody else, does not have that one final shot—that familiar face that somehow got caught reflected in a truck's mirror."

Cavanaugh set the phone down on his desk, sat back in his chair, and glared at Marius. "I suppose there is some point in this, you smartass wop," he said.

Marius just smiled at the ethnic slur. "Well, I suppose that a law enforcement officer who has an open investigation of an alleged terrorist attack might be interested in whether there might have been a *motive* for that attack. Furthermore, I suppose there are authorities, such as Homeland Security and the FBI, who might also be interested in that video." Marius paused for a second. "They might also be curious why it has been sitting on that computer that is in your possession, rather than being disclosed to them." Marius was taking a chance with this last supposition, betting that Cavanaugh had kept quiet about the video because he had no idea of the identity of the boys. Now that he had the identity of at least one of them, he had an even greater dilemma.

"Just what is it that you hope to achieve by your possession of this information, Mr. Greco?"

"What I think we all want to achieve, Sheriff Cavanaugh, is truth, and justice, with a minimum of collateral injury, if possible, especially to young people who have their whole lives and football careers ahead of them."

Cavanaugh now understood that Marius had identified Mick Hudson. "I don't want to see that kid go down for one bad mistake. He hasn't had it all easy since my brother-in-law never came back from Vietnam. He's still MIA. So, my nephew has pretty much grown up with me as his surrogate father. Every year we spend a couple of weeks camping and fishing at Lake Champlain. It's become one the most important things in my life, since I don't have any kids of my . . .".

"Somewhere along the line he picked up some kinky notions, Sheriff," Marius interrupted coldly, assured that he had seized the high ground. "The only thing I know about this kid is that if he falls off your fishing boat and is eaten by piranhas,

I won't give a shit. And I am not unaware of the fact that if he goes down, there's a very good chance you could well go down with him."

The Sheriff straightened up in his chair. "I just want to say that he's not a bad kid. He's never been in trouble before and, now that he has a chance for a football scholarship to a Division I college, he would make our family and my sister proud. I hope you're going to take that into account." Cavanaugh had lost most of his bluster, Marius knew he had to have some further assurances.

"Just between us boys, Sheriff, I think we should have some understanding. First, about Khalid. He could die at any time of course, but you should not want that to happen, certainly by other than natural causes."

"Was it in Iraq that you became an Arab lover? Or, that Jazmeen girl? I don't get it with you and this fucking terrorist kid who killed four people in my town. I'm beginning to think that some people around here have it right about you."

"Yeah, well actions have antecedents. And I have a video tape with some damned incriminating antecedents. Maybe the public will come to an understanding that this so-called terrorist was not interested in establishing an ISIS caliphate in upstate New York, but was driven by vengeance for having been humiliated. Maybe, this whole damn town bears some responsibility for what happened in that school because its hypocritical religious attitudes diminish some people—and I am beginning to include myself among them—to the point where it justifies their torturing and humiliating them. But to shorten that up for you Sheriff, fuck you."

Cavanaugh just glared. "You have other terms, wise guy?"

"Second, if you want this video to remain something that only a very few people know about, your cooperation might be required in a couple of other matters. I will let you know about them later, but you shouldn't be concerned that you will be asked to be helpful in some felonious activity, just be asked to play stupid, or look the other way. In any case, it should be nothing that would be anywhere as bad as what would happen if that video went public."

"You realize that what you're suggesting implicates you in the crime of conspiracy, don't you?"

"I've watched a lot of crime movies."

Marius reached over the desk and picked up the mobile phone. Cavanaugh made no effort to prevent him. "Lastly, nothing unfortunate happens to me either. Copies of this video and explanatory material are also in the possession of two separate people with instructions of what to do should I have an unfortunate accident. So, you had better hope that none of those religious zealot assholes who are throwing lethal bricks through my window is a major league pitcher. And, oh, just in case you can't remember the details of any of this discussion we have had since I came in here [Marius held up the phone] I've recorded our conversation."

Just after he closed the office door, Marius heard a loud smashing sound followed by the tinkling of broken glass to the floor, which he assumed was produced by the small bronze bust paperweight of Ronald Reagan crashing into the picture of Sheriff Cavanaugh and his nephew holding up a large bass in a fishing boat on Lake Champlain.

When Marius left the Sheriff's Department, he sat in his car for a few minutes to reassess what had just transpired. He was surprised that he was feeling a little bit nervous. But he was still thinking clearly, and he wondered why Cavanaugh had not brought up the four other guys in the video. Apparently, the Sheriff had not approached his nephew.

But Marius had.

Two days before he made the meeting with Cavanaugh, Marius summoned Mick Hudson as he was leaving class on *Rebel Without a Cause*. He waited for all the other students to clear the room before shutting the door. Mick mistakenly thought the matter had something to do with his classwork, but Marius quickly got to the point. As he had done with the Sheriff, he took out the phone and asked the young man to look at the video, and watched the blood drain from the boy's face. Mick obviously knew that there was a video, but he had no idea that his face had been exposed in that corner of the side-view mirror.

Mick said nothing, his face a mixture of guilt and shame. Marius didn't ask for any explanation, or render any opinion or judgment. He got right to the point: "Now, you're going to tell me who the other guys are, or I will leave you to guess how many people are going to find out about this video. Write their names on this piece of paper."

Mick printed the names: Jacob Johnson; Ross Eckard; Pete Vionovich; Andrew Borden. He handed the paper to Marius and then elaborated: "Jacob is the brother of Abner, one of the guys who was killed. He's the one wearing the ET mask. And Ross is Brent's brother, who was wounded." He looked like he was about to cry. "Please don't . . .".

But Marius interrupted. "Shut up. Here's what you're going to do now. You're going to go to the rest of your gang and let them know about this video and that everybody's identity is blown—but it's currently under wraps. Two of these guys are from families who are bringing a lawsuit against the Aziz family. You were going to tell these guys that if that lawsuit is not dropped the whole fucking universe is going to get to see this video and there are going to be credits that roll at the end with everybody's name in them. You're going to send me an email within 24 hours that the suit has been dropped and a letter to that effect is being sent to the Aziz family. Agreed?"

Hudson nodded, said "yes, sir," and shuffled out of the room.

Back in his car, Marius thought again that he could have just packed up gone back to LA, or some other place, and be done with it. But there was that side of him that just did not like being pushed around, that Italian insistence on *respetto*, that demanded respect. He also felt he had something to prove, to himself as well as to others, about morality and atheism. He needed to prove his secular humanism was not a withdrawal from the world, but an engagement, principled and preferable to conventional religious hypocrisy. Even so, he might have left it all behind—were it not for Jazmeen.

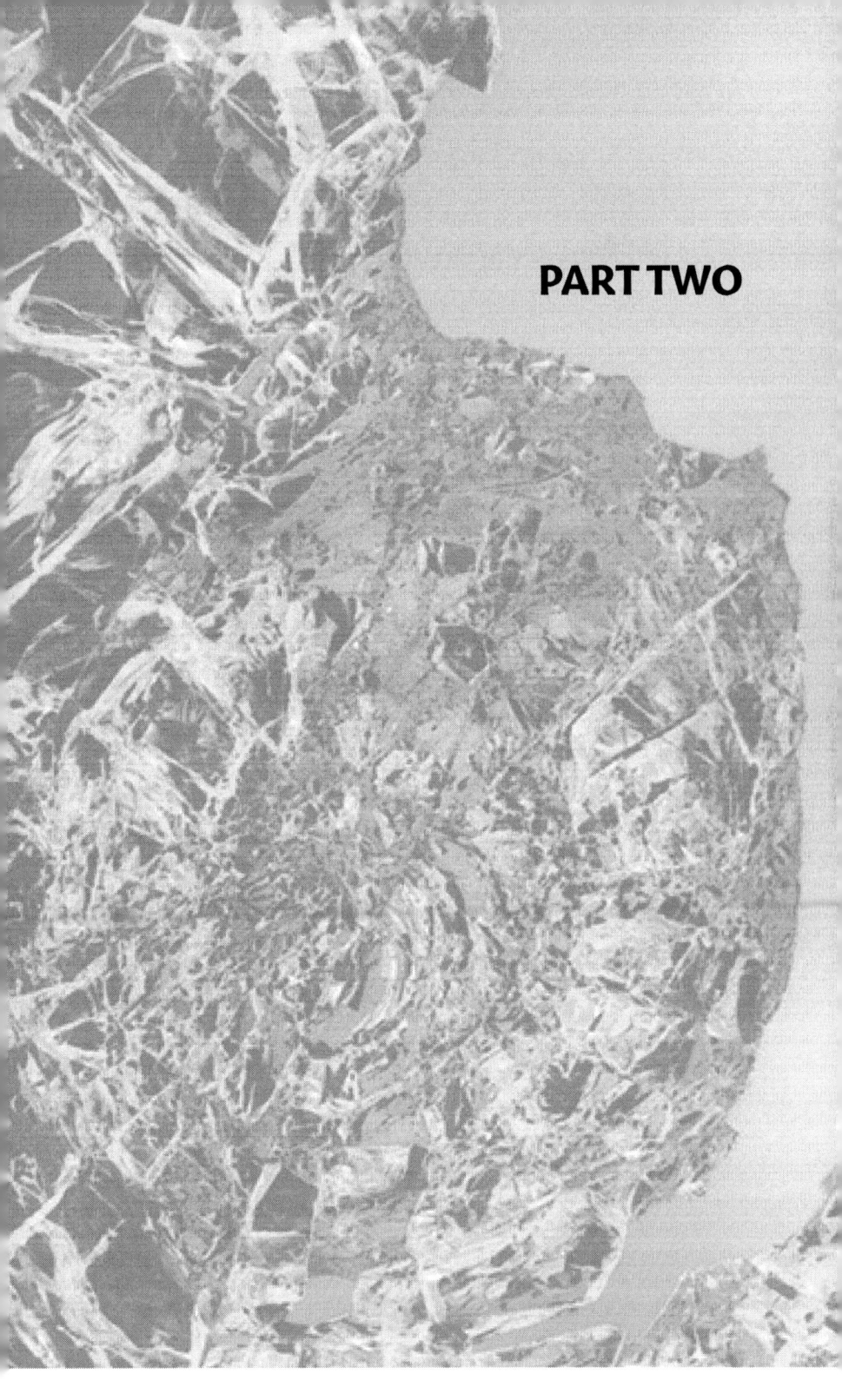

PART TWO

XX

Samarjidid

Marius arrived at Lupita's just as Josh was torturing Jesus with a joke.

"Hey, Zeus. The Past, the Present and the Future walked into a bar."

Jesus stopped mopping the bar rag and stared blankly at Josh.

Josh said nothing, just stared back, resisting a grin.

After a few moments of mutual silence Jesus made as if about a to swat Josh with the bar rag. Josh quickly replied: "It was tense," and guffawed, slapping Marius on the back.

"One of these days he's gonna spike your margarita with cyanide," Marius warned Josh.

"Nah, you would miss my sense of humor, right Jesus?" Josh said to the vexed Mexican.

"*Bésame el culo, amigo*," Jesus replied in a good-natured tone.

"See, I caught that 'amigo' part," Josh said.

"You need to work on your Spanish—amigo," Marius responded

Marius and Josh seated themselves at their usual table. Jesus brought them a pitcher of beer. Josh and Jesus exchanged smiles.

"I still think your idea is *mshuge*, Marius. Have you considered the legal implications? You have to be breaking some law, probably several," Josh said.

"I've thought it through. I realize that there are risks. This thing could go wrong at several stages. But the only reason I am worried about that is not my getting caught, but that the purpose of all of this won't succeed. Anyway, I have a couple of cards to play if things go south."

Josh winced. "Ya know, all I can think about when you explain this thing to me is that baptism scene in *The Godfather* where the heads of all the other New York Mafia families that compete with the Corleones are simultaneously wiped out while the priest is going on about renouncing Satan and all his works."

"A perfect illustration of what Coppola meant when he said that the essence of filmmaking is editing."

"Yeah, I just hope you don't end up on the cutting room floor."

"So, did Rachel find out anything?" Marius asked, jumping to the subject of their meeting.

A few days before, at school, Josh had told Marius that Rachel sold some of her produce to a store in a small village about seventy miles to the east called Samarjidid, or New Samar. Marius learned that the village population was less than six hundred—all Muslims, with a Shia mosque. They were mostly Shia, although there were also some Sufi Muslims living there as well. "Amazingly, they seem to get along," Josh said. "They have been scared shitless since 9-11, and since Americans don't know one from the other and have it in for anyone who's Muslim, they seem to be hanging together. Now there are some right-wing organizations in the upstate area that have been alleging that the village is a training camp for some terrorist group called 'al-something' and want to literally wipe the place off the map."

"I've been in upstate New York for a year and a half and never heard of the place. What's the real story?" Marius asked.

"Apparently, it's typical American xenophobia, with a dash of Islamophobia. The Muslims seem to be law-abiding citizens. They're mostly from New York and New Jersey and took over this old dead village that used to make barrels and wagon wheels. Most of them commute to jobs in the region and some work for the State, mainly in Parks and Public Works. The men still wear beards and *taqiyah* skull caps, and the women head scarfs, and nobody seemed to mind or show much concern until 911. Apparently, the FBI checked out the sermons of the two imams and didn't discover any anti-American expressions, although there was some anti-Semitism, or more accurately anti-Zionism."

Marius refilled their glasses. "So how did Rachel connect with these people?"

"Yeah, you're wondering how a Jewish woman . . . right? Quite by accident. The guy from their produce market, a Mr. Alibadi, happened to be driving through Palatine and stopped at Rachel's little roadside fruit and veggie stand and fell in love with your eggplants and some yellow squash."

"And probably Rachel, too, huh?"

"I wouldn't know; they speak Arabic together. Anyway, they've become friends and she's made deliveries of her veggies to Samarjidid a few times. Alibadi has shown her around the village a little, not that there is much to see. But she did notice that there is a cemetery near the mosque and she asked if she could read some of the headstones that dated back to the time of the Civil War, some of which were inscribed in Arabic script. And he introduced her to the imam. She's become sort of the token Jew of the village."

"Of course; she's gorgeous, grows superb *melanzane*, speaks Arabic . . .".

"And her surname is not Netanyahu," Josh laughs.

"I'll let Hisham know," Marius said.

"I still can't believe you're going through with this, Marius," Josh said, bringing up the subject again. "You are acting like you are fated to carry this out."

"Yeah, fate, right," Marius said sarcastically. "Everything I seem to do, these days seems to be my fate. You're keeping this between us, as I asked, right?"

"Well, just Rachel knows."

"Shit, Josh, I said 'nobody'."

"She's not gonna tell anybody. She only talks to her veggies and those two goats that she loves more than me," Josh replied.

"I mean for her protection. What she doesn't know is her protection. What if something goes wrong and the authorities get hold of her? Who knows what the fuck they're capable of?"

Josh smiled. "Rachel Pasternak is an Israeli, IDF-trained. I think you'd have a better chance of making those goats give up information than her. Did I tell you about the two guys she caught stealing some watermelons from her stand? They gave her some shit and she beat them up. That *krav mag* martial art they use. One guy ended up in the hospital with a scrotum swollen to the size of a watermelon. Appropriately, she visited him out of concern, and brought him a nice, chilled watermelon."

"Really?"

"Yup.

"I feel reassured."

"You should, . . . the goats are Israeli, too." Josh smirked.

"Well, thanks for the story. But my nuts feel a little tingly now."

Josh laughed. "She has that effect in many ways. But seriously, Marius. You know Rachel. There isn't much that will scare her off, which is why I should be anxious about her getting involved in this. We're Jews for Christ's sake—well, not really for Christ's sake—but trouble seems to seek out Jews and not only are we a little uneasy in this Christian conservative town, but now there's this Muslim business. People in this town don't need an excuse to fire up the ovens."

Marius made a pained expression. "Fuck, man, I don't want to get anybody in trouble. But it was Rachel's idea to make this connection. And it was her contacts there that made this all possible. Think I can work out a way of making the delivery that keeps her out of it. Last thing I wanna do is fuck up my supply of *melanzane*."

Josh took a gulp of his beer. "*Melanzane* is not the vegetable that worries me, amigo."

XXI

The Urban Alien

I ronically, it was a drizzly afternoon that Marius backed up the DVD to replay the ending scene in *Bladerunner*. Rutger Hauer as the muscular, white-haired Nexus 6 "replicant," Roy Batty, dripping with the night rain off his face and body, chooses perhaps random images from his installed memories. "I've seen things you people wouldn't believe," he coldly says to Rick Deckard (Harrison Ford), a bladerunner tasked to "retire" replicants but whom he has just saved from a fall to certain death, "attack ships on fire off the shoulder of Orion. I watched C-beams glitter in the dark near the Tanhauser Gate. [he pauses, rain dripping from his hair] All those moments will be lost in time . . . like tears in rain." He gives a wry smile of resignation, then announces: "Time to die." Batty's head droops into a final bow and a white dove flutters off from the building ledge on which they are perched, leaving a perplexed Deckard.

"I wanted you all to see this scene again," Marius explained to the class. "It remains a hotly-debated scene in a movie that has become a classic of its genre. Remember, our theme is "alienation," and this scene is full of material for debates. One of them is whether Deckard himself is a replicant, but just does not know it. Replicants are not real humans, but creations of humans that are given a specific lifespan. But if they somehow evolved to the point where they continue living beyond that lifespan, then they must be "retired." So, one issue that is raised by this application of technology reminds me of the words of German Sociologist Georg Simmel, from his classic 1903 essay "The Metropolis and Modern Life": *The deepest problems of modern life flow from the attempt of the individual to maintain the independence and individuality of his existence against the sovereign powers of society, against the weight of the historical heritage and the external culture and technique of life.* Today, nearly 120 years later, we might see this same concern expressed by those who wonder and worry whether we will be surpassed by what is called 'artificial intelligence.'

Kenny, as had become his habit, and perhaps from an introspection that owed to his infirmity, took something different from the scene. "I think the writer is really intending to say something about memory, that when we die our memories are like tears in rain, that memories are what our lives actually consist of and when we go, our existence is just washed away."

Marius wondered whether the boy had a memory of when he could walk.

"Yeah, but he doesn't even realize that they are not really his memories; he was just programmed with them because they gave replicants their biographies," Armand said.

"How sure can anybody be that their memories are really true? People often remember things the way they wish they had happened, or let their dreams become their memories," Caitlyn offered.

"Maybe that's why Deckard looks so frightened. He's unsure of his own memories," Kenny said.

Marius was impressed. This was the sort of film discussion he enjoyed. But it was tangential to the direction he wanted to go. He pushed it back toward the main theme.

"This is great stuff, but I'd like to address alienation. Is it that we don't trust what is alien to us? Look, you've all seen *King Kong*, right? Probably one of the crappy new remakes—I prefer the 1933 RKO version with Fay Wray—but it doesn't matter. Consider the final scene, it's neither as well-known, or horrific, as the searing memories of the last hours of the World

Trade Center towers, but it has been screened often enough that most everybody knows it. When Kong finally succumbs to the bullets of the warplanes and plunges to the streets of New York below the Empire State Building, the showman who brought him there, played by Robert Armstrong, delivers the line that is supposed to sum up the poor creature's fate: "Oh no, it wasn't the airplanes. It was beauty killed the beast." Very poetic, but the message is that we humans are creatures of technological ingenuity, with guns, planes and bombs."

"How come King Kong seems to always be attracted to blond women?" Melissa, a blonde herself, asked.

"There's always hope for you for a date to the prom, Missy," Jeff chided.

Marius shut it down, "Please, no blonde jokes. More than a classic tragic love story, *King Kong* is classic antagonist conceived in the womb of an offended Mother Nature. The film is a part of a smaller, but still significant, genre that began with Frankenstein movies and a lineage may be traced forward from *King Kong*, to *Godzilla*, to *Jaws*, to *Jurassic Park*, and one may confidently assume on into the future of mass entertainment. Such contrasts allow for plots that exploit the "natural" against the urban, honesty versus guile, simplicity versus complexity, and other dramatic dualities. It is a message that proclaims that the City is a distinctly human invention that exploits and menaces Nature with the result, these cinematic parables aver, of periodic and dramatic retribution exacted by Nature's supersized creations. The underlying message is that humans themselves are not immune to the negative influences of the City. In short, humans have been the authors of their own alienation from Nature."

"I'm still not getting the point," Bobby said. "Are you saying that Hollywood makes these movies to tell us that we are alienated, Mr. Greco?"

"Yeah, I'm kinda lost, too," Justin chimed in.

"Okay, Hollywood is firstly interested in entertainment. But its writers get their ideas out of the zeitgeist, the culture of the times that will connect, even if only subliminally, with an audience. So, a movie that might seem on first glance as just a 'monster movie' can end up being allegorical for something deeper, more philosophical. Alienation is a theme that is traceable all the way back to the biblical story of the expulsion from Garden of Eden when Adam and Eve become alienated from the god that created them. Since then it has been one story after another about how we are supposed to relate to our gods or Nature as well as each other. Take technology, for example. It was New York City that German director, Frittz Lang, took for his model of *Metropolis* (1926), a futuristic science fiction film depicting the giant city in the year 2026. Influential on numerous subsequent science fiction films set in imaginary cities, *Metropolis* created the notion of the city as some human-created, but only tenuously human-controlled other: the city itself as monster. The urban counterpart of the scientist gone mad, became the administrator-gone-mad with the power of his own creation. The metropolis's needs for endless productivity become the alienating force that divides the producing working classes from the consuming elite classes. In Thea von Harbou's screenplay the only solution to an imminent clash between the City's workers' netherworld and the exploitative uber-world of *Metropolis* is not a return to Nature's ways, but to religious ways. This model (and its visual icons) for the over-developed, over-controlled City as a place of social alienation recurs in films such as Chaplin's *Modern Times* in 1936, George Lucas's *THX 1138*, in 1971, and Ridley Scott's *Bladerunner* in 1982."

Marius paused, wondering if he might have left the class behind. He didn't want to lose his main points in a ramble.

"I've seen some of these movies," Justin interjected, "and they are all dystopias. That place in *THX1138* is some underground hell where people are required to take drugs and are turned into cyborgs or dwarfs. That city in *Bladerunner* is all pollution and cyborgs, too."

"Yeah, and in that *Metropolis* most of the people seem to be working like drones so that the rich people can live it up," Helene added.

"Most sci-fi is dystopic, largely because, I think, there is more drama in the strife, social discord, warfare. Perfect societies would be dramatically boring. But, then, competition, violence and such might be our true nature." Marius felt that he was in his "zone" now, making connections that had been forming in fragments in his mind for some time, but now were finding coherence and improvisational relevance.

"This is the paradox of cities, is it not?" He continued to develop the thought, more for himself than for the class.

"These portrayals of the influences the big city are representative of the effects of the characteristics of urban life upon the individual and the resultant "urban alienation" that has come to be expressed in the American cinema. For almost all of human existence, people have had some personal, or biographical, knowledge of those with whom they had social contact. The great part of human existence has been spent in the small social circle known as the clan, a large, extended family, or small groups of "families" that might not have averaged more than twenty to forty people. In rural and small village societies as well, people tended to have some degree of biographical knowledge of those with whom they came into contact. The city changed that condition and, as cities became larger and more socially heterogeneous and economically complicated, the number of people who were strangers, and literally "alien" to one another, increased commensurately and exponentially. These days city people share their urban environments overwhelmingly with people of whom they have no biographical knowledge; people who they scarcely and incompletely "identify" by the clothing they wear, the cars they drive, and other superficial variables. In urban societies, urbanites are mostly "alien" to one another. This is why surveys show that many people crave living in small towns like Palatine, where strangers are few and far between."

"I think when you go to a big city you are forced to, like, become some sort of fake—the way you talk and dress, and stuff. Maybe you have to join a gang, or to get into entertainment or modelling, become a slut, or a homo. I think big cities take away your freedom to, be who you really are, your true self," Melissa offered. Her injured arm was now out of its cast and just in a sling.

"Are you saying that we are not expected to behave in certain ways in Palatine?" Kenny countered. "I think that at least in the big city, because hardly anybody knows you, you have the advantage of anonymity and can reinvent yourself to whoever you want to be. At least you won't be judged by people who already know you."

Marius saw an opening for a sidebar. "Actually, it probably cuts both ways, at least the way Hollywood sees it. Take *Midnight Cowboy*, for example: this guy from Texas wearing a cowboy outfit with hat and boots goes to New York City thinking he's going to be a well-paid gigolo for rich society women, but he ends up being regarded as some sort of a joke that he doesn't quite get. Then a few years later, we get a movie like *Crocodile Dundee*, where a character dressed the same way is portrayed as a hero. The difference might be that Dundee, an Australian who was visiting the city, is not trying to exploit it."

"It seems to me from the movies that I've seen that there aren't any moral rules in the city. It seems like it's all about what you need to do to get money and sex. I think there is way too much sinful temptation in big cities. People see other people doing immoral things and they've become perverted by bad example. My father calls it moral relativism," Armand Gaites said. There was the usual amount of snickering when Gaites referenced his father.

"So, you're saying there is only one moral code?" Amy Brinke challenged.

"I'm just saying that if you look at the Judeo-Christian tradition, you will see that cities in the Bible with few exceptions, were almost always regarded as dens of iniquity. Jericho, Babylon, Sodom, and Gomorrah, were places of sin, depravity or godlessness."

"That's probably why we small-towners are suspicious of you big-city types, Mr. Greco," Kenny kidded.

"I'm beginning to get that feeling," Marius responded. "But if you check, you will see that I arrived here by bus from Syracuse airport, and not by flying saucer. Believe me, that suspicion of aliens goes both ways. Have you ever wondered why movies about UFOs and alien abductions are always set in small towns? Zombies, too. Is there something weird about these places? What you should take away from this topic is that what makes drama work is conflict, and aliens make for conflict. In this country, aliens come not only from immigration from abroad, but also from small towns to big cities, and more rarely the other way round. Frankly, it is easier to fit into the big city." If only they knew, Marius thought. If only they knew, and dismissed class.

As usual, as he left campus, Marius passed by the memorial fence near the main gate. It had been several weeks now and the candles were burned down, the balloons deflated or sagging; rain and moisture had blurred the signs and warped the photos. Here and there a fresh bouquet or candle stuck out. Today there was only one communicant, an older man, perhaps in his eighties, but large and bulky, standing erect and seemingly deep in thought. Marius had seen him there a couple of other times but never engaged him. Marius was a few feet past the man when he heard him speak

"You're the teacher, aren't-cha?" he said raspy-voiced, still focused on something on the fence.

Marius knew it was being addressed to him.

Marius stopped walking. "I'm a teacher here," Marius answered.

"The teacher that took down the shooter," the man said, still not looking at Marius.

"Yeah." Marius started to walk again. The raspy voice had a slightly aggressive undertone.

"My boy," the man said.

"Excuse me?"

"My boy," the man repeated, nodding toward a photo attached to the fence.

Marius turned. The man was standing directly in front of a photo of Mr. Bouscaren, the security guard who, was the first victim of Khalid. "He's your son, sir?" Marius said.

"Was. Was my son. He's gone now."

Marius was one of the few people in Palatine who would not have recognized the elder Mr. Bouscaren, or Maj. Ted Bouscaren, as he was more commonly known, the town's best-known military veterans. The Major had earned a Bronze-Star and two Purple Hearts for combat in the Korean War, where he distinguished himself as a 7th Marine infantry division gunnery sergeant at the Chosin Reservoir. It was the Major's singular life-shaping event; it was his identity.

The Major had hoped to pass on his Marine Corps experience to his son, Alexander. Unfortunately, around age eight, Alex exhibited a diffident personality and a tendency toward obesity. His father sent him to the Catholic elementary school in the hopes that its discipline and orthodoxy would provide a better framework for his maturation, when apparently it was not the most suitable environment. As things turned out, his shyness and excessive weight prevented him from being accepted in the Marine Corps and possibly adding another chapter to the family record of valor by serving in the Vietnam conflict. His son's failure to pass muster was an aching disappointment, and an embarrassment, given the Major's war record and subsequent service on the town draft board. The closest Alex could get to a military uniform was the kit of a local security guard company, an occupation he most likely took to satisfy in some modest and minimal way his father's hopes for him.

Now, the elder Bouscaren might well have been wondering if his son might still be alive were it not for his compensating behavior. The boy seemed to have little interest in the opposite sex and never dated.

"Gunned down by some Islamic terrorist punk before he had a chance to be a man," the sad old soldier said, finally looking Marius in the eye.

Marius made no reply.

"Shot in the back. A cowardly execution," he added.

Marius made no mention of the fact that the coroner's report also said that there had also been a shot to the head, apparently administered as a *coup de grace.*

"I'm very sorry for you, sir," Marius finally said.

The old man looked back at the photo. He took in a deep breath and without turning back to Marius said in a choked voice, "He just couldn't control his weight. It would have been better if he got it in some fucking rice paddy in Nam. Something happened to him when he was a boy, something spoiled him," the Major just let the words trail off, leaving Marius to wonder what the old man meant.

"I need to be going, sir," Marius said, "Sorry again for your loss."

"I saw you on television. Is it true that you didn't know that Iraqi kid was still alive?" Marius was surprised at both the man's change of subject and tone.

"I didn't know. I need to get going, sir."

"He's just layin' there in that hospital, getting the best medical care. How do you feel about that?" The Major's voice took on an edge.

Marius could feel the hackles rise on his neck.

"I was a soldier, too," the Major continued. "We didn't leave any Chinks laying around alive at Chosin . . . ."

"Look, we can trade war stories some other time, sir. Right now, I'm not in the mood, especially for the implication of your question."

"Sorry. I just think that justice doesn't get done. It's something that bothers me, that's all. I didn't mean to offend."

Now Marius had no idea where this old man's mind would go next. "Let's leave it at that, then, sir. I really am very sorry about your son."

Marius hurried off to the parking lot.

XXII

Abduction

The excessively flashy intro-graphics and music of WPAL-TV's "Valley Morning News" opened to a frantic-looking Bradford Inman, the program's usual presenter, but this morning he was beside KGK, anchor for the more popular "Evening Edition." The two news persons rarely appeared together, having never got along since KGK came to the station years after the long-serving Inman and displaced him from the evening anchor slot.

Watching his TV while folding his laundered underwear from the laundry basket, Marius immediately knew that the appearance of the two of them together signaled the "news" he anticipated.

Inman's face was graven, and immediately there was no way Marius's mind could avoid referencing William Hurt's faux emotionalism in *Broadcast News*. "At 6 am this morning WPAL received information from local authorities that the body of Khalid Aziz, the student shooter who killed four people and injured several others at Palatine high school almost three months ago, and has remained in a coma in the IC Unit of Palatine General Hospital, has been reported missing. Hospital authorities at first thought Aziz might have been removed for some diagnostic testing such as CAT scan or MRI, but his body was not returned to the ICU and could not be-found anywhere in the hospital."

Visuals came up of flashing lights from the Sheriff's vehicles, as well as the WPAL remote vehicle. There was a bustle of activity around the entrance to the hospital.

Inman's voice-over continued. "Nurse Claudette Paley, the ICU nurse on duty was told by an alleged radiology technician that Aziz was to be taken to radiology for an MRI. When the patient was not returned after about an hour, nurse Paley became concerned and made some enquiries. That was when she discovered that Radiology had no knowledge of a scheduled procedure, or that the patient had ever arrived in the department. She immediately notified Security to undertake a search for the patient, but after almost an hour-long investigation of the hospital it was determined upon checking with security camera footage that Aziz had been removed from the premises."

Inman turned to KGK. "Karen Gagan-Kemp has more on this breaking story."

KGK appeared to Marius a little frazzled, with her hair and make-up not done to usual perfection. But Palatine was not a place where many big stories broke in the middle of the night. A further indication was that she began by consulting her reporter's notebook; there had been no time to prepare the teleprompters.

"Thank you, Brad. I am just back in studio after having been at the scene at Palatine General, where I spoke with Sheriff Cavanaugh this morning."

The screen switched to video outside the emergency entrance of the hospital. Reflections of the flashing response vehicle lights gave the scene an emergency ambience. KGK asked Cavanaugh what his assessment was at that point of what had transpired.

"Thus far it is looking to me like this was a professional operation. There was a vehicle that arrived just in front of the entrance at approximately 2:17 am this morning. Footage from the security cameras showed a white Ford mini-van. We were able to read the license plates and are currently running them through DMV and other sources. However, beyond the fact that the two persons who emerged from the van were dressed in hospital scrubs, they managed to keep their faces obscured from any possible identification by the cameras. It appeared that a third person remained in the driver's seat of the van. Sheriff's Deputy Leary, who stood security outside the ICU room of Khalid Aziz, said that he was approached by two members of the hospital's Radiology Department—or at least who claimed to be—who said they needed to remove the patient for about an hour for an MRI procedure, and that the deputy could take a break from his duties. Leary said he went to the cafeteria for a cup of coffee. It appears that only nurse Paley got any kind of a look at the two persons who claimed to be from Radiology. She admitted to us that she did not pay particular attention to the appearance of the pair, noting that one of them, the male, wore a baseball cap and had a blonde ponytail, and that the female had a blue color streak in her hair. That is the extent of what we know at this time."

The screen returned to the studio with a one-shot of KGK. "Since that report we do have this one item of further information from the Sheriff's Department. Apparently, the license plates on the white Ford van were false New York State plates from Onondaga County. The Sheriff's Department has indicated that false plates can be easily generated with a computer Photoshop application and a color printer. 'Noon Edition will return to this breaking story with further updates."

Marius muted the TV and returned to his soggy breakfast cereal. He was about to set out on his morning run when his cell phone rang. It was KGK.

"Marius, have you seen the breaking news this morning?" she began.

"Yeah, I was just watching you, and now here you are on my telephone, apparently thinking that I might have something to add to your news story."

"And do you?"

"Sorry, I don't have anything for you on the matter."

"I'm a journalist Marius, and that sounds like an evasive reply."

"I'm an anthropologist, Karen, and I found out what happened on the story when you did, this morning. Why, obviously, are you making me your first call after you got off camera?"

"I'm sorry, I'm not suggesting you had anything to do with it, but I do know that you have visited Khalid Aziz's hospital room a couple of times during the night— there is footage of you on the security cameras—and so one could reasonably conclude that you have some sort of an interest in him and his condition. I just thought that you might have seen or heard something that could be associated with whatever it was that took place last night."

"Sorry, I can't help you, Diana," he said, referring to the reviled television executive in *Network*.

"Please don't be angry with me, Marius," she pleaded. "I'm just trying to do my job."

"Then don't give me reason to be angry with you, and keep me out of this. Now I need a shower." He hung up without saying goodbye.

XXIII

"Isis Takes Credit"

Gloria Sexton was in the middle of a meeting with Fr. Joseph Manley, Associate Dean of Le Moyne College's Office of External Relations, when she saw the email alert flash on her cell phone that was recording the priest's answers to her questions. Courtesy and professionalism required she ignore the alert for the time being. She had driven down to the liberal arts Jesuit College on a hilltop in Syracuse that morning in an angry frame of mind. Earlier she had seen the WPAL newscast about the strange disappearance of Khalid Aziz. Once again, the journalism gods had favored broadcast news over print, and by extension, Karen Gagan-Kemp over Gloria Sexton.

Moreover, the Khalid affair would likely smother interest in what she considered would be the best story that had come her way of both local and national interests in some time. Which was why she was now sitting in Fr. Manley's office: mounting public pressure had forced the New York Province of the Society of Jesus—the Jesuits—to release a document listing Jesuits in the Province who, over a fifty-year period, had committed abuses of students in their high schools and colleges. There were names, dates, and schools, but only vague references to types of abuse as being "admitted" or "credible."

Sexton had done some homework. She had kept files, read history, seen movies, and scoured the Internet since revelation of clerical abuse of children exploded in the media in Boston. In the years since, more about these maltreatments had come to light as victims had become emboldened to come forward about abusive incidents that had taken place when they were children in catholic schools, at orphanages and other charitable facilities. She was not entirely surprised at Manley's response to her question of why now the Society of Jesus, a successful and highly respected educational and missionary order around the world, had decided to go public with this embarrassing information.

"We Jesuits have been tortured, murdered, and otherwise abused by peoples to whom we have endeavored to bring the words of Ignatius Loyola, and the salvation of Jesus Christ, all over the world. For the most part we have prevailed, made converts for the Roman Catholic Church, and established institutions of education and charity on every inhabited continent. Nothing, not even the Vatican, when we have been at odds with our own Mother Church, has brought us down. But now, our very own human weaknesses, our own flesh, our very essence, threatens our annihilation. We must now publicly admit our sins, and we must exorcise them with full transparency and zero tolerance, and submit that they are crimes subject to secular authority, adjudication and punishment. There is no earthly acceptance without justice; no eternal salvation without penance."

Christ! These Jesuits, she thought, what spin-meisters. They will rise above their own mother institution and proudly scrub their dirty laundry in the public square while implying that it was a slag byproduct of their ample meritorious deeds. No wonder they privately refer to, themselves as 'the company,' they are as wily a corporation as any multi-national that pollutes entire countries, then runs commercials extolling their committment to of environmental research. They are the most formidable public relations firm in history. And they don't even have to pay taxes. But she went in a tangential direction with Manley.

"Father, you act as though these abuses are a rather recent phenomena in the Roman Catholic Church, but historical records show that this has been going on for centuries, that it probably has been a byproduct of priestly celibacy, and has been swept under the rug by ecclesiastical authorities for all this time. According to records of the Piarist order that began schools for young boys in Rome in the 1600s, these sorts of sexual abuses have been impossible to eradicate from the very beginning of clerical *loco parentis*. So, it appears that the Church fell to managing the problem with an administrative version of musical chairs."

The priest just smiled back at her. So, she went directly to the point of her visit.

"Your list, Father, names of priests and where they have served and whether they have admitted or have been credibly accused of committing abuses the Church would regard as mortal sins and secular society regards as felonies. It also indicates whether they are deceased, and I note that several of them are still alive, and that some of them have been expelled from the order. My question is this, is there or are there any priests on this list, in or out of the Society of Jesus who were in the search, in Syracuse or the upstate New York area?"

Manley was no longer smiling. "And why are you seeking such information, Ms Sexton?"

Now Sexton smiled. She surmised that the priest was unused to being spoken to with her assertiveness. "I am a journalist, Father, and I am interested in doing a story, or stories on this subject from all points of view. We have heard much from the victims, far less from the Church, and pretty much silence from the perpetrators. Are there any relevant subjects in the area to whom I might speak?"

"Are you a Roman Catholic, Ms Sexton?"

"Yes, Father, I am currently a Roman Catholic. I am attempting to determine whether my Church regards it to be a greater sin to be an atheist or a hypocrite."

The priest smiled again, but more tightlipped. He resented being spoken to by lay people in such a condescending manner, especially by a female. "I think for the present that the Society . . . the Order, feels that the amount of information in our report is sufficient to let the public know that we are committed to dealing with this problem. It is our mess, if you will, Ms Sexton, and we hope to clean it up with a minimal of exploitation by the media."

"When it comes to exploitation, Father, we media may well have met our match."

Actually, Sexton's line of questioning was to test the secrecy of the Church. She had already been informed by another source that there indeed was at least one, perhaps "de-frocked," priest on the list residing quietly in Syracuse. Jan Birkowski, (formerly) S.J., had admitted abusing several boys while a theology teacher at high schools in the New York provinces years before. His admissions had been confirmed by several adult men that had been his victims. Fr. Birkowski had never been arrested for what amounted to serial felonies that would have resulted in decades of incarceration had he ever been brought to secular justice, but was now protected by statutes of limitations. Sexton had learned details of the priest's predation from a member of SNAP (Survivors Network of those Abused by Priests). Birkowski especially interested her because he had occasionally said mass in Polish at her mother's parish church when he was a teacher at Cardinal Cleary Prep. But when she inquired where she might contact Birkowski for an interview, Manley stonewalled. That information "was not available to the public by direction of a Vatican office connected to the Congregation for the Doctrine of the Faith," he said, as if reciting a settled dictum of canon law.

Sexton's original intent, which she hoped would provide an interesting read for a small-town newspaper, was to do a case study delving deeply into the psychology of both predators and victims of clerical abuse. She even entertained the idea of bringing together some priests and their victims in interviews. But lately, after interviewing a man who admitted to years of fantasies of killing the priest that ruined his life and his faith—and then killing himself—she had begun outlining a dark murder mystery novel. She had wondered why there seemed to be no revenge murders for priestly abuse, a *lacuna* she aimed to fill that would be the ideal story to liberate her from Palatine.

But that was before the email on her phone.

Back out in her car in the parking lot, Sexton decided to check her email before heading back to Palatine. There, among the usual annoying number of unsolicited messages was one with a strange address: harb19i@aa.com. She hesitated; opening it might expose her phone to a virus or malware, but could not resist.

To Gloria Sexton, Reporter, Palatine Sentinel newspaper

By the time you read this email, the jihadi of ISIS America will have completed their mission to free the body and soul of our brother, Khalid Aziz, from his imprisonment by the authorities of Palatine, New York. We are making this announcement through you and your newspaper because it was you that it exposed the teacher, Marius Greco, who raped an innocent Muslim girl in Los Angeles, and now has assaulted our brother Khalid. ISIS will deal with the infidel Greco. But first we will return our jihadi brother to his homeland, where he will receive medical treatment to release him from an induced coma. You will know that this is a true message by the attached photo. Let the people of Palatine know that we can strike anyone, anywhere, anytime—in America. Allah is Great!

She hesitated again, this time to open the attached photo. But she took a deep breath and double-clicked it. It opened a jpeg photograph of a New York state license plate on the back of a white vehicle.

Maybe the journalism gods had neglected her, she thought, but Allah might have different intentions for Gloria Sexton. The clerical abuse novel might have to go to a back burner. Back at the office, she had her favorite hacker run down the email which appeared to have been sent from an Internet café in Compton, California. Confident that it wasn't all a ruse, she set to work on her article. News went stale fast.

Sexton's article came out the following morning, a day behind the story by WPAL of the disappearance of Khalid Aziz, but it purported to answer a journalistic question the television station could not—*who?* Sexton had the email to back her up, and in a sense, the ISIS attribution was no less "authentic" than claims made by many Islamic militant organizations opportunistically taking credit for terror attacks.

The Palatine Hill
By Gloria Sexton

"ISIS Takes Credit"

The day before yesterday, startling news on WPAL gave our town—only a little over a couple of months from the shock of the shooting at Palatine High—yet another blow. The perpetrator of that attack, Palatine high student Khalid Aziz, who has lain in the Palatine hospital Intensive Care Unit since that day, *has suddenly disappeared.*

As of this writing, no new information has been added to the newscast that reported a team of two or three unknown individuals masquerading as radiology technicians managed to convince the ICU charge-nurse as well as the Sheriff's deputy on guard outside of Mr. Aziz's room that the patient needed to be removed for radiological scans. The technicians, and Mr. Aziz, on a gurney, were last seen by security cameras leaving the hospital at approximately 2:12am.

Yesterday this reporter received an email from a source identifying itself as "ISIS America" taking credit for rescuing its "... *brother, Khalid Aziz, from his imprisonment by the authorities of Palatine, New York."*

The email, sent from a computer on the West Coast, further indicated that ISIS would be repatriating Khalid Aziz to Iraq, where he would be "released" from his coma. As proof of its authenticity, the email also included visual evidence that corresponds with evidence obtained by security cameras at Palatine Hospital. Currently, that evidence, as well as other information contained in the email, in addition to its address, are being retained by Homeland Security and may be released at a later time.

Even though all the essential journalistic questions seem to have been answered—who, what, when, and even why—there remain perplexing issues; essentially, how could this abduction have been accomplished so effectively and almost completely undiscovered in a small town like Palatine? How could a terrorist organization make its way into our community undetected, and invade a local hospital, remove a patient, and escape undetected without some local accomplices? Was Khalid Aziz a member of ISIS? Is Palatine vulnerable to some sort of massive terrorist act of retribution?

Where is Khalid Aziz now? Is he already back in Iraq? Has he been "released" from his comatose state? Has he evaded justice? There were those who proposed that Mr. Aziz simply be unplugged from his life-support as a form of capital punishment. But there were also those who maintained that he should be kept alive for the possibility that he might regain consciousness and that something might be learned as to his motives, or even if he was acting on behalf of some international terrorist organization. It now seems unlikely that he will ever be available to assist in answering these questions.

It is not the purpose of this column to point fingers towards anyone in this community regarding complicity. However, conspiracy hypotheses are already being circulated by local talk show hosts, and at least one national media company has shown interest in the possibility of a reality show based on the story. There has been speculation that, from an economic point of view, this might be a positive circumstance. On the other hand, there are those who value the insularity and solitude of their small town that regard this as a disaster.

The Sentinel contacted mayor Vreeland before the completion of this article. The Mayor said that "Whatever the speculation, Palatinos want answers, and that a grand jury will likely be convened to address questions from ineptitude on the part of hospital staff to the possibility that such crime could not have been successfully executed without the participation of local accomplices. Palatine used to be a peaceful, law-abiding, God-fearing, and patriotic community until a few months ago when our high school was attacked. I am determined to lead our community back to its better days, whatever that takes."

XXIV

Bonfire of the Vanities

Marius knew it was going to be a busy day as soon as he entered the classroom. It was only two days since "the Vanishing of Khalid Aziz" had hit the news and stunned the community, and Palatine buzzed with a stew of opinion that included outrage, fear, and wild speculation. It was immediately obvious that the disappearance of Khalid was the subject that fueled animated debate and conversation amongst the students. Marius jumped right in over the conversational racket.

"Good morning everyone. I have a good idea what all the buzz is about this morning and I am sure that you would like to make that the subject of today's class. But I do not want to do that. We still have material to cover before finals week. I gave you two movies to watch this week, which probably cut into your videogames and social media applications. Sorry about that."

"Today, we are going to be talking about politics and I want to begin with this statement: America was never meant originally to be a place of big cities. Remember, we started out as a colony for several European countries, principally the English, but also the Dutch, French, and the Spanish. We were a place that was supposed to be exploited—as all colonies are—for our resources, our ores, timber, furs, crops, and could use slaves and indentured servants to do much of the work. We just needed some small towns, and roads connected to ports."

"And canals, don't forget the canals," Kenny said.

"Good point," Marius responded, "because that introduces where I'm going next, to the immigrants. After emancipation, we had to start getting workers from elsewhere. The English and rotten potatoes drove the Irish out of Ireland and other Europeans had bad governments, religious oppression, economic miseries, and other reasons to emigrate. Some of them passed on through the ports of entry on the east coast, but a lot of them chose to remain in those cities. Some built canals and railways and settled on farms, but many built buildings, subways, streets and sewage systems, schools and urban governments. But because America was not supposed to be a country of big cities, the founding fathers neglected to devise a form of government to run them. That is why one of the movies I gave you is *The Last Hurrah*, a story that is about what we call 'the political machine'. Political machines were built on immigrants because the bosses controlled most of the public jobs, and some private contractors as well, and these could be turned into votes from immigrants. But 'bosses' were not always elected themselves, but were the power behind elected offices."

"But that Mayor Skeffington in *The Last Hurrah* is elected, isn't he?" Justin asked.

"Yeah, in the movie it allows for better exhibition of the easy charm in Spencer Tracey's portrayal. He plays a politician that has come up in the world from the scrappy Irish tenements, not unlike the Roman Catholic Cardinal and some other leaders of the community. But he has been unable to achieve public office and retain it without making his share of enemies along the way. Principal among these are the old-line Yankee WASPS who assemble in their private club and plot ways to overthrow the mayor. It is these enemies who provide the melodrama that drives what otherwise might be a soporific narrative. Skeffington finds ways to frustrate the crusty vengeance of newspaper owner Amos Force (John Carradine), who years earlier abused a relative who was in service in his house for stealing a piece of fruit. He outfoxes the leading banker who is holding up on bonds for a low-income housing project by enticing his dim-witted son to be fire chief, a post at which he is very likely to cause embarrassment. Skeffington attends funerals and other social events, using his charm and cleverness to endear himself to various constituencies. There is even a little lesson in the art of political compromise when, at a dinner with his nephew and his wife, he explains how he managed to get a statue erected in the Italian ward where different groups there wanted to honor different Italian historical figures."

"Yeah, but that didn't work out all that well did it?" Kenny commented, "he ends up losing his last election and it kills him."

"Well that's what this movie is about, the end of the political machine in American urban politics, or at least the end of it being local and personal. All of Skeffington's political acumen is doomed against the rising forces of the new politics. The jobs of policemen and firemen are still beholden to the mayor, there are still favors he can bestow and patronage jobs to distribute, but many of the ethnics have moved on into the middle class, suburbs now encircle the city, which increasingly is home to the poorer elements of society, and politics is being re-shaped by the medium of television. His political opponents nominate a dolt to run against him, seen almost exclusively in television and, in spite of obvious ineptness, he prevails over the old political warrior.

"The undoing of the Skeffington machine is not the opposition of the old English-based elite of the city, but the demographics of the new metropolitan area, and television. The emergence of the suburbs, in which issues were different, or competitive with those of the older parts of the city, placed limitations on the old, ethnicity-based grassroots politics. Residents of suburbia were often the children of the residents of the ethnic neighborhoods, but the ethnic mixture of the suburbs, based more upon concerns such as the quality of schools, home-ownership, and the commute to work, was more diversified. Unlike the neighborhoods of the inner city, the suburbs were not predominately Irish, or Italian, or Polish, but as likely to be a mix of these and other ethnic backgrounds.

"Television became a means by which candidates could be presented more like products than personalities. They could be "packaged," shown only in the best of "photo-op" circumstances, and engage in a non-interactive form of communication with their constituencies. While Skeffington was telegenic, he was at his best in small groups and one-on-one political relationships. While his opponent would have been ineffectual in such a context, he could be "packaged" sufficiently by TV handlers to make an effective candidate, enough to deprive old-time political operative Frank Skeffington of his last hurrah."

Banning broke in: "I couldn't stand that interminable death scene in which Skeffington's heart has given out and his political deeds are re-hashed as if to determine the direction his soul should go. I kind of liked this guy, but it got so tedious I couldn't wait for him to die."

Marius kept his agreement with that opinion silent. "Well, at least take away that *The Last Hurra*h did not spell the end of political chicanery, rough stuff, and other behavior that is reminiscent of machine politics. As often happens, political power can be relocated by social changes and communication technology, but its capacity for corruption goes with it. Now, what about *Bonfire of the Vanities*? That was one of the other options I gave you. How about somebody who watched that movie giving us a synopsis?"

The class was silent.

"C'mon, this could be a good chance for somebody to really improve their final grade."

The class was still silent. But Marius noticed that Prescott and LaGuarde were looking at each other.

"Edward and Hélène. Did you guys screen *Bonfire of the Vanities?*"

Hélène fessed up. "Yes, we watched it together in the multimedia room the other day."

There was some immediate teasing; remarks more than suggesting that some sexual escapades had taken place. "Hope you cleaned up afterwards," Banning said.

Marius ignored the wisecracking, although Hélène seemed slightly upset about it. "So, how about you two giving us your perspective on what that movie has to say about American urban politics."

Edward stepped up. "Like in *Last Hurrah,* an accidental death also figures into this story. It's about a Wall Street investor whose financial success leads him to refer to himself as a 'master of the universe.' He's Sherman McCoy, played by Tom Hanks, whose millions bought him a socialite-wife, a Park Avenue duplex apartment, and a mistress, Maria . . .".

"Played by Melanie Griffith," Hélène interjects.

"Yeah, she's pretty hot, and after picking her up from the airport McCoy's perfect existence starts to come apart when he makes a wrong turn off the expressway and finds himself in an unfamiliar area of the South Bronx. That mistake results in him and Maria panicking and running his car into a Black youth she thought was attacking them. The boy's death, with the assistance of a greedy mother and an opportunistic Black preacher who reminds me a little of Rev. Thorne, turns this not particularly special event in a big city into an overnight sensation. McCoy's car is identified by the police as the vehicle that killed the boy and very soon all of the various political interests in the city which might profit from his arrest and punishment descend on him like vultures on the fallen master. There's a district attorney who needs a sensational case to fire up his political campaign, various attorneys, racial activists, and political opportunists. There's this Peter Fallow guy played by Bruce Willis, a boozy, out-of-work reporter who functions as narrator for the story."

"That's a good start, but let's give Hélène a chance to improve her grade," Marius interjected.

Helene was ready to go. "Sherman—that's the Tom Hanks master-of-the-universe character—becomes the center of a media circus. He ends up indicted for the death of the boy after trying to cover it up at the urging of his selfish, oversexed mistress, and loses his job and his wife, and is about to be evicted from his fabulous apartment complex. He learns that the real masters of the universe in New York City are cops, sleazy politicians, newspaper hacks, publicity hounds, cynical lawyers, and ambitious civil servants. For all of his business knowledge with stocks and bonds and big international trades, he is ill-prepared to deal with such characters. In the end he is only saved by a lucky coincidence that produces a tape recording that counters his mistress's perjury that would surely have convicted him and put him in jail."

"What did you take away from the film?" Marius asked.

Helene thought for a moment, then answered, "I didn't like anybody in this movie. Everybody was out to get something and didn't care if the next person was harmed by it. They were all self-serving. Maybe the only person I could like was the boy who was killed."

"Do you think there's a message to this film?" Marius asks the class. "It is based on the book of the same title by Tom Wolfe, but Wolfe borrowed the title from an incident that happened in Florence, Italy back in the 15th-century when a crazy monk influenced religiously zealous people to burn artworks that were considered to represent their heretical vanities in an actual bonfire."

"I rented that movie a few years ago," Kenny said, "when I thought I wanted to become some rich hedge fund manager and live in Trump Tower. I think I was compensating for getting stuck in this chair. But I kept having nightmares of rolling off express ramps into some neighborhood in the Bronx."

"Really?" Jeff snickered.

"Nah, I'm just kidding. But I do remember the movie and I think that, in some ways, Palatine is getting like New York. There's that guy from that cable crime program, *Case Closed*, who has been poking around trying to do something with the vanishing. There's more Homeland Security people than there were before. I heard that some of those crazy UFO types were out checking that crop circle and have even wanted to get on top of the hospital to see if the spaceship that Aziz escaped on to a planet with seventy-two virgins left any burn marks on the roof. There are all sorts of conspiracy theories going around and people arguing about them, even mixing them up with the usual conservative versus liberal ideological positions. There are even a bunch of wackos from out of town who are sleeping in that crop circle because they think the Martians were going to return."

"So, what are you getting at, Kenny?" Jeff challenged, "that we are becoming like New York? God forbid!" There was an ironic inflection on his last two words.

"Yeah, and who is the Master of the universe in Palatine, Mr. Greco? He's the most famous guy right now," Ed chimed in.

"I'm just trying to draw some parallels, that's all. Anyway, Mr. Greco doesn't look anything like Tom Hanks."

"I'd prefer that you keep me out of this," Marius said, his hands raised up in the surrender position. "I am barely master of this classroom, and you should see where I live."

"Now that Kenny mentions it, you could say that Khalid is sort of like the Bronx black kid that gets killed," Hélène offered. "That's what started the downward spiral in this town, and what spells the end for what's-his-name, Sherman."

"That might be stretching things a little too far," Marius said. "I think that what both Kenny and you might be referring to is more contextual. That is, that sometimes all it takes is a trigger event to expose characteristics of a community that lie dormant or repressed under normal circumstances. But then, just like a movie needs an action to activate the narrative and to upset the status quo, the underlying character flaws of a community, be it as large as New York, or as small as Palatine, are exposed when the status quo is upset."

"Isn't this exactly what happened with the election of Donald Trump?" Amy Brinke asserted. Amy rarely participated in class discussion, except when the subject matter prompted her interest in the prevailing political culture. Her Jewish father, a widely-respected professor of South Asian Studies at Syracuse University, was separated from her Anglo-Indian, Mumbai-born mother with whom she lived in Palatine, but Amy's liberal approach to her personal life and politics handled the arrangement quite well. She was an active member and spokesperson for every liberal cause and organization at Palatine High. Her leftist enthusiasms would ignite her luminous grey-blue eyes in her tawny face, flashing wider when she raised her voice for emphasis. "In America, when you're a *halfie*, like me, you are always regarded as the half that White people can feel superior to. And with Trump, America finally got a leader who would rip off the mask of two centuries of racist denial, of slavery, genocide and social oppression, and declare almost with pride that this is a land that was founded by and should always be ruled by White Christian men."

Amy would have added several more paragraphs had Armand Gaites not jumped in. "Come on Amy, we've all heard you on this before and we know that you'll always find a way to criticize this country, as well as the religion that is responsible for guiding it to its greatness. What about that caste system that you have back in India? Why don't you go back there and fix that Hindu mess?"

"Thank you for underscoring my point, Little Reverend," she responded, referencing his father, 'Pearly' Gaites, who had announced from his pulpit that Christ would have voted for Trump who was preparing America for the Second Coming. "You just can't accept a mixed race, Jew/Hindu, as an American. Even when we are born here, you regard us as immigrants, as intruders, as people who will adulterate your fabled 'American way,' your culture that you cannot even define. Like you, I was born here, which makes me just as much American as you. But when you can't handle my ideas and my arguments, you resort to my heritage, which is nothing more than the accident of a sperm meeting an ovum. Your kind are the personification of these little burgs like Palatine that regionalist writers and painters celebrated as the so-called 'real' America, while immigrants building the big cities and the railroads and canals to connect them were doing the real work. What you are incapable of seeing is that there is a similarity between Trump and Khalid Aziz, that they both, in their own way, have ripped off the mask of denial of this country, forced us to look at the history behind it and see that it was never great, but just pragmatically hypocritical."

Gaites apparently decided to yield the field with a dismissive wave of his hand. Marius was impressed with Amy's putdown of Armand, almost wishing he had said it himself, but glad that he didn't have to. "Well we've ranged quite a bit from these movies, haven't we?"

"Except that we seem to have skirted the pressing subject of the day—what everybody is now referring to as 'the vanishing' of Kalid Aziz," Kenny said.

"It has been referenced, where it has been relevant." Marius responded.

"That's my point, sir. But not in the sense that it might have political implications."

"Alright, we have a few minutes . . .". Marius felt it best that there be no appearance at all that he had reason for avoiding the subject. He made eye contact with Kenny and held out his hand to signal "go for it." A couple of students groaned, but most appeared interested.

Kenny gripped the arms of his wheelchair and pushed his body more upright, shrugged his shoulders and stretched his neck. "Right now, I think this just looks like an Agatha Christie mystery, or something from the twilight zone, or the X-Files. Or just a prank. But I think it might be something more serious than that, or something with serious implications. That caper took some doing, some clever planning."

"Maybe he just died and they shoved him in the incinerator," Jeff suggested. "Just to be done with it, and he doesn't get buried someplace where you can be worshiped as an Islamic terrorist martyr. Case closed; it eliminates any fuss." Some murmuring around the class seemed to suggest it was a scenario that made sense.

"Fuss? You mean like people who would want to hang his body to rot in a gibbet at the entrance of town, like they did in Europe in the old days? Then why the secrecy? The hospital has a story, and they also have security cam video of people going through the halls with a gurney, even though you can't make out their faces."

"Still don't get why we should be so concerned about all of this because the guy is gone one way or another and what he did is done and can't be undone," Logan Wilson said.

"I agree with Kenny. This doesn't give us closure, it just drags it out, and that has consequences," Amy countered.

"Like what?" Logan shot back.

Amy's face took on the expression of something between anger and distress. "Like suicide."

"Suicide!" Logan responded with an incredulous tone.

"Yes, suicide. Perhaps you don't know it, but there have been numerous suicides of students who have been survivors at school shootings around the country. There have been suicides of several students in Columbine and Parkland and even a parent at Sandy Hook. These incidents are called 'ripple effects' of the original attack, and also include mental effects like PTSD."

"Are you saying something like this could happen here in Palatine?"

"It already has."

"You mean a suicide? I didn't hear of anything."

"All I can say is, not quite," Amy replied.

There was quite a bit of murmuring in the class and Marius took it as an opportunity to adjourn. But before he could, Melissa Nolan stood up. "I thought I might be okay after my arm healed up," she said, raising the arm that had been hit by a bullet but did not shatter any bones. "But I have been plagued by nightmares for several weeks now, each time I dream that Khalid Aziz awakens from his coma and comes after me to finish the job. I wake up in a cold sweat and am afraid to go back to sleep. Now I'm afraid to sleep at all. Why does no one consider that maybe he actually did come out of his coma, and his friends, or whoever might be behind all this have rescued him, either to escape his punishment, or to return and continue murdering us. Why does no one consider that possibility? We are going to be haunted by that until he is found and brought to justice."

Marius could not tell whether she was going to break into tears, or rage. He quickly finished adjourning the class.

When he arrived at his car, there was a man wearing a Fedora and smoking a cigarette leaning on his front fender. He seemed to Marius ridiculously out of place.

The man stubbed his cigarette under his foot. "Mr. Marius Greco, I presume?" he said coldly. The guy was outfitted so film noir that Marius thought he might have wandered off the set of *The Maltese Falcon*. He immediately did not like him.

Marius thought of answering "not necessarily," but said "yes."

The man quickly reached into his breast pocket, extracted an envelope, and handed it to Marius. "You've been served, Mr. Greco." The process-server strode off without saying another word.

Marius got in this car and immediately opened the subpoena. It commanded him to appear before a grand jury at the county court house a week hence to testify in the matter of the disappearance of Khalid Aziz.

When he checked his phone, there was a text message that Hisham had also been subpoenaed. He wasn't surprised.

Marius pulled over at his favorite phone booth on the way home and called Hisham, "So I guess they're rounding up the usual suspects, which is pretty much what I suspected they would do," he said to the nervous Hisham. "Just don't lose those receipts and you will be fine. And I assume that you are on the security camera at the truck stop. You did stop and buy something, didn't you?"

"Yes. I am just afraid that I will appear nervous and they will catch me in a mistake."

"Just imagine that you are being interrogated by one of Saddam Hussein's sons."

"Uday and Qusay?" Hisham replied with a tremble in his voice. "They are dead, are they not?"

"Yeah, they still are. But it's okay to use them for some good purpose. Don't worry, you'll do fine."

"Inshallah."

XXV

Grand Jury One

The bailiff held out the Bible for Marius to place his hand upon, and handed him a card to read to swear himself in, but the teacher did not comply. The bailiff looked over at the Chairman of the Grand Jury.

"Do you refuse to give testimony under oath, Mr. Greco?" the Chairman asked.

"I try to generally tell the truth, sir. But I do not need the fear of divine punishment to make me do it. Your Bible has no compulsion for me and I won't swear on it.

"On what then, will you swear, Mr. Greco?" the Chairman asked wearily.

"The Constitution, if you have a copy handy, would do. If not, Moby Dick, which is my favorite book, or a DVD of *The Godfather*."

"No need to get cute about it, Mr. Greco. Counsel has just handed me a note that says you can swear on your own honor."

"I do so swear to testify truthfully," Marius said, and sat down in the witness chair.

"You make no pretense to be a religious believer. Do you consider yourself a patriot, Mr. Greco?" The interrogating attorney, Calvin Barrington, was maybe only a couple years older than Marius, although the sandy receding hairline that meticulous comb-work struggled to conceal might have added years. The dark, pin-striped suit struck Marius as right off some costume department's "lawyer" rack. With an accent from somewhere in New England and Calvin Barrington sounded ready-made for some eventual law partnership.

"It's not the type of word I'd use to describe myself," Marius answered. He had already scanned the sixteen-member grand jury and recognized at least five people he had seen around the small town. They were arrayed around a table in a tight room that reminded Marius of the jury in *Twelve Angry Men*. The supermarket manager looked a little like Lee J. Cobb.

"Why is that?" Barrington asked from the other end of the table, without looking up from some notes.

"Let me say that I am an anthropologist, and I am perhaps too familiar with the anthropological history of this country, too much to allow me the feelings that I expect you would ascribe to patriotism."

"What anthropological history?" He was still looking at his notes, which Marius took as a put-down, like the guy was taking some warm-up shots.

"A national history that includes the subjugation and destruction of its native peoples, the enslavement of African peoples, the Chinese exclusion act, the incarceration of Japanese American citizens, in short the pervasive and endemic racism that is the social foundation of this country precludes any patriotic sentiment. I think that patriotism—at least to the extent that it can take on a cultish fervor—is tantamount to chauvinism and a cover for national hypocrisy."

"Yet you fought for your country in the Middle East." Now Barrington made eye contact with Marius as he said this.

"That's one way of looking at it."

"Then who, or what, were you fighting for Mr. Greco?"

"Excuse me, have I been summoned here under the possible threat of indictment for possibly being insufficiently patriotic? Should I have worn my lapel flag pin?" There were some squirms among the jury who recognized the two men did not like each other.

"No, Mr. Greco, this grand jury is not concerned with attitudes, but with deeds. But we also recognize that one can lead to the other, and sometimes it becomes necessary to ask such questions in order to establish a line of further inquiry. So, let me get to a more specific question. Can you tell us what you were doing between the hours of approximately 1am and 3 am a week ago Sunday?"

"You mean, where was I when it has been reported Khalid Aziz disappeared from the hospital."

"Yes."

"I was home."

"Were you alone?"

"Just me, and the cat."

"So, there is no one that can corroborate that you were home alone. What were you doing during those hours?"

"I should've been asleep, but I wasn't. I was working on my doctoral dissertation and was on my computer almost all that time, except for a text I received from a friend in Los Angeles sometime around 1:30 am. So, if you want, you can check the records of my phone to confirm the exchange I had with him, and I can also supply you with my computer, which will have time and date stamps for all the work that I was doing on my documents, as well as the history of my Internet searches."

"We might ask to do that," the Barrington said, his expression slightly vexed.

"Oh, my neighbor's car alarm went off for some reason, I think around a little after two. I went out to take a look and saw him come out to disarm it. I'm pretty sure he saw me. You could check on that."

"Thank you. Can you please identify the person with whom you had the exchange of texts from Los Angeles?" Barrington asked, pen poised over his legal pad.

"Yeah. Tom Villa, a guy I know from the Center for Rational Discourse."

"And what is that center about?"

"Mostly atheism and skepticism. It sponsors lectures, does fundraisers, and several of us appear at debates and forums dealing with subjects like the separation of church and state."

"And you are an atheist, then?" Barrington already knew the answer.

"I cannot see the relevance of that question to the purpose of this grand jury."

"You refuse to answer that question then?"

Marius could feel his anger rising. "I'll make you a deal, Mr. prosecutor. Since you are a person concerned with evidence; if you can provide me one piece of evidence—just one that would stand up in an indictment from this grand jury— that God exists, anything, anything at all that would stand the test of reasonable doubt, that would pass the doctrine of habeas corpus, anything from a smoking gun to DNA under fingernails . . ."

"That's quite enough, Mr. Greco."

"No, please Mr. prosecutor. Answer the question of the ages. Prove that God exists, and I'll answer your question for you."

The lawyer ignored the taunt. "One last question, Mr. Greco. What was your friend Tom, from Los Angeles, calling you about at that hour of the night?"

"Well, first of all it's not that late on the west coast, you know. He was calling me about the Pope."

"The Pope? The Pope in Rome?" The prosecutor asked incredulously.

"Yes, the Pontiff, the Vicar of Christ, the Pope. Tom called to tell me the news that the Pope had just had his annual physical exam and the doctor said that there was an issue with his prostate . . ."

There were a few snickers from amongst the jury.

"Wait a minute, Mr. Greco, where are you going with this?"

"I am just trying to answer your question truthfully, sir. So, Tom said that the doctor says to the Pope, 'your Holiness, I must recommend that you, for your health, must have sexual relations with a woman'...".

"That will be quite enough Mr. Greco," Barrington snapped. "You might not have sworn on the Bible, but lying to this jury does have consequences."

"Tom and I always call each other when we hear a good Pope joke. You'll love this one if you'd just let me finish." Marius noticed that there were a few members of the jury who seemed curious about the punch line.

"You're excused, Mr. Greco, but please make yourself available should the jury have further questions for you."

"Yeah, like what did the Pope do about his prostate." Marius mmbled, with a slight grin as he got up from the witness chair.

XXVI

Sic Transit Gloria

Gloria was right where Marius was told she would be when he entered Wally & Mary's Diner. In fact, everything was just as he was told it would be, and it seemed that it always had been, at Wally & Mary's Diner. Since there was no one else in the place Gloria was enveloped in the cloud of cigarette smoke and hunched over her notebook scribbling determinedly. Even her notetaking in longhand seemed consistent with stepping into the 1950s time-warp of this establishment.

Mary, in her 1950s period waitress outfit straining at her girth, and shuffling her wide orthopedic shoes, was almost instantly at the booth with the coffee pot and thick mug.

"Thanks for coming," Gloria said, head still down and finishing a sentence.

"Maybe I just fear the power of the press," Marius responded, taking his first sip of coffee.

Gloria screwed her fountain pen into its cap and set it on her notebook. "Not so powerful anymore in the age of social media and enemy states hacking into our electoral processes. You have a better chance of being destroyed by some troll on Facebook than by an old-school reporter."

"The mouse is mightier than the pen now, I suppose. No more *Gloria in excelsis scribus*?

"More like *Sic transit Gloria* . . . , " she added with a wry grin.

"See, that's why I showed up; you're the only person in this town that I can have a good Roman conversation with."

"Actually, it's take an atheist to lunch week, so the Latin must remind you of those good old days of Roman Catholic guilt."

"Funny you should mention that."

"Ya know, one of the things that I strangely, maybe perversely, seem to miss from my boyhood days in the church, is sin."

"Sin?"

"Yeah, sin. There was something about the danger of it, playing a game of chicken with mortal sin, with the prospect of eternal damnation. Sin was the forbidden fruit. For some reason those burgers that I ate at Pappas Brothers on meatless Fridays always tasted better than other burgers. Feeling up your girlfriend maybe was only a venial sin, but those boobs were forbidden fruit, too. I liked getting away with it, playing the Church against itself with its own rules for forgiveness and salvation, which for it was a system of control, of course. But for me, it was sort of a game. Once I quit the Church and all the rules were gone, it wasn't as much fun any longer. Everything seemed to be a little bit blander without all the high drama and danger."

"I think I was always too scared of mortal sin to ever do anything like that," she responded.

"It's probably more of a 'guy thing', like cliff-driving or doing wheelies on motorcycles, a male compulsion that helps cull the herd. Anyway, these days I have better things to do then play chicken with the Lord." Marius took another gulp of coffee and shrugged.

Gloria caught it. "Which brings us to . . . ,"

"Are we on or off the record?" Marius interrupted.

"Okay, off until you say otherwise," she answered. "But you should remember that lying is a sin, and you are always on the record with the Lord," she teased.

He nodded.

"You know, Marius, there are people in my office who insists that none of this vanishing business could possibly have taken place without your knowledge. That you must know something about it."

"Why should I? I have no connection with him. I put him in the hospital. I didn't take him out."

"Well, some of that association might be my fault. I published that piece about your issue with that Iraqi girl back in LA. And people know about your military service. And apparently you have made a visit or two to the hospital. Maybe some people thought that you were 'casing' the place."

"You're leaving out that I am now a known atheist, which means in these parts, I am always included among the usual suspects for any immoral or criminal deed. What is it with people around here? They are usually convinced by their religious beliefs that there are easy supernatural explanations for things, like angels rolling back stones from the tomb of Jesus, or just up the road in Palmyra of believing that some guy who was handed golden tablets by an angel just found a new religion. But when they need somebody to take the blame for something, they always find a nice human culprit. Why don't they believe that the so-called 'vanishing' of Khalid Aziz was some supernatural occurrence? Maybe those unidentified people that they caught on the security cameras were angels? Maybe there were some sort of messengers in an alternative metaphysical narrative?"

"I honestly don't know how people here couldn't believe anything like that given the horrendous act that started all of this," she said.

"And maybe people around here don't know all of what might have prompted that act in the first place," Marius responded.

"Might you know something about that, Marius? Are we still off the record?"

"Still off."

"I'm not asking you to incriminate yourself, Marius."

"Then don't. Any implication that I knew anything prior to the attack and I would be subject to accusations that I was sent out here from LA as part of some sinister plan of Al Qaeda or ISIS, or the illuminati—*that I was behind the fucking attack.*"

Mary arrived at the table to refill their coffee cups while Gloria silently considered that Marius did in fact know something of the sort. But what did he know about 'the vanishing'? She was about to see whether there might be a line of inquiry that he would allow to go on the record.

"You know that your 'what did you know and when did you know it' line of questioning reminds me of Gethsemane," he said as he watched Mary shuffle off with her pot of coffee.

"Gethsemane?"

"Yeah. What did Christ know in Gethsemane, and when did he know it?'

"Did Mary put something extra in your coffee?" she said with a squint.

"I think that Christ was a bit of an agnostic at Gethsemane. Remember, he asks God the Father—which, by the way, is supposedly the same person as him—if the 'cup', his impending crucifixion, might be lifted from him. He's thinking of getting out of the deal. Why? Maybe what Christ is exhibiting in that is that he himself had to *believe*— didn't really *know*—that he was the son of God and would be resurrected. If he was who he was supposed to be, the progeny of an all-knowing supreme being, there would be no reason for him to have any doubt. I don't know whether the whole damn story is just fabricated by the authors of the Gospels, but it just doesn't hang together."

"Well, he was a man also," she said.

"I don't want to replay the whole monophysite heresy thing with you."

"Forgive me, but was there a point of bringing this up?"

"I don't know. But it seems to me that it is the '*when* did you know it question that can make you responsible for its consequences." But Marius couldn't explain to her that it was just such a decision he had to make not to have Chamsi see the video of Khalid's humiliation, that he needed her to see him only as a perpetrator, not a victim.

"I thought you were saying that, maybe, it's that Palatine needs Khalid Aziz dead and safely entombed to put closure on this whole business," she said. "Having him hanging around in some ghostly, resurrected manner keeps the matter unresolved."

Marius remembered that's exactly what Melissa Nolan had said in class. "Well, you are a reporter looking for a never-ending story that keeps paying narrative dividends, like where are the Lindbergh baby, Amelia Earhart and Jimmy Hoffa. Then, of course, there is the risen Jesus, the mystery of that empty tomb. Khalid Aziz just might join these unsolved mysteries and you can milk them for speculative stories *ad infinitum*. People never seem to tire of it. Every few years we drag out Jesus for a new onscreen crucifixion with the same old speculations: Did he really die on the cross? Did he die and then was resurrected? Was he really the son of God? Is he really coming back? Or is this just a story of a first-century rabbi who got caught between the Jewish orthodoxy and the Roman procurator and got himself crucified?"

"So, what is the atheist's story?" Gloria asked.

"I'm afraid you have wasted your lunch for not much of a story. If there's one thing I have learned about teaching movies, is that they are nothing without a story. The story is the essence of a movie. And it doesn't matter if the story is true or not, because with movies we willingly suspend our disbelief. Perhaps that is why it might be a long while before you have to worry about the atheists taking over the faithful. It seems that people always liked a story in place of the unknown, something to believe in. We atheists don't have a story; no scripture, no narrative, no plot, probably just mathematics.'

"That sounds terribly boring," she said, pulling a cigarette from the pack.

"Maybe to everybody but mathematicians and physicists. That's why we make up stories; we are desperate to have reasons for everything that happens. I'm okay with that. It makes life interesting because most people can't handle the complexity of the universe and the questions of why and how it came into existence. They don't understand Einstein or Hawking, but they can relate to the story of some prophet, gospel author who basically puts things in a perspective they can appreciate. God, Marius emphasized by making air-quotes with his fingers, "is not some cosmic force, like gravity, operating in a vast dynamic universe of gases, ice, and geological elements. It's easier to accept the idea of God as some white-bearded ancient father, who is so engaged with his earthly creation that he actually has his own son, and even a pet bird called the Holy Ghost. And more important than that, he has a purpose and a plan for all of it, a narrative that has a beginning, middle, and end, which is eternal salvation, and that is a story in which we all have a part. We are not some cypher and a mathematical formula that is totally beyond our ability to comprehend. It is no small wonder to me that the vast majority of people in the world believe in some kind of a story like that. They need something simple to answer their questions, to deal with their fears, to give them a sense of purpose that is beyond their just being a temporary arrangement of carbon atoms in space and time that may mean absolutely nothing."

Gloria had a look of wide-eyed innocence on her face. "Wow, Marius, you have almost talked me back into being a believer. Or, believing that you might be an apostate atheist."

Marius laughed. "Apostate atheist; I like that. And I almost get what you mean. That human need to believe, even believe stuff that, if you really stop and think about it, is total bullshit. But, it is immensely powerful. It almost comes naturally, whereas being an atheist is a lot of work. It takes a constant diligence."

"What do you mean by that?"

"Okay, let me explain by illustration." Marius continued, "A couple of days ago I'm driving some nails into a wobbly bookshelf and I slam the hammer right on my thumb. Instinctively, even before I get to some of my favorite four-letter words, I shout out 'god dammit!' And then I actually call some vague deity a 'sonofabitch'. I'm not cursing some principle of physics, some law of motion, or some aspect of metallurgy that made my hammer slide off the head of that nail and bash my thumb. No, I need, I want some being to blame, somebody who can understand how angry I am with my invective. Atheist that I am, I can almost see that god laughing at my pain and my swelling thumb. What I am saying is that these gods that I allege we humans have invented are always at the ready to take advantage of the good, the bad, and the inexplicable of our lives. They are so much like the default to a metaphysical position, almost in the very air that we breathe, that they and their minions, the angels or the devils, are ever at the ready to explain every aspect of our existence. So after I bashed my thumb, and reflexively cursed the gods, I had to take a moment to reset my atheism."

"And what do the believers do when they hit their thumbs?" she asked, although she knew the answer.

"They say goddammit, too. But then they apologize for their blasphemy."

"And perhaps explaining away the bashing of their thumbs with the notion that everything happens for a reason," she added.

"Ah, now we're on the same page."

Gloria lit her cigarette and took a deep, satisfying drag. "well, I guess I got nothing newsworthy for my lunch. But now I know a little bit more about nothing."

Marius excused himself. But on the way out he stealthily handed Mary a twenty-dollar bill to cover the lunch.

XXVII

The Vanishing Show

The Auditorium filled quickly. "The Vanishing," as it had now come to be called, a title that had a Stephen King horror-thriller-soon-to-be-a-major-motion-picture ring to it, refreshed interest in thePalatine High tragedy that, in the intervening weeks had lost national media coverage to three more recent school shootings and two workplace and one church slaughter. All, but two, had involved assault weapons, and all but one of the perpetrators were White, Christian American citizens. There were now local rumors that Islamic terrorists were planning a revenge attack on Palatine.

So, Mr. Schmidt, School Principal, elected to introduce the subject of the convocation, "A Safe Education," with a reference to the Somali man who killed three of his coworkers, and wounded two others at the Domino's Pizza place in Detroit where he worked as a delivery person. American mass violence was pretty much on schedule, and all the other incidents happened in states in what was typically known as the Bible Belt.

Marius had insisted to Mr. Schmidt that he did not want to be part of this discussion that he knew to have been instigated by a group of parents and a couple of fellow teachers to broach the subject of arming teachers themselves in the school. He stressed to the principal that he had given his opinions on the subject enough times in television interviews and that he had nothing more to say about it.

But Schmidt was adamant, and knew as well that he had a pressure point on Marius that he could leverage with the budget cuts the school was facing for the following Fall term to make Marius partake in it. Marius was unsure whether he would need to be there for at least another year to complete his dissertation research. To cover his options, he consented to be up on the stage with three of his colleagues, the president of the PTA, Sheriff Cavanaugh, and a young woman from South Carolina who was the survivor of a school shooting in Greenville, and a leader of a growing national student anti-gun organization.

Marius was locking his bike when he encountered Josh and Rachel walking onto the campus from the parking lot.

"*Inshallah* and smiley face," he said to the couple by way of greeting," They knew immediately what the code meant, and Rachel gave him a reproving scowl.

"So, what are you going to regale the good people of Palatine with this evening, Mr. Greco?" Josh said, slapping his colleague on the shoulder.

"I told Schmidt that I've done enough of this shit, but he's squeezing my nuts with the budget cuts."

"Well I imagine you want to get back to LA as soon as possible," Rachel said.

"I do. I just want to be covered if I need some extra time here, and not rushing allays certain suspicions. Tonight, I just might tear off my human identity and let Palatine see me for what I really am: a grey extraterrestrial with spindly arms and big, black, almond eyes, who whisked Khalid away to my planet."

"Shhhhhh," Rachel admonished, "there are people here who would actually believe that."

KGK was waiting by the door when they entered and snagged Marius's arm. "Hi stranger. Have you stopped drinking chianti?"

"Just busy with my school work," he lied, having other reasons for not wanting her and her probing journalistic nature around. "Maybe I should have said that I was abducted by one of those ET visitations that your station appears to have given a surprising amount of coverage," he said. Your staff seems to have been very diligent in digging up an enormous amount of blurry footage of frisbees, pie plates and other allegedly flying saucers that are part of the UFO cottage industry. Have you managed to obtain any new information about them?"

"Only that they seem surprisingly obsessed with human genitalia," she responded, squeezing his arm suggestively. "Gives a whole new connotation to *Fifty Shades of Grey*."

"Cute. But the little buggers don't seem to have a monopoly on that."

"Yeah, but they're not much into Chianti," she said with a wink. "Beaujoulais Nouveau."

"Ah, well, they've landed in the wrong place for that, haven't they?"

"So, can I interest you in a little abduction, with chianti of course?" she said.

"Actually, you have me imagining the taste of the young, piquant flavor of Beaujoulais Nouveau. But I think we might have just missed the season."

"Wine-snob."

"Let me get back to you. I may have to get out of town quickly after this evening." Marius walked down the side aisle toward the stairs to the stage.

"Faculty, students, parents, and citizens of Palatine," Principal Schmidt began, adjusting the microphone at the rostrum to his height, "thank you for coming this evening to discuss a matter of the utmost importance regarding the safety of our schools in this community. Let me say before going further that I realize that there are many members of this community who deserve to be onstage to share their views with us, but obviously we could not accommodate everybody, and so have tried to get a representative panel."

There were some murmurs and inaudible shouts from the audience, which the principal ignored. "This does not mean we are not prepared to take questions and comments from the very large audience that has assembled here. So, please try to be patient and understanding. We will do our best to hear all the points of view. I will try to act as moderator and begin now with putting a few questions to the panel we have assembled. You already know most of these people but we are also pleased to have Ms. RayeAnne Bascom from Greenville, South Carolina. Ms. Bascom, some of you might know, is a survivor of the school shooting in Greenville that took place just a month ago and resulted in seven deaths. She is the founder of a national student's association in response to gun violence that is being funded by a major liquor distillery that has paid her expenses to attend our assembly."

There were some flickers of tentative welcoming applause that grew louder and gradually tapered off. The blonde pony-tailed young woman had a pretty, ingénue-ish, face above a full body that also made her the star center of the girls' basketball team at her high school. She sat upright, hands folded in her lap, muscular legs demurely crossed at the ankle, as though she were president of the local chapter of the Junior League. "The remainder of our panel consists of Sheriff Cavanaugh, Mrs. Blair, President of the Parent Teachers Association, Mr. Pascal, mathematics teacher, Ms. Garofalo, gender and child development teacher, and you are by now familiar with Mr. Marius Greco, our teacher of anthropology and urban studies."

Schmidt paused for a few seconds. "We also have two students with microphones in the audience to take questions. But we will try to first center this discussion on what a group of parents has brought to our attention, a question which I am sure is being considered in many school districts around this country, given some of the horrific attacks that have taken place. And that is the matter of how we can make our schools safer, and whether one of the means by which this might be accomplished would be with arming, or allowing to be armed, our teachers in their classrooms. I think it might be appropriate to begin with Mrs. Blair. Mrs. Blair?"

A student onstage rushed over and handed a wireless hand mic to Mrs. Blair. She began to speak, but the mic was not working and the student rushed back to turn it on and check it by gently tapping the top, producing a cardiological thump-thump sound.

Mrs. Blair, a rather bovine woman in her early six-ties—"cowly" was Josh's adjective for her—was also a Republican committee woman for a few years. She was everywhere in Palatine Republican Party politics, active in the county town-ship and village level. Despite the fact that her son had grad-uated from high school, she remained active in the PTA. She was the one who was behind the armed-teacher proposal. She knew local politics.

"Palatine used to be a safe community," she began in a tenor that could almost be considered masculine," but Khalid Aziz has taught us that small towns like Palatine are no longer a community isolated or insulated from the troubles of the larger world that we came here to escape. I am not going to attempt to paint a bigger picture but to get right to the point of why we are having this assembly. Our children need to be protected in our schools. As Ms Bascom can attest, we are not alone in being victims of this horrible new trend. There does not seem to be a perfect answer. Some schools have turned themselves into what looks like the TSA security we now en-dure at every airport, while others have turned their campuses into walled camps, or have tried to turn classrooms into panic rooms. I think that perhaps the least expensive and maybe the most effective deterrent to these incidents might be allowing our teachers to arm themselves. Teachers with proper training in the use of such weapons, if they are not a deterrent to those bent on mayhem, will at least be in a position to bring things swiftly to a stop."

Mrs. Blair appeared to have more to say, but many were surprised to hear Mr. Pascal break in. Horace Pascal barely spoke in his own classroom, preferring to let his equations on his blackboard speak for him. Short, bald except for a fluffy fringe of hair that gave him the appearance of a koala, the mathematician had the unfortunate sobriquet, "the Picker," owing to his habit of nervously picking his nose when he did have to articulate his thoughts. Pascal had come down from Canada many years before, It was rumored he had been a prize-winning mathematician in Montréal destined for a university post, but something had gone wrong in his personal or professional life and he washed up in Palatine. He might've been put on the panel by Schmidt more as a potted plant then a participant."I look at arming our teachers as creating a situation that can make matters worse rather than better," Pascal began, a slight residue of Canadian accent in the squeaky voice. "Imagine what happens when you break a rack of billiard balls with the cue ball. Now imagine the cue ball to be a gun shot by a perpetrator. You get sort of a chaos chain reaction where you cannot predict the trajectory of each ball. The same thing can happen in a room full of armed people when the shooting starts and then if you bring in law enforcement people who do not know the difference between a perpetrator and a protector—well, you can just imagine. I could lay this out in a mathematical equation for you, but I can just tell you that a prediction of a positive outcome would be folly."

There was a little burst of applause from a knot of math students in the audience.

"Ms Bascom, has the same question come up at your school?" Schmidt asked.

The mellifluous southern accent was a bit of a surprise. "Oh yes. South Carolina is a very Second Amendment state as I am sure you are aware. I think we have some teachers who are already armed with concealed-carry permits. But the students in our organization are opposed to this idea because we feel that it only exacerbates the problem of there being almost no regulations on the possession of firearms in our society. Presumably, just because teachers are teachers doesn't mean that they are not subject to the same problems as other people in society. A year ago, we had a history teacher, a young man who left behind a wife and two young children, when he commited suicide with his own gun. What if he was mentally ill enough that it caused him to take out whatever troubled him on some of his students? We never found out what it was that caused him to take his own life."

"Mr. Greco?" Schmidt asked, "you stopped an atrocity without the use of a firearm. Do you have a point of view on this matter?"

"Yes, but I'm not sure on how helpful it would be. If I had access to a firearm, I probably would have used it to stop Khalid Aziz. I probably would have behaved as I was trained to in the military. Nevertheless, I am opposed to the idea of arming teachers. I agree with Mr. Pascal that there can be a lot of chaos once the shooting starts. It's not a video game. People don't become teachers to serve as security personnel. And if they're the armed ones in the room and a perpetrator knows that, then they will be the first to be targeted.

"That just seems contrary to reason, Mr. Greco," Mrs. Blair objected without the microphone.

She did not get to explain further when Sheriff Cavanaugh decided to join in. "You're also forgetting one critically important thing, madam. The perpetrator is the one with the initiative. He decides when and where the attack is to take place. He is the one deciding what position he wishes to be in in order to effect the most successful attack. He only has to be ready when he decides to attack. Armed schoolteachers, in effect, must be on alert all the time if they are going to have even a chance to counter attack. I think that it is impossible to do that and be an effective teacher at the same time. So, what I am saying is that the advantage of initiative, of surprise—and that's a big advantage in a gunfight—is almost always with the perpetrator. By the time your armed teacher can respond he, or she probably would not be able to hit the side of a barn."

Schmidt looked a little frustrated. "It looks like arming our teachers is not getting much support. The consensus seems to be that firearms are the problem, but not the solution." A man in the audience stood and shouted without the benefit of a microphone: "If the men who seem to have the most experience with guns do not think they are the answer, then what is the alternative, just put our hands up and be slaughtered?"

Marius considered for a moment that it might turn out to be a short evening if he could just keep his mouth shut. But he could not, and motioned for the mic to be brought to him. "I don't blame guns for killing people any more than I blame forks and spoons for obesity (although guns will kill you faster). They are just efficient instruments, especially those that are specifically designed for killing people. The more they are made available, the greater the potential for more people to be efficiently killed." He paused to let that sink in. "But the *causality* lies elsewhere, and this is where, as a society, we like to lie to ourselves. It continues to amaze and amuse me that every time one of these mass murders takes place, the first thing people seem inclined to do is pray. We pray for the dead, sometimes even the perpetrator, who is usually among the dead. People turn to religion, or I should say, their religion, when, too often, a case can be made that the root cause of the violence is some religious injunction, like anti-abortion, or a racial superiority, or alleged moral superiority over non-believers. We refuse to admit that religion is about power, the power of fear of the other. When others, like Muslims, commit violence, we ascribe it to their religious zeal, their violent culture—it is evil. When the perpetrator is one of our own, we disguise their crimes as mental illness."

"So, if the problem is religion then, Mr. Greco, are you suggesting the answer is atheism? Thanks to that article in *The Sentinel*, we are not unaware in this Christian community of your infidelity," Mrs. Blair said with fire in her eyes.

"I am no apostle for atheism, Mrs. Blair. It was *The Sentinel* that made public what is my private, personal information. But I think you can rest assured that an atheist will have no cause to kill you because it will earn him a higher place in the eyes of his god and in the heaven in which he does not believe. So, I will no longer allow you to use me as a scapegoat and as a distraction from where you should really be looking as the cause of violence that you putatively abhor. We need to do something about religious prejudice, racial superiority, and social and gender inequality. They are ultimately the causes of someone finding a gun or making a bomb because they are either the abusers, or the abused victims in a society that is unwilling or incapable of confronting the reality is that we are our own worst enemy."

"So, I suppose you do not regard the atheistic communists as our enemy either, Mr. Greco?"

"I don't think communists are responsible for any of the violence against our children. Nor, so far as I am aware, are atheists responsible for the most contemptible of crimes like the sexual abuse of children that is evident now across all faiths and denominations. We seem to allow this to be defined as *sin*, not crime—I think because our society is inclined to accord excessive respect and privilege to religious institutions—and the perpetrators go on to preach and prey—that's *p r e y*— another day."

Marius was probably a little less surprised than everyone else when his student Melissa Nolan rose from her seat, asked for the mic, and began to speak. Principal Schmidt interrupted her to say that she was out of order, but Marius intervened to ask if she be allowed to speak. Schmidt relented, and Nolan, who had continued to remain standing, continued, directed her words to Marius. "We are grateful for the courage that you exhibited on the day of the shooting, Mr. Greco, but I think you should realize that your West coast liberal ideas about religion and the second amendment are not compatible with the way we think about such things in Palatine. We believe in God around here, and we also believe in the right to protect ourselves with guns."

"You seem to think Ms. Nolan, and I would agree that probably the majority of the people of Palatine would agree with your statement, that it is my intention to somehow undermine the fabric of your community by preaching atheism— which, by the way, I do not—just some critical thinking that is willing to address the negative role that religion has played historically. You won't find me calling for the abolition of gun ownership either, which I find hopelessly idealistic, since it is America's preferred mode of suicide. I regard myself as a guest here and, other than some nasty things that have been spray-painted on my garage door, some disapproving scowls, and a truck that tried to run me down as I was jogging one night, I have felt reasonably welcome, and my views on metaphysics have been tolerated, if not accepted."

Left with no other challenges to Marius, Melissa sat down. But she had emboldened others in the assembly to speak directly to the stage. A middle-aged man stood. "I think we need to get back to the original purpose of this meeting. That is, how safe are we now in Palatine? The school shooting was one thing, but if they can come into a hospital and steal a body without anyone being able to do anything about it, who knows what else they might be able to do. Now they have deprived us of perhaps finding out what made that Aziz kid take a gun to his classmates. I think they came and snatched him because they were afraid he might wake up and talk. I think he was supposed to kill himself, like most of these terrorists do, and he didn't get to do that."

Marius glanced over and caught Cavanaugh's eye for a moment.

Another man stood. "I think you are having an emotional reaction. People have become paranoid since 9-11, running out and buying guns, fearing that terrorists are everywhere."

"So, you think we are safe, then." The first man said.

"Yes, for the most part. But we are making the terrorists more successful by making us suspicious of one another, and especially suspicious of outsiders and immigrants, by undermining our sense of community. That *is* the whole point of terrorism. We had to come up with the term 'homegrown terrorists' because we now have many more indiginous terrorist attacks, or just plain mass murders, than from foreigners. I think this is the way that Osama wins; in a perverse way he has unleashed the tendency to violence that has always existed in American society."

Ms Garafalo asked for the microphone. "We have to admit the fact that there are many of these people who are not terrorists but are motivated by something else—racism, grievances against their workplaces, or people they don't like, or prejudice against some other religion, some political ideology, or whatever. Or maybe they're just people who we say are mentally ill, which is the conclusion we often make when we have no basis for determining their motivation because the final person they kill is themselves. How do we deal with mentally ill people in our communities? We don't even have an agreement on that. We used to put people in mental institutions and try to care for them there, even though they weren't always the nicest places to be. Then when we discovered people's mental illnesses could be controlled by drugs, we eliminated the institutions and gave them pills, which was less costly. But that has its side effects too. People overdose, or commit suicide with their drugs."

"You're making it sound like we are the problem, not the terrorists," Mrs. Blair countered.

"That's not my point; just that foreign terrorists are not the whole cause of our problems, or that guns are the obvious solution. We are always trying to find appropriate answers to the problems that we have, and we make mistakes along the way, often finding out things by trial and error. My point is that we have a lot of problems going on in our communities that when we add a lot of guns into the equation we run the risk of making them worse. Of course, there are people who say that we need even more guns to protect ourselves and I think this is the insidiously wrong conclusion. Simple situations of conflict that might be resolved with a shouting match—there was one the other day in the express checkout line at the supermarket when somebody exceeded the limit of 12 items— could end up in a gunfight if everybody is carrying a weapon."

"I think you're exaggerating," the middle-aged man in the audience shouted, "now you are blaming guns for our problems."

"No, she's not," Ms Bascom objected. "That very thing happened in an argument over a parking space outside a supermarket down in Georgia just last week, and a man was shot and killed."

"I didn't hear about that," the man responded.

"Why would you?" Ms Bascom, who now had the mic, said, "that stuff hardly makes the news anymore since we average a mass shooting in this country about every ten days. The media are almost bored with these incidents unless they're as big and flashy as that Las Vegas massacre."

A tall, bearded older man in farmer's coveralls shouted from his seat. "I don't care what you say. The second amendment says it's my right to carry a gun for my own protection and that of my family . . .".

"That's bullshit, Amos," another man who apparently knew the farmer, shouted from a few rows behind. "It says if it's necessary for a militia. It doesn't say anything about you needing to feel safe, that you like to go hunting, or something like that. That's what the NRA and the gun manufacturers have cocked up, something for you to perhaps compensate for some personal diminished capacity."

The farmer completely missed the provocative reference. "Say what you will, Karl. I say it's my right."

"Yeah. And the next thing you're going to tell me is that you'll shoot me if I try to take that right away from you, even if it's by democratic means."

"If you force me to."

"Gentlemen, please," Schmidt said.

"So, you get to decide when you're unsafe," the farmer continued. "You would even regard yourself in danger if you feel that your so-called right to bear arms is threatened, even though you can't make a good case that the second amendment was written so that every frightened jerk can get himself an AR 15 . . .".

"Gentlemen. I don't think we should let this get out of hand," Schmidt pleaded.

"I think he makes my point," Karl shouted. "I don't even know if Amos is armed. I don't even know if he's on meds, or off his meds, or whatever. I just know that if he doesn't have a gun and this is just a shouting match, I wouldn't end up getting killed because I don't agree with him. Ask yourself whether you feel more safe or less safe when you don't know who is carrying a gun," he said to no one in particular.

"I think we have had allowed for a range of opinion," Schmidt said, trying to regain control of the proceedings.

"Unfortunately, today so much of our politics runs on fear. We prefer to live in a small town because we wanted to be someplace safe, away from the violence, crowding and filth that we have in the streets of our big cities. Now you're telling me that I'm no safer here then I was there; maybe even less so. I refuse to accept that. That is defeatism, and frankly, un-American."

"You tell 'em, Mr. Mayor," someone shouted from the audience.

"Do we have any further points of view from the panel?" Schmidt asked.

Mrs. Blair had been quiet, but apparently not inattentive. "I think there is a question that we have been avoiding and that we need to know the answer to, and that is we still have no idea of the motivation behind the shooting that took place at our school. We do not know the reason why Khalid Aziz, a student that everyone I have spoken to seemed to regard as perfectly normal, took a gun and began killing his own classmates. I also keep hearing people repeat that saying that 'all it takes to stop a bad man with the gun is a good man with a gun', and I still support the idea of arming teachers. But from what I have heard this evening, I think we also need to know what it takes to prevent somebody from picking up a gun in the first place. Now that Mr. Aziz has disappeared, we may never know the answer to that question."

Mrs. Blair's slightly more enlightened position encouraged Marius to express some thoughts he had held in abeyance. He signaled for the mic. "I'm not a believer in the notion that everything happens for a reason, but that does not mean that effects do not have their causes. To get to the truth of that, you have to be able to ask yourself the questions that are not clouded by presuppositions. Something caused Khalid Aziz to arm himself and attack his schoolmates. Now that he is gone, we might never know, his not having left anything behind as clues to his motivations." Marius paused to glance at Cavanaugh, again catching the Sheriff's eye. "This unfortunately, leaves an informational void that invites all sorts of narrative speculation. But when we delve deep into the question of causality, we might find many diverse sources of blame in a society with a history of racism, bigotry, gender inequality, not to mention clerical sexual abuse and trafficking of women, spousal abuse, immigrant children torn from their parents, religious and ethnic discrimination. Add in our foreign wars, and the wonder might be that there is so little homicidal slaughter. The more we don't face these sources of anger, discontent, or justification for vengeance and lethal retribution, the more we will be left with explanations based only on rumors, speculations and prejudices that are usually inspired by the same cultural faults. Maybe Khalid Aziz did what he did because he wanted to be a martyr for his faith or some other stupid reason. We have no certainty of that. But it is hard to think of a noble reason for such an act."

Schmidt, who had his own mic, took this as an opportunity to adjourn the proceedings. "Well, it seems this might be the place for us to conclude the discussion, if not the question that brought us together tonight. The council will be taking up the question as well at its next meeting. So, I would like to thank our panel for their insights and Ms Bascom for coming a long way to add her valuable input. Please . . .".

"What about the UFO?" someone interrupted from the back of the room.

"Yeah, what about it?" called another voice.

The was a general murmuring in the audience and some quizzical looks among the panel. Schmidt looked confused, and said, "I think we can dismiss that UFO story as having any relevance to the issues we have before us."

"Nobody has a good answer for what happened to that shooter kid. He just disappears." It was Mr. Eckard, the truck driver who claimed he saw something that was not "earthly" in the snowy night sky above the hospital the night Khalid Aziz disappeared. "I know what I saw."

"If it's *unidentified*, then how can you know what you saw, Mr. Eckard?" Schmidt responded.

"You're just like all those government people, Mr. Schmidt. You want to keep these things secret, classified. This ain't the first time this has happened and been covered up in Palatine, and you damn well know it."

Schmidt looked over at Cavanaugh in desperation. The Sheriff knew exactly what Eckard was talking about—the time that Ronnie Loomis disappeared but that his clothing had been found at the center of a crop circle on that farm off Route 31. That was twenty-three years ago and Ronnie's body was never found. All sorts of UFO and alien abduction stuff was in the national media and the vanishing of Ronnie Loomis, a mentally-retarded teenager, was like a made-for-TV special. There was every sort of speculation about it, from his supposed murder by his parents, to his being used in a ritual sacrifice by a cult of Satanists, to kidnap by a sleazy carnival that came through upstate each Fall to feed off the paychecks of migrant harvest workers. The body was never found, but an unidentifiable mess of flesh and bone eventually turned up in a canal lock over a year later that a DNA analysis certified as the remains of Ronnie Loomis. It could have been suicide, homicide, or a fatal accident, but not likely a returned alien abduction.

Cavanaugh at first just shook his head in the negative, but when Schmidt gave him a pleading look he reconsidered, thinking that at least the alien thing was a welcome distraction from searching for a plausible reason behind that incriminating video with his nephew. But as he was considering how to approach the subject, Pascal signaled for the mic.

"What do we think when we hear about or see a UFO? You automatically think something extraterrestrial. You automatically imagine little gray men with almond eyes. Despite the fact that the term means something *un*-identified, maybe not even an object, maybe not even something that is flying, maybe just some insubstantial illusion that only exists in your own mind. No, we have become accustomed, maybe even conditioned, by the people for whom what has come to be called "ufology," that carries no more reason for being a science than does theology, but has become sort of a business and, arguably for some people, a psychological need, a need for the attention that comes with being an abductee, or of being subjected to some sort of curious physical examination. Somehow the un-identified perversely becomes identified with considerable specificity. And here we are, even myself, talking about it as if it were reality, because we have this need for an answer to something that is unknown. So, for some people it seems, if the vanishing of Khalid Aziz does not have an evident explanation, we are quite ready to accept his abduction by extraterrestrials as a plausible explanation."

"Yeah, well you can't prove they don't exist either," someone shouted from the audience.

"I think the burden of proof lies with the one who says that something is there, when it might be nothing more than illusion, or have a perfectly rational terrestrial explanation," the math teacher fired back as though he were admonishing a student in his classroom.

"Don't piss off the Picker," one of his students in the audience whispered to another.

"Any final observations?" Schmidt asked.

Ms Garafalo took the mic: "And why are extraterrestrials— Steven Spielberg's ET excepted—seemingly always evil creatures bent upon exterminating us and taking over our planet? Is this yet another expression of our fear or suspicion of the outsider? And why are we turning this young man who, it appears, does not get accorded the explanation that he might be mentally ill, or affected by drugs, because he is not a white Christian, why are we turning him into some kind of a space alien recruit, a potential bogeyman, with whom we can frighten our children into eating their vegetables or finishing their homework? Doesn't that just make Khalid Aziz some sort of mythical figure to always haunt Palatine? If that was the intention of those who kidnapped him, we need to keep our wits about us, our rationality, as Mr. Pascal has said, or we will never get past this horror."

<hr />

Marius did not linger after the assembly, but quickly slipped out through a side door leading to the parking lot. KGK was leaning on the fender of his car.

"I'm going to have to report to Cavanaugh that I am being stalked," he said as he approached.

"That's what newshounds do," she replied with a grin.

"I'm yesterday's news; you know that, and I didn't add anything newsworthy tonight."

She pushed herself up against him, slipping her hands on his hips. "I just want to check a few facts, that's all," she said looking up into his eyes and moving her hands together.

"Yeah, like what?"

She looked right and left and behind her. They were off in the corner of the lot, out of the penumbra of one of its lights. Then her hands found his belt buckle.

"Hey," he meekly protested.

She kept about her business. "You claimed your opposition to being armed, Mr. Greco. But I am, not convinced, so I am just checking to see if you are 'carrying' a weapon."

"Look, I'd just like to get home and make some notes and get some sleep and . . .". Marius shuddered as she found what she was seeking.

"Yes," she said, "You definitely are 'carrying' something, Mr. Greco. Definitely."

"Hey, this isn't fair," he protested, then emitted a pleasurable moan. "I need to make those notes.

KGK was now applying more pressure and motion. Marius placed one of his hands on the fender to support himself, and the other on her shoulder as she gained more command of the situation.

"Oh, c'mon now. What notes? You can tell your favorite journalist while she finishes her investigation," she said mockingly. "Oh, my, this is quite a weapon I have discovered. I wonder what caliber it is."

"This is going to end in a mess if you keep this up," he said.

"Not so quick on the trigger there, soldier. Tell me what these notes are about."

"Just dissertation stuff. Nothing you'd be interested in."

"C'mon, tell me," she insisted, more interested in controlling him than what he had to say.

Marius hesitated, as though to collect his thoughts from the effect of her manipulation. "I had been thinking that there is an insularity to small towns that is provided by their being surrounded by open territory. They are sort of like islands in seas of hinterlands. In fact, they remind me of islands in other ways as well."

"Really? How interesting," she whispered with mock sincerity, now employing both hands fully on his genitals. "Is that all?" thoroughly enjoying his awkwardness. She did the same to him one time when they were in bed together and he received a phone call; recalling with mischievous delight how he had difficulty putting his thoughts together and speaking.

"No. . . . ahhh," he moaned, but continued with a wavering voice. "When I was an avid reader of accounts of whaling voyages in the 19th century because I was so taken with *Moby Dick*, I learned that whalers were some of the first white men, the first aliens of any kind, to be encountered by remote island people in the Western Pacific."

"Moby Dick?" she said, stressing the second word. "I'm not sensing anything 'moby'. Continue."

"I don't know if I can."

"You like this, don't you?" she teased.

"I was always curious that their reception—the whalers that is, at least in the beginning, was often quite negative and violent. And this was for good reason. Encounters with strangers were more likely to have bad results than good. Strangers brought diseases to which there was no local immunity and this, as it did in places like Hawaii, resulted in wiping out large segments of the population . . . I think I am about to . . . ".

"Not just yet," she released slightly, "this is fascinating, about the diseases and all." She was mocking, but she was also enjoying being in charge. More notes?"

He was breathing heavily. "They brought in new "gods," especially in the cases where missionaries followed commercial interests. These diseases, physical and metaphysical, were incredibly upsetting to these traditional societies, not to mention what commercial interests, like copra for example, did to bring on colonialization. So, the best thing an aboriginal society could do when it encounters strangers was to kill them, much for the same reason that we attempt to kill a deadly virus when it invades our body. —Oh, yeah, right there, that's it— Strangers are frightening, threatening to the established social order and culture. It is true that the encounters with different cultures might also bring good things, new technology and medical science, and these have often been used to the advantage of religious conversion and colonialization, but the original society is never the same. Oh, no, can't hold back any longer."

Marius convulsed as KGK giggled. "Now look what you've gone and done. You naughty boy. You know how having those thoughts about colonialism and diseases in aboriginal societies gets you so sexually excited. It's a good thing mama brought along some tissues."

"Jesus, why do I feel so satisfied and foolish at the same time?"

"That sort of describes the look you had on your face," she said, with a smug look on her own. She finished with her tissues, just tossing them on the ground, and buckled him back up.

"Hey, my DNA is all over those tissues," he complained.

"So? You think they're going to track you down and fine you for littering, or discovered that you have extraterrestrials in your genealogical heritage? Now how about you return the favor by driving me home since I got a ride over here."

In the car she remarked, "I must admit you did rather amaze me the way you were able to keep your thoughts about your notes together. Why were you thinking about that stuff?"

"I have to think about this stuff; it's all related to my doctoral dissertation. I think this is somewhat taking place in Palatine. It is not a social island that has developed over thousands of years, perhaps a little more than a century; but its relative insularity has been penetrated by mass communications, principally television and now the Internet. And now, with this incident of the school shooting, something that is known to be happening elsewhere in the United States, Palatine has been pulled into a wider universe against its will. And in an allegorical sense, it is a microcosm of the nation itself that now has a political element highly opposed to immigration. Globalization has spread economic benefits and brought elements of modernization to many areas, but it has also initiated backlash political movements to protect traditional cultures. Moreover, this response is often couched in a resurgent nationalism in many places that has resulted in the oppression of nonindigenous subcultures, for example by the Uighurs in western China, the Rohingya in Burma, and resistance to immigration from erstwhile colonial territories."

"Wow, you do have a dirty mind," she joked.

"I just kind of see the stuff being connected. You should appreciate that because you media people are very much a part of it."

"Yeah, well my bosses and our sponsors are rather more myopic about it all. Their scope is the 24-hour news cycle. So what bearing does any of that thinking of yours have to do with what transpired at that assembly tonight?"

"I don't think they even got close to the essential question."

"And that is?"

"The essential question they need to ask themselves—we all need to ask ourselves—is what it would take: what humiliation, what degradation, what level of physical or psychological debasement, would it take to get any of them to do what Khalid Aziz did. That's the question they are afraid to ask themselves. What the Nazis did to the Jews? What the Japanese did in Nanking? Why Hutus massacred Tutsis? What the Burmese are now doing to the Rohingya? What would it take? The answer to the question of what made Khalid Aziz is not just inside Khalid Aziz; it's inside all of us."

"How can you have such a question, right after what I just did to you?"

"How can we understand the most excruciating pain without having understood the most exquisite pleasure?"

"Marius, sometimes your complicated mind frightens me."

"Me too," he responded as they pulled up in front of her place. "Here you are, Miss helping hands."

"Don't forget to shower, Mr. sticky pants."

Dear Marius,

I am typing this in the middle of the night after a furious couple hours of packing. Yes, packing. I received a call from corporate headquarters earlier this evening saying that they want me down in New York by tomorrow afternoon. Adele Kastenbaum who, as you know, has been the co-anchor of the evening news from the city for several years, has resigned over a dispute with her producer over sexual harassment. You will hear more about this in the coming days from yours truly, if you are watching. I will need to get past the focus groups and such, and hopefully no groping of my body, to be her replacement. In any case, as you know this might be my big break, the one I have been hoping for and, now that it has arrived, I have mixed feelings about it, no small part of which relates to you. Should I hold onto my fantasy that one day you and I would head over to France in the Beaujolais nouveau season? I'll keep that one tucked away.

Ironically, you are partly responsible for this, as corporate made several references to the interviews I did with you after the school shooting. I certainly didn't feel so at the time, but they thought I really knew what I was doing and might even become one of the hosts for their investigative reporting programming. Of course, I did not let on that there were any other dimensions to power relationship, which I am sure they would have seen as a tendency on my part to breach principles of objective journalism.

As to our relationship, I came to think I was just a place marker. I don't know whether all women have the capacity to understand that they are not really 'the one'; but somehow I could tell that in the most intimate contact with you, there was something missing, something that you just could not express in words or touch. There were those words, of course, that neither of us dared to utter, despite the fact that I was getting close to wanting to say them, but knowing at the same time that I would almost be obliging you to repeat them back to me. And I know that I would be able to detect that they would not be truly meant, that these were words that you really have reserved for someone else. I know who she is, Marius, because the dots were not all that difficult to connect for someone with a journalist's instincts. But I continued without resentment to regret of my own volition, and I think we played together beautifully, without deception, without exploitation or obligation—and that is beautiful and memorable, a loving friendship.

I was not without my doubts that things could progress any further. You are West Coast and I am East Coast. You are public university and I am snooty private girls' school. Religion, we both agree, would not have been a problem, although I incline to be what you would regard as one of those New Agey types that falls for that spirituality stuff.

Which brings me to that other ironic element that plays into what might be the next stage of my career: Khalid Aziz. I probably would not be writing this email at all were it not for what he did—and what you did as a result of it. Don't you find it rather curious, Marius? I know that you don't see connections between things the way I do, but I can't help but wonder whether this was meant to be.

Marius cringed at reading those last three words: "meant to be." He instinctively began to mentally compose a response. "No, it's not meant to be, it's just that you happened to be a newsperson and school shootings are newsworthy events—this one was a national event—and you are likely the reporter to be seen on TV, and somebody in corporate authority liked the way you looked and sounded. What's so unusual about that? A terrible thing happened to several people, but one of the results of that was that you got a kiss on your sweet ass. This kind of shit happens all the time and for 99.9999 percent of the people it has little existential significance. This was your significant event. That's why language had to create the word 'coincident', if you will. You happen to think that it was meant to be, foreordained for some reason. You pluck it out of the randomness of life and give it a story. On a given day somebody might get hit by a bus. Or they might not and they get on the bus and sit next to a person who becomes the love of their life. They don't stop and think, I guess this was not my day to be run over by a bus." Marius stopped, realizing that he was elaborating these thoughts more for himself. Her next paragraph seemed to anticipate the point he was trying to make.

I'm not using this as an excuse, Marius. I don't want you to remember me as Diana Christensen, as somebody always seeking her own advantage. Believe me, I am not unaware of the chance that I am taking. I remember you telling me that LA is full of small-town beauty queens with dreams of making it in Hollywood only to find out the place is full of beauties even prettier than them. I expect that New York will be much the same for people with ambitions in media, the arts, and finance. See, I picked up a few things about my illusions between killing bottles of Chianti and amorous escapades with an urban anthropologist. Alright, at first it was just about the sex, but it got to be much more interesting than that.

Well, I need to get a couple of hours of sleep before that early flight from Syracuse, or I will look like a zombie in front of those New York corporate pooh-bahs. I will miss you saying "just put the money on the dresser and get out." I hope she is worthy every bit of having me be . . .

Your placeholder,

Karen

Marius felt a little pang. There was more to KGK than literally, and pleasurably, met the eye, he admitted to himself. She at least had a sense of herself beyond "being in the moment," and beyond the commodification of the type of journalism she practiced. But he also felt a sense of relief that circumstances had taken the responsibility of ending the affair out of his hands, even if it wasn't meant to be.

XXVIII

Grand Jury Two

Rachel Berman settled into the Grand Jury witness chair and threw a glance over at Josh, who was reading a subway-folded *Sentinel* newspaper. She examined her "farmer's hands," her only feature that might betray that she was not a cover model for a fashion magazine, especially since the waning light that streamed through the windows of the jury room lighted her auburn mane like a burning bush. With the addition of some makeup, and the right dress, Rachel could be intimidatingly beautiful. And she knew it.

"I need to know—and we ask this of everyone—where were you and your husband at the time of the disappearance of Khalid Aziz.

"What time would that be?" she responded, instinctively suspecting that it was a trick question to determine how she knew the time.

"Approximately 2:15 a.m.," Barrington answered.

"We were in bed."

"The reason we have asked for testimony before this jury is that photographs that we have of the perpetrators show them getting away in the same make and model of vehicle as your husband's."

"Actually, I own it," she corrected.

"Are you Jewish, Mrs. Berman?" Barrington asked.

There was an audible snort from Josh that turned heads in the room and also made Rachel smile.

"Have I said something that amuses you, Mrs. Berman?"

"You might know the answer to that question if you yourself were Jewish, Mr. Barrington. But since you apparently need to know, my answer is 'not necessarily'."

"Excuse me?" Barrington asked.

"We Jews have learned over the ages that we need to know who, and why, somebody wants to know if we are Jewish. It matters greatly. So, the ambiguous reply 'not necessarily' means 'it depends who's asking'. Therefore, if your name happens to be Himmler . . ." Rachel just let the sentence trail off, knowing it should be sufficient, but kept direct eye contact with Barrington. She reached back with one hand fluffing her hair as though she were stoking a fire, but the motion was undeniably sensuous.

"I hope that you are not implying that these proceedings have some sinister intent, Mrs. Berman," Barrington remarked.

"If you knew my family history, Mr. Barrington, you would know better than to imply that I should ever relax my abiding suspicion of sinister intentions."

"Well, I hope you are able to relax sufficiently here to answer a few questions."

She just smiled.

"I asked about your faith and/or ethnicity because, as you know, Khalid Aziz is an Arab and a Muslim and there exists, shall we say, considerable enmity between Muslims and Jews. Therefore, it is not unreasonable to consider how you feel about Mr. Aziz."

Rachel looked over at her husband. Josh hiked the newspaper he was browsing to cover his face, wanting very much to be sitting in that witness chair.

"Can you tell us where you and Mr. Berman were on the evening in question, Mrs. Berman?"

"Yes, I can. Earlier that evening we were at a lecture at Syracuse University, then we had dinner at a Chinese restaurant near the campus that we like very much, and, because of the snow storm and the warnings about black ice, we spent the rest of the night in a motel on Erie Boulevard rather than risk the to drive back to Palatine."

"I see," Barrington said, a little surprised. "Can you tell us what the lecture was about?"

"Of course. It was a lecture on the Myth of Judeo–Bolshevism."

"The myth?" Barrington asked. He might have been asking to determine whether Rachel had added the term to the title, or perhaps because he was among the believers. Rachel couldn't tell, but it left an opening.

"Well, the myth of Judeo-Bolshevism is Europe's most pervasive and influential 20th century manifestation of anti-Semitic thought. It emerged before the rise of Nazism and has continued to have a curious life long after the Holocaust and the defeat of Nazi Germany. Of course, it had suited the Third Reich's aversion to communism that it regarded anyone of Jewish origin as a Bolshevik. Even many prominent non-Jewish revolutionaries, Lenin and Karl Liebknecht, for example, were mistakenly identified as Jews."

"What about Trotsky?" Barrington asked, reaching back into his undergraduate history major.

"What about him? He was of course a Jew, but an internationalist and he didn't fit with Stalin's scheme, so Stalin murdered him, as he did several of the small number of Bolsheviks who actually were Jews. Non-Jews were always finding economic reasons for persecuting Jews as subversives wherever the diaspora spread them. In the Middle Ages they were hated for the practice of usury, after Marx they were regarded as communist revolutionaries, and in the 20th century rapacious capitalists. I think it doesn't matter what label you combine with "Jewish" a political ideology is only an excuse for the anti-Semitism."

"May I ask how you'd label yourself, Mrs. Berman?"

"I am a social agriculturalist vegetarian."

"Could you elaborate on what you mean by a social agriculturalist?"

"Well I suppose it comes from my having been raised as a child on an Israeli kibbutz, which I am sure you are aware is quite a socialistic concept organizationally. That experience gave me a love for agriculture so after I immigrated to the states and married my husband, I prevailed upon him to move where I could have a small farm. We were able to afford the one we have just outside of town."

"Is it a good business?" the lawyer asked.

"I think there is no worry that I will be dominating agriculture in the Mohawk Valley, Mr. Barrington. I sell some of my produce from a roadside stand, and I supply small amounts of fruits and vegetables to the Aziz Market here in Palatine, and a small Muslim market to the east in Samarjidid."

Barrington smiled, resignedly. "Do you have your receipts from your Chinese dinner and your motel in Syracuse?"

"My husband would have them."

"We'll just take your word on that, Mrs. Berman. Thank you. You're excused."

"I hope I have been of some assistance to this grand jury, Mr. Barrington," Rachel said as she rose from witness chair.

She had nearly joined Josh, when she heard Barrington reply: "Not necessarily."

Outside Josh said, "Do you think it was a good idea to volunteer that information about you're selling vegetables to those Muslim markets?"

"Why not?" she answered. "First of all, if I volunteered the information, he would think that I have no worries that it might lead to something incriminating. Secondly, should he decide to check it out, he'll find out that I had told him the truth about my doing business with them. It just adds to my credibility. Nobody's going to disclose anything else, because we're all in on it."

"I'll just take that as Israeli logic," Josh replied as they got into the car.

"Do you realize that he never asked me if we were practicing Jews?," she said.

"Are we?"

They looked at each other for a moment. Then in unison they shouted, laughing: "Not necessarily."

XXIX

THX 1138

"This is our final class of the term," Marius announced to the students as he dropped his lecture notes on the rostrum. He waited a moment longer to allow them to settle down and silence their mobile phones. "I think it is appropriate that I reserved our movies have to say about the future for this final class, because the end of something is always the beginning of what's next. You are going to continue with your studies, then off to college, jobs, or whatever is to be the next phase of your life, and I, . . . I will be heading back to Los Angeles to finish my own studies." This was his first mention that he would be leaving Palatine High.

There was a lot of murmuring in the class and, as Marius might have predicted, it was Kenny who spoke up first. "Save a spot in LA for me, Mr. Greco, I'm a rebel without a cause like that Jim Stark guy."

"You didn't pay attention to the last line of today's movie, Kenny," Jeff said.

"Let's not get ahead of ourselves here," Marius said. "There's a lot of territory to cover with this subject, but I think Jeff has hit on the reason that I chose *THX 1138* as the main film for today. But first I want to spend a little time setting up the theme." Marius placed a thumb drive into the computer connected to the classroom projection system and opened his notes. He opened the drive and clicked on the first image. "What we call 'science fiction' allows us to speculate across a broad spectrum of imagination. This is a picture of the actor Orson Welles from his famous, or infamous, *War of the Worlds* radio drama on October 30, 1938 that caused many people to run screaming in terror from their homes at the 'arrival' of vicious Martian invaders. From that seed sprung a "little green men" genre of film and pulp literature has expanded almost exponentially. With the Roswell incident in 1948 and the subsequent NASA programs, interest in exobiology, extraterrestrial creatures, in fact and fiction grew enormously. Invading aliens from space haven't ceased to activate our imaginations and generate conspiracies since."

Marius clicked open a black-and-white photograph of a man in a silver space suit. "Not all of those space aliens were scary monsters bent on extermination of the human race. In the 1951 movie *The Day the Earth Stood Still*, probably the science fiction film that influenced me most when I was growing up, a single alien visitor named Klaatu and his powerful robot, Gort, land their saucer-shaped spaceship in a park in Washington, DC. To demonstrate technological superiority, they turn off all electrical and mechanical power on earth, illustrated in a montage of cities brought to a halt by stalled modes of communication and transportation. The 'message' of the film is that unless humans find a way to live peacefully with one another—the film was made during the days of the Cold War and the proliferation of atomic weapons in the US and USSR—even more technologically-advanced aliens might have to step in like a parent among squabbling children and slap some sense into them. Since then, we have tried to show some of our neighbors from other galaxies as more favorable to us in movies like *Close Encounters of the Third Kind*, and *ET*.

Justin Cummings raised his hand: "Klaatu barada nikto." Several of his classmates gave him curious looks.

"Ah, I recognize another *The Day the Earth Stood Still* aficionado. Yes, that film became somewhat of a cult favorite. I will let you explain to any curious classmates what those words from the movie mean. The movie's central message is a forewarning that has been sounded by cool heads and Jeremiahs from cinemas, books, political podia, and pulpits since the first technology expanded humans' control over Nature, and over themselves: beware what you make; it might re-make you."

"I always thought there was something religious underlying Klaatu and Gort, like they were some god's messengers warning humans with possible punishment," Justin added.

"I think you will find a good deal of religious allusions in science fiction if you look into its subtext," Marius responded. He found it gratifying that's some of his students took the material to another level. "Mary Shelley's *Frankenstein*, or the *Modern Prometheus*, which she wrote in 1818, questions the concept that it might be possible for man to conduct the most godlike of all wonders: the creation of life itself. It's a view of man's relationship to nature that has been revisited many times, right up to *Jurassic Park*. So much for background. Let's get to why I chose the main movie I assigned for today's class."

"You wanted to make us all depressed that you are leaving?" suggested Kenny. There was murmured agreement.

"Yeah, you're leaving for La-La land and we're gonna be stuck here in boonville," Edward Prescott chimed in.

Marius laughed. "Well, maybe subconsciously. But now that you are showing yourselves to be such perceptive students, I'm probably going to miss you—a little. But, really, what George Lucas—who you already know as the creator of *Star Wars*—was trying to do with this earlier, and far less well known and, in my opinion, far more socially perceptive *THX 1138* is address the overriding concern of serious sci-fi. So, what do you think that might be?" Nobody seemed to want to hazard a guess.

"Why are extraterrestrials so fascinated with our genitals?" Jeff suggested.

"Why are *you* so fascinated with *your* genitals, Jeff?" Kenny said.

"Wrong movie, you guys," Marius said. "I maintain that the overriding concern of serious sci-fi is the emergence of an authoritarian over-regulated society—the kind of society that scares the bejeezus out of political conservatives—yet, at the same time is an expression of the paradoxical extremes of conservative regulation."

Robert Schermerhorn raised his hand. "I have a feeling that you're getting ready to do a farewell dump job on conservative Palatine, Mr. Greco." Schermerhorn rarely spoke up in class, but often telegraphed his feelings with frowns and grimaces whenever it appeared that Marius came off as a "left coast liberal." Schermerhorn was known as "The Aryan" among his classmates owing to his barely-disguised White supremacist sympathies and some ambiguous sinister tattoos. He was also almost always seen in the company of Richard Ferdette, a big farm kid he'd befriended as a shield.

"I think it would be inaccurate to confine Lucas's point of view to places like Palatine, Robert," Marius responded, although he could not help thinking that the kind of society portrayed in *THX 1138* probably met with this student's approval. "The nameless subterranean city of the movie was actually shot in the under-construction tunnels of the Bay Area Rapid Transit system in San Francisco. Workers in this subterranean world are suspiciously drone-like as were those of *Metropolis*, the 1926 silent science fiction film by German director Fritz Lang and written by his wife, Thea von Harbou." Marius thought the reference to the Germans ought to, please Schermerhorn. "In fact, the film is an homage to other science fiction luminaries as well, borrowing a god-like figure from Orwell's *1984* "Big Brother," and stunted dwarf-like people from Aldous Huxley's *Brave New World*. Released in 1971, it is full of allusions and references to contemporary TV programming, to the infamous House Un-American Committee phrase 'Are you now or have you ever been . . .', which, of course, is a reference to the Communist Party. All of these movies, and the books from which several of them are derived, are concerned with fears about the evolution of societies ruled and regulated by authoritarian regimes that are powerfully assisted by forms of technology ranging from police state control, to drug-induced sex and reproduction control, to the use of media to control political thought and education, even to the creation of false deities to foster a spiritual allegiance between people and the state."

"Sounds a lot like Palatine to me," Kenny joked.

"Quite the contrary, in fact," Marius said. "These are imaginings of states that swallow up, in the way city state centered empires of the past did, towns and villages like Palatine and forced them to adopt languages, customs, and religions and other dimensions of subservience to their overlords."

"This is the same as the stories in the Bible," Armand blurted as if he were struck with some sudden revelation. He was met with a few groans.

"No, wait," Marius insisted, "Armand has hit on an important connection." He was pleased that the preacher's son had led the discussion right into an area that he had considered avoiding altogether. Armand was delighted, and not just because his grade in the class needed a boost.

Marius elaborated. "I presume that you were referring to the Bible's stories about the Hebrews, who were really a pastoral nomadic people more than villagers, always being thrust into captivity by the Babylonians, or the Egyptians, and in the New Testament, by the Roman Empire. They were always being enslaved and forced to do the bidding of their rulers."

"But they always held onto their faith, to their god," Melissa Nolan joined in.

"That's how you survive against these . . . these, these *bastards*," Roger Flanagan half-shouted, plucking up his courage to express himself with an expletive.

Marius thought that his class was beginning to take on the spiritual fervor of a revival meeting. He had been anxiously awaiting the end of the semester, but classes such as this, in which students interacted with the subject matter in ways he could not have predicted, in which a special, improvisational relationship between teacher, the material, and students seemed to emerge spontaneously, were what he loved most about teaching. It was, he felt, infrequent, but "intellectually orgasmic." He had been a participant on such occasions as a student, as a teacher, and he hoped with his research and its eventual publication, as a contributor to the material that stimulates it.

"But the New Testament changes all of that," Melissa said. "Jesus was the revolutionary. He was the Messiah who was willing to take on the Roman empire."

"You are leaving out that he was also taking on the Sanhedrin, the Jewish religious establishment. He was a new covenant," Armand added, sounding like he would be ready to take over for his father.

Logan Wilson waved his hand franticly. "I'm getting confused about what all of this has to do with the movie. So, what's the point?"

Marius did not want to lose the chance to make some significant connections. "I think it is important to remember that when movies like *Metropolis*, *The Day the Earth Stood Still*, or *THX 1138* express concerns about the over-regulation of life in autocratic societies of the future, they are referring to the power of technological control that is god-like, that can be employed to control the moral and spiritual dimensions of life. These movies are therefore recognizing what the rulers of autocratic societies extending back to the time of ancient Babylonia claimed: they were gods as well as kings. So, religion possessed great power for order and obedience. Combining bodily fear of the police with fear of divine punishment has historically proven an effective method of manipulation and control."

Marius realized that he was stepping dangerously close, if not already over, a line he had managed to avoid thus far, a line that was inscribed by the fact that most everyone in Palatine knew he was an atheist, and that some regarded him as the antichrist. While it should hardly concern him now that he was only a matter of days from finishing his contract from Palatine, future teaching assignments could be jeopardized by a negative recommendation from his most recent employer. He was also mindful that the power that teachers possessed in the classroom extended only to the assignment of grades and that students could turn on him as well. But he couldn't let what he regarded as his most essential historical reference slip away.

"Moreover, it seems that organized religion has been just as eager to cozy up to political power for the security and influence it affords," Marius said, throwing discretion aside. The class was ominously attentive. "Consider the early Christians, who are mostly portrayed, as Hollywood loves to show them, as a persecuted sect always being thrown to the lions. But then, in the 4th century, Christianity became the official religion of the Roman Empire. For a thousand years, it was the most powerful faith, often the only acceptable faith, in Europe, before spreading to the New World. It has achieved its enormous wealth and power through crusades, inquisitions, persecutions and holy wars, but these days it is still retaining its power by playing the 'we're being thrown to the lions' card." He felt like he had just poked some sleeping dragon.

"You're gonna hear from the Pope on that one, Mr. Greco," Kenny said through a grin.

"Yeah, time for a little heretic barbeque," Jeff kidded.

There was some laughing, maybe because it appeared Marius had been singling out Catholics. But there were also glares.

"You can always repent, Mr. Greco," Armand said. "Christ is always ready to forgive and be received in your heart."

Marius smiled. "How about we get back to the main theme of today's movie. How would you characterize *THX 1138*? Anyone?"

"As George Lucas's phone number," Kenny said.

"A bit of backstory movie lore. But I mean as genre."

"To me it's a dystopia," Justin said.

"Exactly!" Marius exclaimed. "The future is not a happy place in any of these post-apocalyptic movies. In *Metropolis* a ruling elite enjoys the sybaritic pleasures of the powerful and privileged. They play and rule from the soaring structures of the upper city, and are supported by a subterranean-dwelling and laboring proletariat living a life of drone-like drudgery that is physically and socially beneath those above ground. The workers of the urban netherworld toil on a ziggurat-like structure that, in a dream sequence, becomes the mouth of the devouring ancient pagan deity, Moloch; the clock serves as a symbol of the crucifix upon which one worker is, so to speak, 'chronified.' In *THX 1138* we see the same drone-like work, now assisted by mandatory drug dosage, sex is restricted and punished, and entertainment consists of mindless brutality by Blacks. In *Blade Runner* 'replicants' have advanced to possess powers greater than humans and must be hunted down and 'retired'. In 1984 the degree of control exercised by Big Brother is pervasive and sinister. Drone-like labor is also a central element, together with surveillance, and in *THX* there is a constant exhortation to produce and consume, although we don't know what. This, according to Hollywood, is what you have to look forward to."

Philip Armitage raised his hand and waited for Marius to recognize him. He was generally regarded as a nerd and was a member of the Young Republicans Club. Marius wondered why he was taking his urban anthropology class, as it was well known that Armitage had his ambitions firmly in sight—to Yale undergrad and law school, then some high-ranking position in the State Department of a Republican administration. He was only in Palatine, he was too eager to explain to anyone who might be curious, because he was spending his high school years with his aunt, a piano teacher, while his parents were in Brussels doing something with American relations with the EU. The answer to the question of why he wasn't with his parents and establishing a European educational pedigree was less forthcoming. Perhaps it had something to do with Philip's gender dysphoria, which was not the right kind of baggage his parents cared to drag around. "I remember that a lot of people were worried when the year 1984 finally came around, as if the Orwell novel had predicted what would actually happen. Instead, the places that were supposed to be most like what Orwell had written about, particularly the USSR and Red China, were falling apart politically. A few years later and the USSR was finished and China had gone capitalist— none of which would have happened without Nixon and Reagan," he added with a satisfied smirk of too-red lips.

That Armitage had an interesting point, but a dubious explanation let Marius to reply simply that "Life does not always imitate art—on a schedule."

"I think Lucas got almost everything right," Kenny said. "Some of the stuff, like the cyborg cops, the dwarfish road workers, and the intravenous educational system, might be a little too early for 2021. But the torturing of prisoners, the violent entertainment and, especially at the end where the cyborg cops stop chasing him because it has exceeded some budget level, that stuff is already here. And I disagree with Philip, a lot of that 1984 stuff is also here, especially that 'newspeak' and the amount of surveillance. I don't buy any of that right-wing crap that these sorts of things only happen in communist countries," he said, flashing a glance at Armitage.

Marius consulted his watch. "Well thanks to all of you for such a wide-ranging discussion, perhaps the most interesting of the semester. But I am curious that no one has mentioned what I found to be the most poignant scene in that film: *THX* climbing up that airshaft to the surface and the cyborgs calling to him 'you have no place to go,' 'you have no place to go.' At the surface *THX* stands there against what looks to be a setting sun in a sky on fire. A bird flies by but there is no other sign of life. Is it no longer habitable on the surface? Is that why they live subterranean? Why does he have no place to go? Will he be dead in a matter of minutes from radiation or pollution,? O will he be greeted by a gorgeous Southern California day, or the one day of Spring you get in Palatine?

"That's not correct," Kenny said, "since global warming, Palatine Spring is now three days."

Marius smiled and continued. "Then, how many of you would take the chance that *THX* took, and climb out of that underworld not knowing whether it meant freedom or death? Or, is there another underlying question raised by this movie. What is the cost to have an orderly world? Why is the society after these guys, controlling them with electrical shocks and drugs and putting them in prisons that are like the inside of a milk bottle? Because they have disturbed the order of things?"

"I think you might be asking us what it would take for any of us to get out of Palatine, Mr. Greco," Jeff said. "Do you see Palatine as some sort of place like that underworld in *THX 1138*? Is that why you are leaving us Mr. Greco? You know something that we don't know?"

Marius gave a tight smile, with a tinge of sadness. "No, now that you have taken my course, you know everything that I know. I'm just leaving because I'm giving you all lousy grades and I don't want my body to be found floating in the canal."

They laughed. "But seriously, I enjoyed teaching this stuff to you guys and I hope you got something out of it."

The students applauded, although there were a few exceptions.

XXX

It's a Wonderful Life

Marius had just sat down on his favorite bar stool at the end of the bar when Jesus said immediately: "Hey Marius, George Bailey, Clarence the Angel and Mr. Gower walk into a bar in Bedford Falls and . . ."

"Wrong," Marius interrupts, "It was Pottersville, and Clarence wasn't an Angel yet, just some second-class stupid intern, or something, because he hadn't gotten his wings. You have to get this stuff right, Jesus. You don't see me screwing up *The Three Amigos*, do you?"

"Who are three amigos?" Jesus asked.

"You, Marius, and me," Josh said, sitting down next to Marius. Is this a Capra seminar? What have I missed?"

Jesus butted back in. "*It's a Wonderful Life* was on TV the other night. I finally saw it, for the first time. Now I can join you amigos in talking about it. Okay?"

Marius and Josh looked at each other, mocking smiles on their faces. "Join in? Join in? He wants to join in?" Marius said sarcastically.

"He's seen the movie how many times?" Josh asked.

"Ah, once," Marius replied.

Josh just shook his head back and forth in mock disgust. "Next he will be wanting us to call him Nick, after the Pottersville bartender."

Jesus, now completely aware that his two amigos were making fun of him, was glad that he didn't tryout his punchline to his bar joke about George, Clarence, and Mr. Gower.

"He doesn't even have the slightest resemblance to Sheldon Leonard, don't you think?" Josh said to make Jesus feel even less informed.

"No, he's more a Gilbert Roland type, wouldn't you say?"

"More Tony Quinn to me."

"Okay, let's go with Quinn. But definitely not Sheldon Leonard."

"Nope."

Jesus slapped his bar rag down on the bar. "Now you two *piñiatas* are going after my heritage."

Marius and Josh smiled at each other. "Okay, we'll stop if you get us a couple of margaritas," Marius said. "How about you make one for yourself, too, as this is sort of a farewell libation."

"Ya know, Jesus, this place is one of the few things I'm gonna miss about Palatine," Marius said when Jesus returned with three mango margaritas and some chips and salsa.

"I don't know why, there's a Mexican bar or restaurant on every other corner in LA," Jesus said.

"Yeah, but none of them will have played a part in a great mystery of Palatine."

"Here's to that mystery remaining mystery," Josh said raising his glass. The three of them clicked their glasses together.

"Ya never know, it might make a good screenplay someday," Marius said, half-jokingly. "Every small town should at least have a story."

"Better it should remain a mystery. Zeus and I have to live here, remember," Josh admonished.

Marius affected a thoughtful look. "Nothing should remain secret forever, or life has even less meaning than it already has."

Josh snorted. "I'm gonna have to suck on that little philosophical gumdrop. Can I email you if I figure it out?"

"Please do, because I'm not sure I get it either."

"So, Marius, you are going to be like George Bailey, except that you were going to leave your town and not marry the pretty local girl." Jesus offered, still striving for acceptance in the *It's a Wonderful Life* Club.

Marius grinned. "George should have left Bedford Falls when he had the chance; a young man with dreams and ambitions. Maybe he wouldn't have ended up any happier, but at least he would know why. Capra's way, he is always going to wonder what kind of adventure he missed out on."

"But that wasn't the American Dream at the time," Josh said. "Soldiers coming back from the war making the world safe for democracy, back to the girl whose picture he carried, to the job and family. You know, the world Norman Rockwell illustrated for him."

Marius demurred. "Places like Palatine, or Bedford Falls, were already in decline by the time that *It's a Wonderful Life* was released. You get a different angle from Wyler's *The Best Years of Our Lives*, released the same year—that world had already changed, moved on."

"Am I going to have to watch another movie?" Jesus said.

"Yes, but first make another round of margaritas," Josh said.

"I always wonder about George, the next day," Marius mused. "The day after that wonderful manifestation of community solidarity, familism and friendship, the Building and Loan rescued, finding Zu-Zu's petals, and Clarence getting his wings. It's just like the day after Christmas—when you have probably watched this movie again—the next day when George is going to have to walk into his family-run business and deal with uncle Billy and his drinking problem."

"How can you say that Marius?" Jesus objected. "It says The End of the movie; so it is over and there is no tomorrow."

"Only in movies do people live happily ever after, with no tomorrows." Marius was about to elaborate, but Josh broke in, addressing Jesus. "You have to understand that a movie isn't just a movie to somebody like our friend Marius. He is an anthropologist and movies are a cultural artform that reflect the way in which we perceive reality. He is interested in deconstructing that perception of reality to determine what it is that we consider wonderful about the story of *It's a Wonderful Life*. Have I kind of got that right?" He asked, turning to Marius.

"Couldn't have said it better myself," Marius responded. "Well, maybe I could have. Most people approach movies as entertainment, a form of diversion from the reality of their lives, and they prefer the time they spend in the willing suspension of disbelief to be kind of neatly contained, with a beginning, middle, and an end that sort of sums things up, answers questions, and seems a plausible conclusion. Its realism is justice served, mystery solved, people living happily-ever-after, and such. But, we know, that is not realism. Reality is that *every ending is a new beginning*. Like the Greek philosopher Heraclitus said, 'everything changes, nothing remains the same.'

"But the ending of that movie is always the same," Jesus protested.

Marius shook his head. "But it does not have the same meaning to those who view it, because they are different, because their times are different. Consider Bedford Falls, or Palatine for that matter, in the American experience. America was founded as a colonial enterprise. It was not foreseen as a place of big cities like Europe, but an extension of hinterland for Europe from which its rich resources could be exploited for the advantage of the old country. It was seen largely as a place of extraction, of farms, mines, and trapping and lumber camps. All that were needed were small towns to provide essential products and services and assembly points that connected to the few coastal large cities that were shipping ports. Sometimes canals, like the Erie Canal running through Palatine, were needed to enhance these connections. When you look at the writings of some of the founding fathers, like Jefferson for example, they did not see America as a place of large cities, of which many of them had an abiding distrust. Small- town folk felt alienated from and looked down upon by big-city people—like they still do today."

"You mean people like you? Is that why they keep writing nasty shit on your garage door, Marius? Because you look down upon us?"

"What do you mean by us, amigo? I hope that you and my bagel friend here are not under the delusion that you are socially integrated members of the local populace. To really fit in and be accepted, your families would have had to float in here on the Canal in the Mayflower a couple of hundred years ago."

"Perhaps you exaggerate slightly," Josh said.

"I'm not just expressing an opinion. I am an urban anthropologist and it's my business, my academic responsibility to study this stuff. Back in New York, or Chicago and LA ,both Jews and Mexicans, like most other ethnic groups that are not regarded as white and/or Christian, tend to associate mostly within their own ethnic enclaves where they are most accepted and comfortable. We are able to operate in big cities because we fit into the economic infrastructure as school teachers and other professionals, or people who perform agricultural or other modest on professional activities. Most immigrant groups settled this way in large cities, and their numbers and utility gained them a certain level of acceptance. This applies even to immigrant groups of currently suspect ethnicities, such as Middle Easterners and Africans. There are loads of Ethiopian and Somali cabdrivers, there are large communities of Arabs not only in Southern California, but also in the upper Midwest."

Jesus set down more chips and salsa. "So how do they get to fit in so easily? And how do you like my modest unprofessional services, gentlemen?"

Marius grimaced at the rebuke, but was determined to get his point across. "It's not always a smooth process, but the size and scale of big cities, and thier social and economic needs, make cities more forgiving. It's like a big ocean; there's more dilution of any ethnographic differences. The culture of the American small town is radically different, and we see now more than ever that small towns and rural areas have played into the cultural, and consequently political rift that has resulted in the kind of electoral politics that produced the likes of Donald Trump. The people of small towns and rural areas are predominantly White, Christian, and conservative. These places used to predominate until the turn of the 19th century. They were celebrated by regionalist writers and painters as the true heart of America, where anti-urbanism prevailed. Cities were regarded as crowded, dirty, corrupt, and a babble of immigrant voices, much of which was true. In 1900, the majority of people lived in small towns and on farms; but, by 1920 the majority lived in cities and have continued to the point where four-fifths of the population now live in metropolitan areas. By 1946, when George Bailey wanted to leave town, because like so many young men like him—and some young women, too, like the girl in *Sister Carrie*, another movie you should see . . ."

"Oh, shit, not another movie," Jesus moaned.

"Are you just practicing your dissertation defense on us?" Josh asked. "I hope there's not an exam before we go home."

"Small towns and rural areas were pretty much on life support," Marius continued. "Today George would have an even bigger problem in that a lot of the farms and businesses he has loaned money to are failing and declining in value because family farms are more given over to agribusiness, local mom and pop store operations are getting clobbered by big-box stores and even more so by Amazon, and the local movie house has been closed for some time now because everybody is streaming their entertainment. And George is going to try to hold his operation together against the machinations of increasingly consolidated big banking operations with their derivatives and subprime mortgages, and other types of collateralized debt obligations. Hell, it was a lot of people in small towns and rural areas that got financially screwed by these slick operators who suckered them into debt. Now these White Christian farmers and townspeople are angry. And most of the people they are angry at come from big cities; Wall Street is screwing them over financially, Washington is a swamp of self-serving politicians that can't or won't keep out illegal immigrants and terrorists, and Hollywood is polluting their culture with LGBT values. They don't trust anybody and they want their conservative, small-town Bedford Falls version of America returned and will vote for somebody who promises it to them."

"And they got him," Josh said.

"Also, they are armed," Marius continued. "And some of them are angry enough, to shoot up their own schools and places of worship."

"But that's not what happened here. It wasn't an angry White Christian who attacked our school," Jesus said.

"Not directly," Marius countered. "They just got somebody else angry enough to do it as an active revenge. I don't see much difference there. We know the story behind that."

"So, you're going to do what George Bailey couldn't do—you're getting out of Bedford Falls," Jesus said.

"Yup, much the only reason for my staying here would be you two guys and these," Marius responded, lifting his mango margarita. But the Mediterranean climate, gorgeous sunsets and my dissertation committee call."

"And isn't there a certain female voice in that chorus?" Josh asked.

"Let's drink to that. A farewell round of margaritas, amigos. But we are still going to miss you."

"I will miss you guys as well, but I have to get out. Circumstances might have cast me as a hero in Palatine, but eventually these people are going to turn on me, as some of them already have, because I have disappointed their expectations of a hero. I am the perennial outsider, with values and ideas that threaten their established and accepted order of things. And my job here is of the most insidious sort; I am a teacher, with access to shaping the minds of their next-generation. And I am an atheist to boot. And since many of them have found out that I am only here for the purposes of my dissertation research, they have come to regard me—and perhaps not without just cause—as exploitative. It wouldn't end well."

"You had better get out of town then, George," Josh said. "what did George say were the three most exciting sounds in the world in that movie?"

"Oh, yeah," Marius answered with a smile of satisfaction, "anchor chains, plane motors, and train whistles."

Jesus just shook his head in defeat.

PART THREE

XXXI

Deception

Eight weeks earlier

Marius was surprised to find Hisham parked in front of his house when he returned from school. He walked up to the pick-up and Hisham rolled down his window. The expression that the Iraqi was wearing on his face signaled a problem.

"What's up, man?" Marius asked, "We weren't supposed to meet. In fact, the less we are seen with each other at this time, the better."

"I want to stop," Hisham said curtly.

"Stop what?" Marius asked, although he had a pretty good idea from the tone, and Hisham's white-knuckle grip on the steering wheel, what he was referring to.

"To stop the plan," he replied.

"Really? You have a marvelous sense of timing," Marius said with as much sarcasm as he could muster. "What is it? The Quran says you can't do it on an odd number date, or has some other prohibition?"

"I know about the girl," Hisham said.

"Of course you do. I told you about her. From my end of things this is the whole reason for this. What's your problem?"

"You didn't tell me everything about her."

Marius stopped leaning on the pick-up door, straightening himself as he looked up and down the street to make sure they were not being observed.

"What do you need to know? How much she weighs?

How tall she is? You know enough. You know the reason I set this up. And from your end of it, you should appreciate that this is a little shot at moral redemption. It solves your problem of honor in the best way possible. So, what the fuck is the deal?" Marius could feel his anger rising.

Hisham looked up at Marius. He almost whispered. "You did not say that she has become an infidel," he said.

"So what! She also likes the Golden State Warriors."

"My brother cannot be joined with infidel."

"What? Is your brother a Knicks fan, or something? Jesus, they're not getting married. This is ridiculous."

"My faith says there can be no contact in any way," Hisham said firmly.

"Well, let me tell you something, you fucking mosque mouse, you're going to have to eat this ham sandwich, because you're in this thing up to your balls and I am not going to let some proscription from your holy book screw things up for a lot of people." Marius again checked up and down the street because his voice was rising.

"I will be sinning against Islam if I allow you to do this. I will be cursing both myself and my brother."

"Bullshit. Your religion is like every other damn religion—it changes its dogma and doctrines to meet any need or convenience. It's about power and market share. It's about controlling your believers and out-numbering your competition. And it doesn't matter if you're a goddamn hypocrite. What about your 'temporary marriages' that allow you guys a little piece of infidel ass when it suits you? Does the Quran say that it's okay to join with some sinful flesh in motels that rent by the hour? You Muslims are no less hypocrites than practitioners of any other faith."

"You should not speak about Islam in this way."

"Well, my friend, as a pre-talking-movie days Jewish singer used to say, 'you ain't heard nothing yet' if you think

I'm going to let you weasel out on some metaphysical technicality."

Still, Hisham did not seem intimidated. "I will go to the hospital and I will disconnect my brother from those tubes and things that keep him alive. I will let him die and go to paradise as a *shihadi*. That is what he wanted; not what you want to do. I should have done that long ago."

Marius could feel his anger rising to the level of violence. "That's bullshit, too, and you fucking know it. He didn't go into that school for Al Qaeda, Mohammed, or in order to screw virgins in paradise. He went in there for payback for what happened to him. You want to get even for all the indignity, the prejudice, the insult of being called a sand monkey, and for what's on that video. And you and I know the only way that video can ever harm him, is if it gets out there where everybody can see it. I've turned that video into an insurance policy. It's an insurance policy that allows us to do really the only thing your brother can do for redemption. And as long as it stays secret, you are not going to have that Sheriff up your ass over anything. Now you want to blow that up? What do you think they're going to do with his body after you pull the plug on him—give him a funeral parade through the center of town?"

"He still will not become someone who serves the infidel."

"First, they will autopsy your brother until he looks like a zipper display, and when they are finished with him they're probably going to cremate him and you'll be lucky if you get his ashes in a coffee can. And that's all going to be done by infidels. You know that my answer to that is different."

Hisham made no response, only twisting his hands over the steering wheel. Marius checked the street again. It was starting to snow and he could not help noticing the beauty of the big heavy flakes as they fluttered through the penumbra of the streetlights. He did not mind the arrival of this type of snow so much. It was that dry powder that blew in on cold winds, winds well below freezing, that turned the roads into treacherous glaciers in these parts, winds that froze gas lines and stopped engines altogether. He didn't need a weather problem to compound the plan that he had made with this conflicted Muslim.

After a minute or so, Hisham broke his silence. "When you were a soldier in Iraq did you kill any Muslims, Mr. Greco?"

Marius just glared back. "You were, what, eleven years old when your family left Iraq, even before your younger brother was born?" Marius said rhetorically. "I liked a lot of the Iraqi people that I met over there. Some of them I liked even more-than some of the Christian assholes that I was serving with. I didn't think we had any good reason to be there trashing your country. I didn't believe any of that American government propagandistic bullshit about WMD. But let me ask you: might you have been one of those Iraqi kids, standing by the roadside as our Humvees and armored vehicles drove by, and holding a cell phone, waiting for just the right moment to punch in that last phone number digit to trigger an IED? I saw a few of those kids. They had usually disappeared by the time the dust, debris and guts settled. I lost a few comrades that way, but actually I lost even more who did themselves in after they came back. Maybe we should've shot every goddamn kid standing by the roadside with a cell phone."

"My father worked for the Americans," was Hisham's only reply.

"I'm just trying to tell you that if there's no good way of getting into war, there's no really good ways of getting out of one either. You're going to have to deal with this little blemish on your route to paradise, brother. Or I'm going to regard you as just another kid standing on the roadside holding a cell phone. I'll shoot you dead in the moment."

"What do you mean by that Mr. Greco?"

"What I mean is this: you do anything that exposes me or places people that I have engaged in any kind of jeopardy and I will be forced to use that video as a form of moral coverage and you can deal with the consequences that it will create between your personal dignity and Islam. You don't have long to decide, brother. You know what your role is in all of this. If you're smart you will recognize that it's the best deal you can get for your family, and that includes your brother."

Hisham looked up at Marius. His face was angry, but his eyes were beginning to tear up.

Marius calmed down a little. "I hope that you will see that this is the only way, Hisham. We need you; not just your consent, but your participation as well."

Hisham said nothing. He just started the pickup, turned on the windshield wipers to clear off the thick, sticky flakes, glancing up at Marius and slowly drove off, his tires muffled by the snow.

Marius stood in the street watching the truck's lights disappear in the falling snow like a cinematic fade to white. "Don't fuck this up, brother. Don't fuck this up," he mumbled to himself.

A few days later, the snow had turned granular, hard, and propelled into drifts by an icy wind when Almaaz collected Chamsi, Saddiq, and Jamal at the Oswego County airport where they had arrived on a connecting commuter flight from Toronto Pearson International. The Californians shuddered against the chill of the hypothermic gusts.

The fact that they all held U.S. passports did not entirely allay their trepidation of a trio of Middle Eastern names crossing international borders. But they had dressed as "American" as possible—Saddiq in a Golden State Warriors jacket,

Chamsi with a little fuchsia streak in her uncovered hair, Jamal did his best to offset his swarthy complexion and thick black hair by shaving off his mustache and sporting a LA Dodgers cap and Vans footwear. They were "back-storied" with a fake wedding invitation in Arabic script from Samarjidid, New York that would allow them to claim they were relatives. Jamal was eyed warily by one security person in Toronto until he asked the agent if he was a Raptors fan and expressed his admiration for one of their players. They made sure to keep speaking English with Almaaz on the way down to Palatine. In the back of the van was the box of medical equipment that had been shipped from LA a week earlier.

None of the three had ever seen weather like this. The snow came down blown horizontally, "like a frozen sandstorm," Saddiq said, that created a "whiteout" effect just a few yards ahead of a vehicle. So much snow had already come down that plows had made several passes on the streets, almost burying some parked cars, and creating glacial walls that obscured vision of the other cars at intersections. Their vehicle's tires made an odd, muffled scrunching sound on the roadway, that sounded, Saddiq commented, "like Styrofoam being compressed."

Almaaz remarked that this weather was not untypical of the region which experienced heavy snowstorms from what was known as "the lake effect." "Some local had even invented an orange Styrofoam ball, about the size of a golf ball, to stick on top of one's car aerial," she added, "to warn of traffic at intersections when the snow was piled several feet high." Each time the car slid in the snow, they yelped and grabbed one another like riders on a roller coaster.

The weather report was that the temperature would drop even further than the twenty-two degrees. Saddiq and Jamal had never experienced snow before and now understood why they had been instructed to bring warm clothing. Almaaz knew that it could worsen very fast and she worried about the icy roads and blizzard conditions that could raise hell with their plans. But so far all was going according to schedule, so she remained outwardly calm to her passengers.

Almaaz also did not want to have a driving problem that might incur any involvement of law enforcement. The minivan was a potential weak spot because the plates might be discovered as fakes, although they were half-obscured by icy slush. Marius had given Rachel the $700 to buy the older van "for her business" and have the name of her farm painted on the sides. But on this day the signs were covered over with adhesive plastic of the same white color as the van. Josh had expertly created the fake license plates, but if they were run through the registration system the ruse would be discovered. If all went well, the sign cover and the fake plates would be removed afterwards and it would just be another legally-registered commercial van.

The trip to the farm took about forty-five minutes longer due to the weather, but by late morning the trio began comfortably waiting out the remainder of the day at the Berman farm. The weather assisted Almaaz in keeping her guests inside the Berman house and out of sight of anyone passing by.

Hisham and Jesus checked to make sure that all of the security cameras at the Aziz market were operational. They then placed two plastic cups of mint tea in the cup holders in Jesus' truck before heading east in the direction of the village of Samarjidid, a little over two hours down the road from Palatine.

Hisham usually enjoyed the occasional trip he made to this village of a little more than six-hundred almost exclusively Iraqi Shia immigrants, many of whom had arrived years before the rise and fall of Saddam Hussein. He could visit the simple little mosque, chat in Arabic about the old country that he only knew as a young boy, and feel the kind of society to which he had never become fully acculturated. But this time he was anxious and unsettled, still not having gotten over that argument with Marius, still bothered by what he was about to participate in as something *mazhur*, something illicit and forbidden by Islam. He worried that he would not see his brother in the afterlife.

Jesus sensed the tension in Hisham's silence. At first, he accounted it to the younger man's concentration on driving the icy country roads. They had slid off a couple of times but merely bounced off the high piles of packed snow that the plows had distributed along the roadside.

"Let me know if you want to take a break and I can drive," Jesus offered.

"You don't think I'm doing very well?" Hisham said evenly.

"You're doing fine. I'm just a sharing sort of guy."

"Neither of us are from places that have this kind of weather," Hisham said. "I never even got to drive in a sandstorm."

Jesus reflected for a few moments on the possibilities for further conversation. He didn't know the Iraqi very well and now had a little idea of what the young man might be going through emotionally. After a few minutes it was Hisham who broke the silence.

"I don't feel like saying very much—or maybe I feel like saying too much—because I am so pissed off."

"That's okay. I understand, amigo. You've been going through a lot."

"I don't know if you can understand everything. Everybody has their own history. People here treat us like shit. Not everybody, but they have us wondering every time they look at us that they are not seeing those two buildings in New York crashing to the ground. It doesn't matter that there was not a single Iraqi in those planes. We are all the same to them.

They don't even understand the different forms of Islam. If we were driving to Cairo or Istanbul around four centuries ago, we would find those cities as tolerant and multicultural places, where Sunni and Shiite Muslims, Christians, Armenians, Copts, Jews, even Zoroastrians or Hindus were living side by side in relative peace. There were disagreements and riots, and there was religious discrimination, but they would be a tolerant, liberal paradise compared with Europe at the time. If we were driving around the same time to Paris or London, we would find cities full of religious bigotry, in which only those belonging to the ruling faith would be safe. In England they killed Catholics and hunted their priests like dogs; in France Protestants were the prey; the Jews were always caught up in religious wars and inquisitions; and everybody wanted to keep those dangerous Muslims out of Europe. And now, just like the Christians, and other faiths, because we have some extremists who use their religions to justify their political motivations, Islam is not wanted anywhere. Yet, in many respects, our politics are a result of the way we have been treated by Christian Europe and by the Zionists. Sorry, I told you I can talk too much."

"I should know more of your history," Jesus said. "Shit, I don't even know my own very well. You should hear Marius on that subject. The first time I met him he hadn't even finished his first margarita before he told me that my people are the original people of America and that the Christians who came from Europe, Catholic and Protestant, basically enslaved us and forced us to accept their religion, ands language. They wiped most of us out with their diseases and stole our land and, now if we try to come across their border, they will take our children away from us. Then he asks me if I can find any good reason for worshiping their god."

"Yeah, that sounds like Marius."

"He really messed up my head. What was I supposed to do, start worshiping snakes and lizards like my Indian ancestors probably did? I didn't dare talk about it with Lupita; she would've strangled me with her rosary."

"She's Catholic religious?"

"More than the Pope. She doesn't mind too much if I don't go to church. A lot of Mexican men are that way. But if she thought I was giving up my faith I would be in big trouble with her. The problem is the way Marius describes things. I feel either like a sucker who has been abused by these gringos, or a revolutionary who wants to take my land and culture back from them."

"Maybe we have more in common than you think," Hisham said with a chuckle, then added, "but Marius is an atheist. When he dies he will have no place to go to. He will have no Paradise. I don't understand how he can do that to himself."

"He says that he can't believe what is not believable to him—that he does not choose to be an atheist."

"But God chooses us. We do not choose him."

"Then He seems to choose some of us to get the shit," Jesus said.

"We believe that God is great."

"Yeah, but we are driving in a snowstorm to . . .". Jesus left his sentence unfinished.

"Now I'm going to have to put my brother in a grave that is not even his own."

"If we don't end up in a snowy grave ourselves," Jesus said as they nearly sledded off the icy road.

Samarjidid had been founded apart from the town of Islamberg, a small settlement of Black Muslims down near the Pennsylvania border. Islamberg had been settled by Sunni Muslims, whereas Samarjidid was mostly Shia. Islamberg was actually founded earlier by some ex-slaves who were Muslims in Africa and never got caught up in the Christianization of

Blacks who filtered into Protestant denominations. They were descended from the very first Muslim slaves brought to Caribbean plantations by the Spanish in the 1500s. Since then there had been some addition of Middle Eastern Muslims, but most of them have gone on to big cities.

But both communities, despite their small size, were the subject of suspicion by Homeland Security and Islamophobes of being in some way connected with international terrorism. However, Hisham's father had decided to settle in Palatine when he came to the states because he preferred his children to be in an environment where they could acquire fluency in English and have better prospects for assimilation into American society. Many of the residents of Samarjidid nursed a dream of returning to the homeland that Muhammad Aziz did not share. Having worked for the Americans, he and his family would be forever stained as opportunists and collaborators. Palatine had not been an easy place to assimilate, but Muhammad understood some similarities between small-town culture in Iraq and the U.S., particulary the conservatism and insularity, that he could negotiate the way he did with the American soldiers when he served as their translator. It had been going reasonably well until what happened to Khalid.

XXXII

The Long Night

Chamsi and Saddiq, outfitted in hospital scrubs, strode confidently into the hospital, acquired a gurney out of a side hall of the ER and rolled it to the elevators. Chamsi wore fake glasses and Saddiq had donned a false ponytail wig below a baseball cap. Their fake laminated ID badges had been relatively easy to create. Josh got a photo from a nurse with her badge clearly shown from the hospital website and Photoshopped in their photos and fake names.

At the ICU floor Saddiq pushed the gurney on toward Khalid's room as Chamsi approached the nurse's desk and told the nurse in charge that she had come up from Radiology to retrieve Mr. Aziz for a full MRI that had been requested by Homeland Security and authorized by the Radiology scheduler on duty, who had phoned (actually Jamal from a phone outside Radiology) with verbal authorization just minutes before.

Saddiq announced to the Sheriff's deputy outside of Khalid's room that the patient was to be taken to Radiology for a scan and they would have him back in "half an hour, or so." Chamsi and Saddiq then proceeded to switch Khalid and his fluid bottles over to gurney and rolled him past the nurse's station to the elevator. The nurse, chatting with the Sheriff's deputy, paid them no attention. Neither she nor the deputy noticed that the elevator was heading for a floor other than where Radiology was located.

By the time they reached the main floor Chamsi and Saddiq had taken down the fluid bottles and stored them under the sheet that they spread an entirely over Khalid. For a moment Chamsi shuddered at the thought that something they were doing might actually bring Khalid out of his coma.

At that hour in the morning, the only traffic in hallways were people coming into the ER. A woman in the waiting room was rocking in her seat, trying to gentle a crying baby, and going through the door they passed a man in a blood-stained shirt who was being escorted by two other men who appeared to be inebriated. Attracting no particular attention, they managed to push the gurney out the door to the van as if they were removing a deceased patient. They folded the gurney into the back of the van, got in behind it, and Jamal drove them away into the night. They jettisoned the gurney as soon as they were about a mile from the hospital, then, turned around to head in the direction of the Berman farm.

It wasn't until about thirty minutes later that the ICU nurse began to wonder and made a call down to Radiology where the technician informed her that he had no idea what she was talking about.

By the time that Sheriff Cavanaugh arrived at the hospital, the van was already pulling into the Berman barn. Jamal immediately removed the magnetic coverings over the signs painted on the sides and removed the fake license plates.

Up to this point Chamsi had been so preoccupied with the logistics that she had not had time to consider the task that was now before her. It had been one thing to observe videos of surgeries, to read up on procedure, and to actually practice on the surgery dummy. The first thing she did was vomit.

"Are you gonna be okay?" Siddiq asked. "Better to do this with an empty stomach, I suppose."

"It had better be," she answered, wiping her mouth with a paper towel.

"I think I know what's bothering you. The same thing is bothering me," he said.

"Yeah." She nodded.

"This guy's already dead, Cham. Certainly brain-dead. Look at it that way."

"I know, I know. I keep telling myself that. But . . .".

"And he's a murderer. Who knows how much hell he's already brought on our people. Idiots and bigots calling us dirty names and yelling at us "go home, camel-fucker." Saddiq was psyching himself the way he did for his *muy thai* competitions, summoning the anger, reaching into the depth of disappointment with the hypocrisy of a country that was falsely sold to him as a land of equality. Yet he was conflicted. How often he had silently cheered when the Americans lost in battle, when their own kind committed atrocities with their beloved guns. This was not the satisfaction he might get from becoming a *jihadist* himself, but maybe even better. He could sit back and watch them sputter and wonder at what happened, and he wouldn't have to risk being blown to bits of bone and guts. He checked the ISIS and AQ websites from safe computers, but he had come to his own view of strategy. Let the white motherfuckers defeat themselves. Look how bin Laden had put terror in them like a plague virus; he completely changed their society, more powerfully than Bush or Obama. One blow, and they were like ants when as kids they pissed on their colonies. These were not an invincible people because they were soft and self-deceiving with their false notion of being unified. They will destroy themselves as all empires eventually do. Bin Laden put the fear of Allah into them, and their fear has given them Trump, their messenger of death. So, now our project will add to their fear of a ghost.

"Even his brother is on board with this," he said to Chamsi.

"I *know*, I've been over it a hundred times. It's still not easy."

"Look, Cham, we gotta be fast. Try to think of just what has to be done—for her. If I didn't think I would fuck it up, I would just have you tell me what to do and I would do it. I saw enough blood and guts as a kid in the old country."

"No, I can do it. I just need you to assist. Technically, this isn't difficult. It's most important to avoid any sepsis in the organ, so let's get cleaned up and get him prepped. We will do this right inside the van."

Chamsi cleaned and isolated the surgical site following the protocol in any standard surgical procedure. She found a vein and injected a general anesthetic while Saddiq laid out the surgical instruments as she had instructed him. It was her first chance to get a good look at the face of Khalid now that they had some bright light on his body. It was the face of a young, handsome Iraqi boy, she thought, as she double-checked his eyes, lifting the lids to make sure he was out. She wondered what he was like as a person. Could he be anything like the brothers of Jazmeen? They are handsome boys, too, she thought, but they became monsters capable of believing that the honor of their family demanded their sister's death. Perhaps if she thought of them as she performed the task ahead of her it would be easier. But her thoughts always returned to her friend and the suffering that her brothers had brought upon her, not only the physical suffering they had imposed on her body, but the loss of her family as well. Chamsi had come to admire the inner beauty that was behind the luminous green-brown eyes in her lovely face. In the months that Jazmeen had been tended by Chamsi and her mother and aunt, through the court trial and conviction of her brothers and the rejection of her family, Jazmeen had come to understand that first search that took her toward atheism was an attempt to free herself from the shackles that religion imposed, the wall it placed between her and a fuller womanhood and a wider world of experiences and relationships. She could not bring herself to accept that she must endure the imprisonment of conservative Islam for the promise of some *akhirah*, or afterlife on which she would be resurrected and judged for how obedient and dutiful a daughter and wife she had been. She wanted the life she had in hand, to dare to trust her own mind and heart. And even at the depths of her suffering she did not regret that those feelings had intersected her fate with Marius Greco. It was *haram* even to allow herself thoughts of intimacy with an infidel and yet he understood her more completely than anyone, even Chamsi. How far the intimacy of that unlikely couple had gone Jazmeen never revealed beyond metaphor, or once a vague reference to Cathy in *Wuthering Heights*.

Chamsi never pushed the subject, thinking it might be some inexpressible love forged from her shared metaphysics with Marius, and physical attraction. During this period, she had often reflected on the oddity of it all. This Iraqi girl from a conservative Muslim family getting involved with a former American soldier who might actually have killed Iraqis. It was something that should not have happened for several obvious reasons and yet what they came to feel for one another superseded everything. "Love conquers all" was the English saying that seemed the only explanation.

But of the relationship between the two young women Jazmeen managed to find its own closeness in words. Chamsi loved the little poem that Jazmeen wrote in the birthday card she made for her.

What is a friend, you ask?
What is the taste of a fruit
at the peak of its ripeness
What is a friend, you ask?
What is the caress of the sun upon you
when it emerges from the clouds.
What is a friend, you ask?
Ask the beautiful bluebird

as it fluffs its feathers for your delight
And asks nothing in return.

Jazmeen had written it in Arabic script, and Chamsi recited it to herself often from memory. She repeated the verses again, as she hanged the bag of morphine from a hook inside the van and connected it to the port in the IV line.

"I'll call Tom in LA and he can text the pope joke to Marius," Jamal said to her.

"No, wait until it is done. I want to have it safe and secured first. Then make the call," she ordered. Chamsi had been so preoccupied with the logistics that she had not thought for some time of the audacity of this project when it was first proposed by Marius. She had to make up an elaborate story for her mother and aunt, about visiting some specialist out of town with Jazmeen that was only a small part of a complex alternate reality that Marius had scripted. Often, when Marius would be describing the process to her, he seemed to sound just like he was describing the plot of some motion picture and he had a way of making her believe that it was all feasible and would resolve like a movie plot.

Saddiq had been relatively easy to recruit into the scheme. He was just the type, cool and with an adventurous spirit. Under the right circumstances, he might be joining up with some Middle East political cause. He was a restless, picaresque, guy who balled up his fists at the slightest insult to his ethnicity or faith. Jamal had been brought in by Marius, who had served with Jamal's brother, Amir, as an interpreter in the military. Marius had spent a considerable amount of time with Amir and his family up until Amir's PTSD brought him to stick a 9 mm in his own ear in his car one night. Since that time Marius had become Jamal's substitute brother, with a loyalty that he would do almost anything for Marius. He was also absolutely enraptured with Jazmeen.

But now the danger in all of this put a frisson of fright through Chamsi. They had already done enough to probably be deported or incarcerated. But she could not let these thoughts interfere with her concentration on what she had to do next. "Okay, Saddiq," she said, "It's crunch time as the Americans say. We can't wait any longer, especially since that storm outside could really play havoc with our schedule. Grab those sponges and be ready."

Chamsi took a scalpel off the tray, put her left index finger close beside the point of incision, took a deep breath, and without hesitation, cut. Saddiq let out a little sigh of surprise as the blood ran over the stomach and down Khalid's side onto the blue surgical sheet.

"I'm in the right location, but I need to get deeper. I have to be careful here not to harm the organ itself," she said in an almost instructional, authoritative voice. "Sponge some of that blood away, so I can see what I'm doing, and I can do some vascular clamping."

Saddiq complied. She cut deeper, with care, stopping to apply hemostatic forceps. The liver began to appear and she enlarged the opening to gain access to the ducts. "Looks like there is a bit of a bruise here on the top edge of the right lobe," she said.

"Is that bad?" Saddiq asked.

"No, I don't think so. Maybe it was a sports injury, but it looks like it was already healing."

"In *muy thai*, some instructors teach the liver punch and the liver kick. It can be very painful and some fighters will drop and give up if you deliver a powerful and accurate blow. I know this because I have been struck in the liver a couple of times. Do you think I might have bruises like that?" he asked.

"Let me finish this job first. Then I can open you up and we'll take a look."

"No thanks. I'll take a pass on that."

"Maybe you ought to take a pass on kickboxing as well," she said. "Now I'm going to disconnect some plumbing. First, the bile duct; there, like that. Now the proper hepatic artery. Snip, snip, neatly done. There's no going back now; I could never reconnect these. Gimme some sponge right there so I can get a better look at the ligaments. The instructions were not to cut them too tight."

"What's that under there?" Saddiq asked.

"Gall bladder; makes bile, and sometimes stones. Okay, Coronary ligament first, then the Falciform." Chamsi took a couple of minutes, working carefully. "There. Now let's just check around to make sure we've got all the disconnection done—is the carrier ready?"

"Right here," he answered.

"Open that line on the morphine," she said. She took a breath and added, "full open."

Surprised at its heft, Chamsi lifted out the organ. She slipped it into the sterile bag, and gently placed it amongst the freeze-packs in the insulated red carrier with "Human Tissue for Transplant" printed on its sides. Saddiq zippered its top closed and secured it with a small padlock. A label on the lid described the contents with dates and times and contained a pocket with a donor consent form filled out with false names and signatures. It was as official-looking as they could make it.

"Okay, I'm going to suture. You can make the call to Tom now." Chamsi knew that she did not have to do a fully pro-fessional closure of the incision. She quickly checked his pulse and it was weaker than last time. She did not expect that it would be long. In a couple minutes she had it sutured and it looked more like a crude autopsy closure then a proper surgi-cal job. It struck her again that this young man was dying right in front of her, bereft of a vital organ, and with lethal doses of morphine pumping into him. It gave her a shudder, but she knew that if she kept busy, kept with the schedule, the distraction of the process would keep her from thinking about it too much. She called to Jamal to bring the bodybag.

It was 3:27 am when they were packed up and ready to move. Chamsi busied herself making sure that no traces of their activities would be left behind, gathering up the sheeting to be burned in the barrel fire Jamal had set outside the barn. Every few minutes she would stop and check Khalid's pulse and at 3:38 it was undetectable. She knew there was enough morphine in him now to kill a horse, so, according to plan, she called Almaaz to come from the market to pick her up. Her message was a simple *Inshallah 'alb*, "Allah willing" plus "heart," to mean that Khalid's heart had stopped. It seemed a strange way for her to tell her that her brother was dead. But then there was nothing normal about this.

The boys loaded Khalid's body on the floor of the van, arranging boxes of vegetables to cover the body completely. They took about fifteen minutes to burn everything from the hospital, scrubs, rubber gloves, drip bags, sheets with kerosene in a fifty-five gallon drum.

The boys waited until Almaaz arrived before departing. "Don't drive too fast," Almaaz cautioned them. "This is not California, and some spots are very icy. You can't afford to slide off the road into a ditch because there's a good chance you will not be able to get out without the assistance of a tow truck. We can't have that. Have you checked to make sure the GPS on your phones works?" They nodded affirmatively as she rattled off the questions.

As they were about to leave Saddiq whispered to Chamsi, turned so that Almaaz could not hear, "Are you sure he's really dead? Fuck, what if we hit a bump and he wakes up? What would I have to do, smother him or something? I don't know if I could do that."

"Don't worry about it; he's gone. No vitals. I checked several times," she said assuringly, but suppressing the thought that she had many times in nightmares that horrified her—that Khalid might revive once he was sealed in that cold grave. She added: "It was merciful. The only thing we could do. Almaaz and her older brother agreed to this." Even as she said it she knew this night would haunt her. "Get going," she commanded, "and good luck, *bit-tawfiq.*"

Almaaz asked for a few minutes alone with her brother and stood quietly beside the body bag. She said a few prayers over the covered body of her younger brother, wiped a tear from her eye and turned to walk to her car.

After the boys departed in the van, Chamsi and Almaaz conducted a thorough check for anything incriminating that might have been overlooked. Chamsi found a couple of spots of blood on the floor and one of Jamal's cigarette butts. Then she took a few minutes to color over the purple streak she had in her hair. Then they quickly set out in Almaaz's car for Oswego Airport, the organ carrier in the trunk where the car's heater could have no effect upon it.

The women consciously avoided the subject as they headed north in the early morning snow flurries, making small talk instead about being young, unmarried, professional Muslim women in quite different geographical locations. Marius had made sure that neither of them knew about the video, lest any sympathies their knowledge of it might impede their participation in the scheme. For the present at least it was necessary that they only know that Khalid had committed a horrendous crime and that any outcome should he survive his coma would be less just and dignified, indeed, *redemptive.* For the same reason, he had even kept knowledge of the video from Jazmeen.

Almaaz preferred to wait in her car in the airport parking lot with her mobile phone should anything go wrong. After about half an hour she received a one-word message from Chamsi via the LA burner phone, *"wadaeaan,"* and drove off toward her office.

———

According to plan Hisham and Jesus arrived the day before and had remained overnight in Samarjidid with the family of Mr. Alabadi.

Things did not go as smoothly for Saddiq and Jamal. Just before 5am they ran into a Sheriff's road block about two miles outside of Palatine. It was still blowing snow and the flashing lights of the squad cars created a surreal pulsing rainbow that almost got the boys to turn around and make a run for it. But Saddiq quickly rejected that idea and decided they had a better chance trying to fake their way through.

"Where are you headed?" The sheriff's deputy demanded, his flashlight searching the inside of the truck cab even though he had commanded the boys to put their hands on the dashboard where he could see them.

"Samarjidid," Saddiq responded. "A family wedding later today."

"Where are you coming from?"

"Toronto. We flew in last night and borrowed this van from a friend in Oswego."

"So why are you on the road from Palatine then?"

"We had agreed to pick up some fruits and vegetables from there. We kind of got delayed by the storm," Saddiq answered. Jamal was impressed with Saddiq's composure, and said nothing.

"Well, we are still going to have to take a look around in your vehicle. You guys will have to step out while we have a look in the back", the deputy said. Get your license and registration ready for me to examine. I wanna see your passports as well."

There were a total of four sheriff's deputies. As the boys stepped out, one of the deputies stepped back a few feet with his hand on his firearm and the other two made their way to the back of the van.

Saddiq knew that he had to act fast. "Sir, do you mind if I just make a quick call on my cell phone to say that we're running a little late?" He also took quick notice of the name patch on the deputy's uniform.

"Yeah, no problem. I have to phone in your plate and document numbers. So we are going to be a while."

As he had been instructed by Marius, Saddiq called him, began by saying that he had been given "permission to call by Sheriff's Deputy Miller." He then told Marius about being delayed and in the course of that mention the keyword "Hussein."

Fortunately, the boys had locked the back of the van and had to get the keys for the other deputies, which provided just enough delay for Marius to get a call to Sheriff Cavanaugh. In another couple of minutes, Deputy Miller received a call on his shoulder communication device from Cavanaugh. Saddiq was close enough to the deputy to hear. "Miller, you can let those two guys with the van that you are holding get on their way to their family wedding. I know they are okay. One of them has a cousin, Hussein, who is a good friend of my nephew, Mick."

"Sheriff gives you guys a clean bill." Miller said. "Boys, you can close of the van and give these guys their keys," he called to the two deputies, at the same time handing Saddiq their documents.

Jamaal gave an almost audible sigh of relief. "What the fuck was that all about?" he asked when they were back on the road.

"Fucked if I know. Marius just told me that if we are arrested, I am allowed a phone call and I should get the name of the policeman and then call him and say 'Hussein'. It was like magic. I wonder if Hussein works on all police." They laughed.

Sometime later, in the early morning, the Berman van arrived and Siddiq and Jamal connected with Hisham, Jesus and the imam. It was about 6:15am when Marius received an "OpInshallah+ S" text from the LA burner phone via Saddiq to let him know that the van had safely arrived in Samarjidid. Forty-five minutes later he received a message "OpInshallah+C" after Chamsi had arrived without incident in Toronto.

They immediately proceeded to the small Muslim cemetery near the mosque. It was freezing and blowing snow, but there was a fair amount of moonlight and their feet made scrunching sounds as they made their way into the iron-gated precincts of the cemetery. The imam, carrying a broom, led the way as the four men followed, each with a handle on the body bag.

Arriving at their destination the imam swept the cover slab on the grave and with a flashlight revealed the name Imam Hasan Askari, inscribed in Arabic script, 1884-1953. The brownish sandstone, spotted with green lichens, algae and moss, looked more ancient than it was. It took all of the men, pushing on one side to slide the slab open.

When the imam flashed his light into the dark interior, it was evident that the grave was empty. Askari's bones had been shipped to a cemetery in Najaf, Iraq in 1997. The grave's new occupant would be an anonymous sixteen-year-old in a plastic body bag, known only to a few people, among them the five men who performed this secret inhumation minutes before sunrise in a bone-chilling wind that would quickly erase evidence of their presence with fresh snow. Hisham wanted to look at his brother's face one last time, but the imam discouraged it. Instead, he remained a while longer, waited for the sun to rise on the horizon, leaned down to put his hand on the grave slab and said one word: *shihadi*.

As instructed, Jesus texted "OpInshallah+S" to Marius.

Later that morning, after a breakfast of mint tea and a fried and sugared confection that tasted to him very much like Mexican churros, Jesus headed for the airport in Oswego with Saddiq and Jamal. Hisham retrieved some food products that had been shipped to Samarjidid from Iraq, loaded them into the Berman van and set out for a return to Palatine.

———————

By that evening, a quiet, fluffy snowfall was wrapping the town of Palatine in a counterpane of white that Marius associated with that epiphany for George in *It's a Wonderful Life*. Capra cleverly used falling snowflakes as an indicator that George was returned by Clarence to those moments when he was considering suicide by jumping into the freezing river. Capra even paid-off the transition of the scene by having George check in his pocket for Zu-Zu's rose petals and, discovering they are there, burst into a smile of relief. That was all it took to bring the viewer, and George, back to reality. But that fluffy snow descending from the night sky, was the key to it, the use of just the right imagery—fresh snow—to reset the narrative. It was what made Capra a maestro in the art of cinema.

Marius felt an existential reset, too. He could begin thinking about his own return in earnest, about how Jazmeen would feel in his arms, about breathing in her exotic, sweet-spicy aroma, about how it seemed he was unwrapping a new gift with each removal of her *hijab*. He had waited as patiently as he could, allowing time for her to recover, for Palatine to accommodate itself to the vanishing of Khalid Aziz, and for any suspicions of his complicity in it to subside.

But there was Dr. St. George's email. It was a fundamental axiom of the life of the Ph.D. candidate not to ignore the wishes or recommendations of your dissertation committee chairman. "You are wishing to join an exclusive club," St. George had said, "where you can call me Trevor and we can sip brandy together," the gatekeeper of his career had once counseled over lunch. "The Ph.D. admits you to that club," he added to make sure that Marius understood that getting those letters after his name required as much political acumen as academic ability. He needed to take the email seriously.

Marius,

Your last email, in which you referred to the vast geographic interstices whose denizens like to call "the heartland of America" as "Flyover country" got me thinking when I heard the latter term on the television the other day that perhaps there is an opportunity on your return to LA to which we ought to avail ourselves. While I do not wish to gainsay the data that you have obtained from your time in of Palatine, we do have to admit that, through no fault of your own, circumstances have insinuated themselves that significantly infected the context with the consequences of your own actions.

This gives me a little cause for concern too, especially when we get to the defense of your dissertation, particularly from that annoying arsehole on the committee from your beloved Department of Anthropology, Dr. Bartels. There is no need for us to revisit my initial concerns about him, especially because he considers this still to be primarily an Anthro dissertation and that our roles should be reversed. He has enough of an ego that I would not put it past him to torpedo this project, or at least try to make the case that most of the data is irrelevant. I think we need to be prepared for that, and that means we need to buttress the core of the data from Palatine with additional material.

So, what I am proposing is this. That rather than flying back to LA, you make your return by automobile through what we might refer to as "Drive over country," allowing you to stop at small towns and rural areas along the way—pretty much at your discretion, or on the basis of where you think engaging the locals in conversation might prove illuminating—together with observations that might be compared with, or in confirmation of, those you have already registered with respect to your experiences in Palatine. Of course, there need be no comparative information with respect to the cursory account it has been necessary for you to give with regard to your involvement in the Palatine high school shooting.

Reading this reminded Marius that he had deliberately not disclosed to St. George any information beyond what took place on the day of the shooting. He smiled to himself thinking that if the professor knew what really happened subsequently, he might be amenable to a movie development project instead of a dissertation. In an earlier email he had mentioned that Marius's experience had a good "cinematic narrative line".

As you know, the Sanders Chair that I occupy comes with a nice slush fund for travel. I think I can break out enough to cover your fuel, board and lodging costs along the way. I am confident that you will not be anywhere in the vicinity to be tempted by a Michelin three-star restaurant, or a Ritz Hotel.

I realize that you are anxious to return, and that I am dropping this on you at a late hour. But I think it will give us the political insulation from Bartels we might need at the defense, and it would make for a better dissertation, from which we might glean some postdoctoral possibilities. So, try to keep those positive results in mind during those long hours on the road. Where you are able to get online, I expect that you will keep me informed of your progress from Drive Over country.

Cheers,

TSG

Marius had mulled this over for a couple of days, but he knew that he would comply. Jazmeen was not that happy about an indeterminate amount of time—Marius thought maybe three weeks—before she would see him but, coming from a culture that expected obedience to authority figures like professors and women were often required take their meals in the kitchen, she voiced no complaint. He decided on two new front tires, a brake job, and fixing that left rear taillight that, in passing through fiscally strapped small towns, would almost guarantee even White guys get pulled over.

XXXIII

Bouscaren

That morning Marius sat at his desk gazing out the window at the white birch trees. He knew he would miss these trees, which, as far as he knew, did not have roots in California. But the upstate NY sky had its almost omnipresent, tragic, slate grey canopy, the kind of sky, he thought, one almost always sees in scenes of cemeteries in movies.

When he later turned on his TV to catch the morning news over his cereal and espresso. Marius was surprised to see the familiar face of KGK. He had almost forgotten about her since she was elevated from the tiny affiliate in Palatine to its New York station. KGK, looking striking against the New York skyline background, and seeming perfectly comfortable broadcasting from the Olympian Heights of WNYB, announced in her clipped broadcasting voice:

"The upstate town of Palatine New York, still mourning its tragic high school shooting earlier this year, has once again been shaken with this morning's report from the Mohawk County Sheriff's Department that two elderly retired priests were gunned down in the modest former farmhouse they shared off State Route 26. [Video showed the customary scene of flashing police vehicle and ambulance lights, news media remote trucks, yellow crime scene cordon tape and people milling about looking at their cell phones. The house looked rather derelict, with flaking paint and a few cracked windows behind torn screens.] *"In a bizarre turn of events the murder was reported by its perpetrator, whose name is currently being withheld. The shooter, who has only*

been described as an elderly gentleman himself, called the Sheriff's Department from the landline phone inside the home, where he remained until the arrival of police and first responders, and quietly surrendered himself to authorities.

Sheriff Jerry Cavanaugh has released the names of the two victims. They are Edward Cunningham and Jan Birkowski. Both victims were defrocked members of the Jesuits, or Society of Jesus, who have been living in the former farmhouse for seven or eight years, after being expelled from the religious order for serial sexual abuse offenses over a period of decades against boys in Jesuit high schools in both the upstate New York Province and the Eastern Canada Province. The ages of both men have yet to be determined, although they are estimated to have been in their late 70s to early 80s.

Specifics about the manner of their deaths have yet to be released, although Sheriff Cavanaugh indicated that there was "exceptional brutality" involved. It was confirmed through Le Moyne College in Syracuse that the names of both victims appear on the list that the Jesuit's New York Province released not long ago of priests who have been accused of and/or admitted to sexual abuse of both male and female students in New York State Jesuit high schools and postsecondary institutions. The addresses of those on the list are not released.

WPAL will continue to follow the story as it develops in our afternoon and evening editions.

Mary looked up from filling the sugar dispensers to greet Marius with a warm *"buongiorno, bello."* An older man in workman's coveralls seated at one of the counter stools briefly looked up and stared at Marius for a moment, as if trying to identify him, then returned to his ham and eggs.

"Come va, bella zia?" he replied.

He heard Gloria giggling as he approached her favorite banquette. "This place is sounding like the Sons of Italy Club," she said, stubbing out another cigarette in the half-full ashtray and glancing up at Marius through her bangs. "I suppose you have seen the news this morning?"

Marius slid into the banquette. "Yup, and it's all over the radio on the way over here, but I didn't catch anything new. Got anything?"

"Yeah. I just got off the phone with Beverly, my friend on what's left of the city desk at the paper. She was one of the first reporters on the scene. One of the EMT guys, who was also one of the first guys in the door, is a friend of hers. She's only got a description from him, so she really can't use it until she gets some confirmation."

Gloria stopped when Mary came by with a cup for Marius and a fresh pot of coffee and, when she asked he said he already had breakfast at home.

"EMT guy told Beverly he only had a quick look before the sheriff's deputy shooed him out because he said they only needed the Coroner's van. But he apparently saw enough. Nevertheless, what I'm about to tell you is now thirdhand so I would keep it under wraps if I were you."

"I'll be on my way back to LA soon enough. I don't think you have to worry about me getting caught up in this one. So, what did this guy tell your workmate Beverly?"

"He said he'd never seen anything like it before. Apparently, the shooter used a shotgun and shot both of the priests in the groin, maybe more than once, after apparently making them remove their pants—a gruesome emasculation of both of them. The EMT guy reckons that they both must have bled out from those wounds before they died, which might have taken a little time."

Marius winced, then took a swig of his coffee. "The shooter obviously wanted to make a point, aiming where he did. If he shot both of them that way, it obviously wasn't accidental."

"I agree," Gloria said, extracting another cigarette. "Given the history of these guys the message is pretty clear."

"Yeah, and the shooter meant for them to have some time to think about it, and to suffer for it. I've seen that wound, from blasts, in Iraq; it's as much psychological as it is physical. Better that it kills you. Nothing about the shooter?"

"Only that he was wearing a military uniform. But the police aren't identifying him as yet. But, given that Cunningham and Birkowski were longtime sexual predators, there could well be a victim who would want to punish them. Research has shown that these victims carry their psychological wounds well into adulthood. I had wanted to do a book on this subject and visited the priest at Le Moyne who was responsible for making public that list they assembled of pedophile Jesuits. I wanted to do some interviews, but they are very closed-mouthed, even protective, of these guys. Usually they ship them to another location. I imagine they will tighten things up more after this."

"Yeah, where they find new victims."

"They've been doing this sort of thing for a long time. It's baked into the Roman Catholic Church. I can't honestly say that when I first heard of this that I didn't find it a sort of poetic justice. Those priests have been living out on that country road for years, probably supported by the society, and kept as an ugly secret."

Gloria exhaled the drag of her cigarette over her shoulder in deference to Marius. "Every small town has to have an ugly secret I guess," she said, getting to what she really wanted to ask Marius about. "So, what do you think is really the ugly secret about what happened to Khalid Aziz?"

"How should I know? What should we presume? At least we know he wasn't the shooter this time."

Gloria caught the rhetorical nondenial in his response. "Forgive me for thinking that you must know more than you're letting on, Marius."

"That's the problem with these little burgs: they always suspect the aliens because of those *Invasion of the Body Snatchers* movies. Some will believe it was Khalid who shot these two priests, huh? Maybe he slipped out of his coma and took some revenge for being abused," Marius said with a smirk, realizing that he was skirting the truth.

"Now you're just being ridiculous," Gloria said, adding "and that just makes me all the more suspicious."

"Look, Gloria, I just need to get out of this town, or I should say, out of this movie, because that's what it feels like to me."

"You see everything as a movie, Marius."

"What I mean is that I have fallen into almost a classic plot. Out-of-town guy finds himself in a small remote town for some reason, then something happens that draws him unwillingly into its dirty secrets, you know, like what happens to Sidney Poitier in *In the Heat of the Night*, right?"

"I know the movie," she said.

"Well I don't think it's too much of a stretch to say that's what has become my problem. I came here to do an anthropological observation study for my dissertation and being pulled into the history of the town has probably polluted my project. I was supposed to be a fly on the wall, and I ended up being like a T-Rex who attacked their Fourth of July parade."

"I think the reason that you are here in Palatine is a little more complex than that, Marius. Remember, I did some digging in your LA garden."

"Yes, and just between you and me, that's another reason why it's time for me to leave." Marius began to get up from the banquette. "Speaking of which, I still have some packing to finish up."

"I'm going to miss our little chats," Gloria said. "We don't get that many weird alien types in Palatine."

"Marius, do you remember from our first lunch together when we were discussing atheism?"

"Yes. I said something about God is always lurking around for his chance at being credible, and you thought it was strange that I was an atheist and yet seem to believe in his existence."

"Yes."

"I don't believe in his existence; except that I believe that he exists as an idea, and as an idea he is forever dangerous because ideas are more powerful than gods. Just like fictions can become more powerful than facts. That is the power of the human need to believe. When they can't really know the facts they just make shit up."

Marius sat back down. "Listen, Gloria, maybe it's time for you to get out of here too. I'm sure you want to get out of having to find eight hundred words of gossip to write three times a week. If you get to a city where you can get to work on that book you want to do, let me know."

Gloria nodded. "It might not end up being my choice anyway. *The Sentinel*, which will be 121-years old this year, appears to be going the way of extinction of hundreds of small-town papers that can't compete for ads with Amazon and Google and online news. I don't give it more than a couple of years."

"Well, you don't have to be extinguished along with it. I could be in possession of some information that . . . well, let's just say that, like a good wine, it might have to spend some time in the cask. Anyway, for the time being you have that double priest murder. Keep in touch."

"Happy reunion with Jazmeen," she said with a smile.

On his way out, Marius stopped for a word with Wally and Mary. "I won't say goodbye just now, because I will be calling you to make me a couple of sausage and pepper *frittata* sandwiches for the road when I hit the road."

On the morning of his departure, Marius took one last whiff of the sweet aroma of the white birch trees in the backyard. He thought that this was the one scent that he could inhale anywhere in the world and it would immediately transport him to Palatine. He made sure that Mr. Woolley had food and water, locked the door and, as instructed by his landlord, dropped the keys in the mailbox.

He was on his way to Wally and Mary's to pick up his *frittata* sandwiches, stuck his mobile in its holder on the dashboard, and turned on the car radio. Immediately following the weather reports, which he was delighted to hear forecast snowless weather for his westward trip down the New York State Thruway, there was a special news announcement:

WPAL has learned this morning that the shooter in the assassination of two defrocked Jesuit priests who had been living on Route 26 was Mr. Arthur Bouscaren of Palatine. Bouscaren, age 86, who is known locally as "Major" Bouscaren, and is the chief officer of the local VFW. Local law enforcement withheld the name of Mr. Bouscaren for nearly two days while he was being examined by mental health professionals from the Upstate Medical Center in Syracuse. He had been calmly drinking a can of beer in the kitchen of the victims' home when police arrested him. Authorities said that Bouscaren surrendered peacefully, his unloaded shotgun lying on the kitchen floor a few feet in front of him. The former Marine soldier, who had been decorated for valorous service in the Korean War with a Bronze Star and two Purple Hearts, refused to say anything for several hours until he was allowed to read the following statement after he had been read his Miranda rights.

"I, United States Marine Maj. Arthur T. Bouscaren, Retired, hereby admit to the execution of former priests Cunningham and Birkowski, sexual predators who were protected for many years by the Roman Catholic Church. I have therefore hastened these scum to their final judgment on behalf of all the innocent children they victimized, amongst which was my own son, Andrew. Last year, Andrew was shot in the back of the head by Khalid Aziz, the perpetrator at Palatine high school, and died while on duty as the school security officer. For many years I treated my son unfairly because of his failures in sports and his rejection by the military because of his inability to control his weight and other, what were unaccountable at the time, personality issues. I did not discover the origins of these problems until after Andrew's death and revelations in some of his private writings. It was in these that I discovered painful descriptions of the abuse to which he had been submitted by then Fr. Birkowski when my son was a student at Cardinal Cleary Prep. It appears that Father Cunningham was not specifically involved in incidents with my son and so I executed him in retribution for the other children. Now they will be celibate for eternity."

Le Moyne College's Fr. Joseph Manley, the spokesperson of the Society of Jesus, when provided with a copy of the Bouscaren document, made the following statement. "The emasculations and deaths of Fathers Cunningham and Birkowski is a gruesome and unwarranted penance for past transgressions which the Church has long forgiven." It is our hope that this act of vengeance will not be repeated.

Mr. Bouscaren has been taken into custody and removed to Syracuse. Authorities have disclosed that he is calm and cooperative but has declined to make any further statements regarding his actions until he is provided with legal counsel. WPAL will continue to follow the story and broadcast updates as they develop.

When Marius arrived at the diner he found it empty except for Wally and Mary who were leaning over the newspaper on the counter doing the crossword puzzle together, Wally wearing his soda jerk hat, and Mary stuffed into her waitress outfit. They looked up.

"You got a long drive ahead of you, Marius. I don't think these sandwiches are going to last you the whole way," Wally said. Marius could not look at Wally without thinking of the songwriter and pianoplayer Hoagy Carmichael in *The Best Years of Our Lives*. Like Carmichael, he had that gaunt face and wiry frame, but with arms covered with faded military insignia tattoos. He had joked to Marius that he always was very lean and Mary's efforts to fatten him up with pasta had only resulted in her enlargement. "This is also for you," he said, sliding an envelope across the worn Formica counter.

Mary came around the counter to give him a hug. "*Buon viaggio, ragazzo,*" she said. "Drive carefully." When Marius attempted to pay for the sandwiches, she just gave him a stern look of refusal.

Out in the car, Marius opened the envelope and removed the note.

Dear Marius,

When I wrote that exposé piece about an atheist teacher from California that I thought might enhance my column's readership, we almost started out as enemies. I wouldn't blame you if you'd seen me as one. I am certainly culpable for a lot of the abuse you received from your neighbors and other intolerant people in the town. I should have known better. But then again, had you not tracked me down to give me a piece of your mind, I might never have enjoyed those wonderful conversations we had, and I might never have faced up to some of my own metaphysical demons. I will miss that, as I will miss your obsession with cinema allusions. I know there is a book in the circumstances that took place while you were here—maybe fiction, maybe nonfiction. Hey! Maybe even a screenplay, now that I have a connection in Hollywood. But for the moment I have to pay the rent and my tabs at Wally&Mary's. I am enclosing a draft of the piece that will run after you are on the road back to California. Have a safe trip, and best wishes with your dissertation and with your reunion.

Gloria (in excelsis) Sexton

The Ghost of Khalid Aziz
By Gloria Sexton

There are several hypotheses to the vanishing of Khalid Aziz. One hypothesis is that he did not just "naturally" succumb to his injuries but was given an assist in his demise by a person or persons who could no longer endure his hanging around in a coma. He might well have been removed from the hospital by such persons and disposed of in a manner in which the location of his remains would never be found, thus ensuring that his grave would not become a memorial for Islamic extremists (although there is still no compelling evidence that Aziz's attack on Palatine high school was instigated by Islam and extremism).

Hypothesis two is that Khalid Aziz had actually regained consciousness, which was perhaps noticed by his brother, a frequent visitor to the IC Unit and that his clandestine removal from the hospital was planned and arranged by friendly Islamic entities to spare him the suffering of a trial and an inevitable sentence of life in prison.

A third hypothesis is that offered by the putative ISIS representative who earlier contacted this column with an email taking credit for the removal of Khalid Aziz and alleging that he was being taken to receive better medical care and to be repatriated to his home city in Iraq, where he will presumably become a poster boy for ISIS. However, in this age of Photoshop and computer-generated imagery, we must remain visually skeptical.

But the fact is, at present, no one really knows the whereabouts of Khalid Aziz, or of whatever remains of him, and who were the perpetrators of his vanishing. At least no one who knows and is willing to disclose that information for whatever reasons they remain secretive about it.

He is a ghost who will continue to haunt the memories of Palatinos who will remember that horrible day at Palatine High, and will become part of the lore of this town. There will be no closure, no resolution, which will not be good for all of us and will be especially painful for the families who lost loved ones on that dark day when our little town joined the growing list of once safe and placid communities that are reaping the consequences of the love of firearms and the hatred of anyone who is different. Now we have a ghost to remind us of that.

XXXIV

Flyover

There was a time when a cross-country drive took place on two-lane roads that passed directly through small towns and villages. Guest houses and small motels sprung up as rest stops, and gas stations and repair garages appeared to minister to the limited driving ranges and mechanical unreliability of early automobiles. By the post-World War II period that all had changed. Thanks to atomic warheads and the development of intercontinental ballistic missiles, the Interstate Defense Highway System was inaugurated by the same president who had warned the nation of the emergence of the "military industrial complex." Small towns and villages were left without the exhaust fumes of transcontinental traffic, often deprived of offramps from new multi-lane, high-speed limited-access highways. Small towns outside the orbit of large cities in metropolitan areas often stagnated and declined as they were not only driven past, but soon to be flown over. Marius felt very much like an urban archaeologist as well as anthropologist in setting out on a drive-over quest that would take him through the landscape of a time gone by.

The green door to room 401 of the Munsee Motel had begun to flake its maroon paint, revealing that it had once been beige, and even earlier a darker green. It was wood, and there was evidence of a split in it that ran between zero and the one, perhaps, Marius speculated, the result of the pounding of some fist, perhaps an anger, or panic, long ago, the banging sound long since absorbed in some long-forgotten night. Why was there a 401, he wondered, since there were only about twenty rooms in this rundown place that might have been established when this now out-of-the-way country road was first paved. "Bates Motel" he had mumbled to himself when he first observed that the blue neon of the last three letters of the "vacancy" sign was not functioning.

But that was, in fact, the attraction of the place. It was a motel with that spooky ambience that might have been from a Hollywood back lot construction with a dozen film noir stories in its credits. The decor was just blandly creepy enough to evoke any number of noir movie scenes from the 40s and 50s, with a threadbare bed cover that had no doubt seen more than its share of urgent and vigorous sex. The bathroom sink had telltale rusty brown drip spot leading to the basin that said "don't drink from this faucet." Marius did a couple of Bogart lines from *Key Largo* while looking into the mirror that shower steam had decorated with mottled corners. It was the perfect set for a murder, a ghostly apparition, or an alien visitation. Or, of course, a romantic assignation.

Marius had decided he would give Muncie, or *Middletown*, one day, maybe a day and a half, two at most, and be on his way. As he drove into its outskirts, Marius encountered the first of the ruins of Muncie's urban archaeology. Along one stretch of road, what had once been a large parking lot was being reclaimed by high weeds that had pushed their way up through the asphalt to reach for a sun obscured by slate skies. Paint peeled off the stanchions of light poles that once illuminated the cars of the night-shifters. But whatever factory it had serviced was long gone. He pulled over to ask a man pushing a shopping cart, the only person he had seen for a long stretch of road, what factory had been there.

"Chevrolet," the man answered with the single word, keeping his slow pace.

Marius idled along beside him. "Did you work there?" he asked.

"My father did. Chevy set up shop in 1935 to make transmissions. They kept expanding right into the 1960s, then things reversed direction with the recession in the 1970s. By 2006 it was all gone, like you see now. Town lost over 20,000 auto jobs." Marius wanted to ask the man what kind of work he did, but he thought better of it as he looked unemployed.

As he drove around the erstwhile industrial areas of the town, there still were some signs of long-departed tenants: empty BorgWarner and DelcoRemy auto parts plants remained, as did the Marhoefer meat-packing industry that was an important part of the Muncie economy for thirty-three years, until filing for bankruptcy in 1978. And there were still Ball buildings, the factory that churnned out glass canning jars. The Ball family, as the Lynds' *Middletown* studies had disclosed, was a classical homegrown American "company town," with its name emblazoned on much of the town's physical and social infrastructure, most prominently Ball State University. At their peak during the depression, their plants produced thirty glass mason jars per minute that were used to canned fruits and vegetables all over the country.

As he explored the center of the city, Marius stopped to make notes, one of them remarking that some buildings reminded him of a "lower middle-class guy wearing a threadbare out-of-style suit," and "in place with a residue of formerly prosperous land uses among cheaper replacements." Some of the crumbling brick buildings with rusting steel frames and flooded floors reminded him of "the beauty of classical ruins." To get a contemporary point of view, he parked in front of a coffee shop near the university and within a few minutes was disturbing an African-American student who appeared to be wasting his time playing a video game on his computer.

"It was the only D1 school that offered me a full ride," the student said when Marius saw an opportunity to ask him how he liked being a student at Ball State. "So it looks like I'm in this jerkwater town for at least two more years unless I declare eligible and the Golden State Warriors draft me."

"Looking at you, I'd have to say point guard, right?"

"Yeah, I think I've topped out at six-two, without an Afro,"

"Warriors. That's my team. I'm from LA, but I can't stand the Lakers. You're not from here then."

"MoTown, or NoMoTown these days. Kinda like this place, on steroids. What the hell are you doing here?"

"Just passing through on my way back to La-La Land."

He chuckled. "You must be wishing you passed through a little bit further, like about to Las Vegas."

"Naw, I actually want to find out what 'flyover America' is all about. So I'm driving through it."

The student affected a wry grin. "It's like driving through a cemetery. Just about every one of these small towns and villages speckled all over the Midwest— the heartland of America—are on some sort of life-support, hanging on with welfare payments, food stamps, 99 Cent stores, bargain basement healthcare, or not at all, people living in rundown houses or rusting trailer homes, closed factories and shuttered businesses. Schools and their basketball teams are probably the main source of community solidarity and entertainment. It's rural blight. Family farms are hanging on with Federal price support aid, or selling out where they can to fracking companies. Mental health and opioid addiction . . . you name it . . .".

"What about churches?" Marius asked.

"Christian only, and white only."

"So, what's your major?"

"Econ, the dismal science. Perfect for around here."

"Yeah. Who was it that said dismal?"

"Some dude named Carlyle, I think. He must've been from Muncie."

Marius laughed. "Okay, I gotta ask you: what's it like being African-American in Middletown?"

"Well, if you can lead a fast-break, it makes a difference. Remember, this is Indiana. Hoosiers love basketball. I live in a dorm, which is part of my ride. But if I didn't, I'd probably be over on the east side of the railroad tracks which is where most of the Black folk live, probably about ten percent of the total population. I've been told that for a long time there was no fire station and there is still no supermarket there, and if a train is on the line and the roads are blocked, it can slow down the response time for ambulances. If they don't have game Blacks are kind of non-people around here. Like tree decorations."

"What's that?" Marius asked.

"The brother that's my roommate is from down the road in Evansville. He knows a lot of local shit. Like back in the 1920s and 30s more than a third of the white guys in this town were KKK. Indiana had a huge KKK membership."

"Really?"

"Yeah, you know we ain't that far from Dixie. Lower Indiana is sort of like upper fucking Alabama. In 1930 a white mob in Marion, Indiana, a few clicks up the I-69 from here, broke into the local jail, dragged three black teenagers out of their cell, beat them and then hung two of them from a tree by their necks. The third brother must've been quick and managed to get away. The night before, they had been arrested and charged with robbing and murdering a white factory worker and then raping his white girlfriend, who later, by the way, testified she hadn't been raped. I've seen a photograph of that lynching, with a whole crowd of local rednecks, including children, smiling for the camera below the hanging bodies."

"I guess that answers my question," Marius said.

"Damn straight. I prefer being in Detroit or Chicago. I might end up dead there, too, but it will more likely be a bullet from a home-boy, not some white motherfuckers hauling me up by the neck."

"Hey, I don't even know your namee," Marius said.

The student hesitated and Marius thought for a moment that he would decline to supply it. Then he said, "It's Darius." He pronounced it Dar-ee-us.

"Sort of rhymes with mine. I'm Marius. Yours is Persian in origin, I think."

"I was going to change it to some African name. But it upset my mother. She named me Darius after some ancient king. She said an African name might make it easier for me to be deported." He laughed.

Marius smiled. "Yeah, my mother is a citizen now, but she still refers to *los Americanos*. So much for that melting pot bull-shit. It's still the land of 'us and them'."

Darius nodded. "Got to get to my Macro Econ class. Nice meeting you, man. Safe trip home. Be sure to check that you don't have a broken taillight. That's how they get us Black folk. You got those New York plates."

—————

Back at the motel that evening Marius showered, connected to the local WiFi, navigated to YouTube, opened the pizza he had ordered, and settled in to stream-watch *Meet John Doe*. The 1941 Frank Capra film stars Barbara Stanwyck as a cynical newspaper reporter who creates a phony letter to the editor from a man who says he is so despondent over social conditions that he intends to commit suicide on Christmas Eve. When the paper is forced to produce this 'John Doe', the editors engage a homeless man, John Willoughby, played by Gary Cooper, an apolitical hobo who only cares about his failed baseball career.

Marius thought the film was set in a generic mid-sized city, like Muncie, that was also greatly impacted by the Depression, but knew from research that it had been shot on Warner Bros. soundstages and a neighborhood just south of downtown LA. After the opening scenes he paused the movie, which he already knew almost by heart, and switched his computer to his word processing application. He began an email to Professor St. George explaining why his brief Muncie experience put him in mind of *Meet John Doe*. Marius elaborated:

"Capra loved Christmas Eve as a movie motif, and on the occasion in that movie as well, his heroes were threatening to jump to their deaths. I wonder whether that said something about the economics of the times, or maybe about Capra. I like to look for patterns and themes and the way directors approached their subjects. Capra seems to be interested in casting attractive, smart, cynical urban women against simple all-American men. Two years earlier, in Mr. Smith Goes to Washington, *Jimmy Stewart plays a naive boy scout leader from a rural state who runs for Congress, wins and, when he gets there, finds it corrupted by career politicians. Jean Arthur plays a cynical newspaper woman who introduces him to the realities of politics, and romance."*

"Back around 1940 women were relegated to apolitical roles in both film and politics. These films are only two data points, but one wonders what might be made of the fact that Capra chose women to represent "the media" in these movies. Both are urban, sassy and cynical, and almost too smart for their own good. Typically (of Hollywood) they fall in love with the heroes in their films and figure in their righteous crusades. But suffice to say that the media were also vilified by politicians in those days. There is probably more to the media equals women equation that could be distracting. Then, too, Capra also had an interest in corruption—maybe that came from his Italian immigrant background—in casting corrupt older guys: Mr. Potter, D.B. Norton, Senator Joseph Paine. How much was art imitating life back in those days?"

"Where I am heading with this appears to have some small-town connections. What the Sarah Palin candidacy reminded us of is that Americans have not lost their love affair for the rural or small-town politician who aspires for higher office out of the worthy motive to bring honesty and cleanliness and true American mores to governance. Politicians used to invent "log cabin" birthplaces for themselves to connect with this tradition, which was almost as important as a military pedigree. So, Palin invoked her Wasilla, Alaska, (population only about 8000), background regularly to contrast herself with those from evil big cities like New York and Washington. Just an innocent small-town "hockey mom" married to a "Joe six-pack." We saw how that worked out. Who would've predicted Obama? And then followed by Trump? We finally got Potter, Norton, and Paine, all rolled into one. This country needs to go back and watch its Capra movies."

Marius clicked "save," opened another can of Coke, grabbed a piece of cold pizza, and sat back to reread his draft, correcting a typo or two in each line. He had more to say.

"America has long been a country with an identity crisis. Our roots are in the soil; we started out mostly as farmers, not urbanites. Some of our founding fathers deeply distrusted cities. Jefferson called them a "sore upon the body politic." We celebrated small towns because they were places where "everybody knew everybody else," with a gossip-driven behavioral policing system, where you knew who were churchgoers, who weren't. Family values were the norm and people knew their place from their skin color. They were also places where vital farm-to-market roads led; American farmers were not interested in subsistence, but were capitalists who were concerned in producing a surplus for profit. I bet I will be driving past a lot of struggling family farms like that portrayed in Country, *where Jessica Lange and Sam Shepard's—what was their name? Yes, Ivy, nice rural name—marriage is disintegrating*

right alongside with, and because of, their agricultural misfortunes and debts. No wonder that those idyllic farms of the American regionalists are beset today—maybe always were—by higher rates of mental illness, drugs, and familial abuse than are to be found in cities.

Marius clicked save and sat back, wishing he could swing down to go through Kansas. That's where *Picnic* was set in 1955, in some small nameless town not too far from Tulsa. Joshua Logan used locations in five different small Kansas towns that nobody ever heard of to portray a place of limited and predictable prospects. Kim Novak was just radiant as Madge, the town beauty, that everyone sees destined as a trophy for the local rich boy. But she, as well as everyone else in this town, seems confused and depressed. Her father disappeared, leaving a depressed mother. Her sister has big-city ambitions, and the teacher friend has an ambiguous relationship with an alcoholic local businessman. The spark for change, as well as romance for Madge, is provided by the arrival of William Holden as a handsome (miscast, in my opinion) drifter. Their only chance for a relationship was for both of them to get out of the constrictions of that small-town. But the best thing about the movie was the musical score. He would love to pop into one of those towns to see what the contemporary Madge looks like—probably covered with tattoos—but can't afford the detour. He returns to his email.

Cities were beginning to fill up with more rural and smalltown emigrants like Picnic's *Madge and Hal. By 1920, when Americans became predominantly "urban" in habitat, we had moved inexorably into the metropolitan age. In the process we left behind a significant part of the American experience that was shaped by the small town. Scores and scores of small towns have withered and died, abandoned by their youths or economic bases, or bypassed by the freeways that connect the big cities. Others, swallowed by met-*

ropolitan expansion, struggled to preserve what small-town identity remains. Today, for most of us, the small town is a place we know mostly through movies, novels and TV, and whose reality lies somewhere between often contradictory myths. One of these myths is of the idealized small town: an almost utopian preserve composed of Andy Hardy or Our Gang type kids playing happily on elm-lined streets with white picket fences. It has little red schoolhouses, town squares with band gazebos, the requisite general store and a protestant generic clapboard church. Everybody knows everybody, perhaps too well, but it's usually preferred over big-city anonymity. There are, in addition, the small-town social archetypes: the pastor, the school marm, a town drunk and town floozie, the two old maid sisters who live in the big Victorian house on Elm street, the local constable, the publisher of the Elmtown Gazette, and, of course, the chorus of solid, small-town families knitted together by unshakable allegiance to God and his Son, the flag, high school football or basketball, and the Fourth of July Parade. Small towns are the sentinels of American social conservatism.

There's a host of people to whom we can credit these images: Regionalist painters, Samuel Clemens, sociologists of the early Chicago School, and, I suppose, Frank Capra films, among others. But more and more, such places exist (maybe only ever existed) in the myth-misted recesses of the American mind. One reads or hears occasionally of a revival of small towns, of disenchanted stock brokers and Corporate executives (and their wireless routers) emigrating from the hyper-urbanism of New York or Chicago to small towns in Vermont or Oregon in search of the grail of smalltown-ism, with its slower pace, smaller scale, and, if not love, at least know-thy-neighbor values. But the demographics soundly demonstrate that for most of us, the metropolis is the habitat of choice or necessity.

What is certain is that more and more of us will have to choose either myth from less and less real experience with the small-town. More and more, our images of small towns will likely be formed by scriptwriters and novelists with little or no small town experience.

But since myth-making is a proven staple of mass media, it is also fairly certain that, no matter how metropolitan or cosmopolitan we become, politicians like Sarah Palin, and even, ironically, rich New York guy Donald Trump, will always try to tap into, if only in our imaginations, a small town somewhere in each of us.

Almost everything in the current political context seems to have a precursor in It's a Wonderful Life. *There is the run on the Bailey family's savings and loan bank; there is the difficulty of immigrant families assimilating into xenophobic communities and affording homes; and there is the rich and greedy Mr. Potter, the equivalent of President Donald Trump. And, I should add, if you are the wrong color, or have one of those "what-kind-of-a-name is that?" names, you are probably going to get a dose of good old American racism.*

Perhaps, too, the rhapsodic reputation of the American small town has been tarnished by the same sources of myth-making that exalted it. Today, when we assay the bedrock of American self-anointed exceptionalism, we find it adulterated with a mixture of myth, reality, and revenge. While the mass media have given us a skewed romanticized perspective of the small towns of Andy Hardy *and the* Waltons, *they have also fed our imaginations on a staple of* Peyton Place *and the generic small Southern towns of mean-spirited, bigoted, xenophobic, reactionaries.* Andy Hardy *has grown up to knock-up Sarah Palin's teenage daughter or lead a gang of unemployed, sexually-frustrated small-town youth ready to commit atrocities on any alien they can chase down in their gun-racked pickup trucks.*

Maybe this negative imagery has come about in the same way as the idealized myth of small towns—a modicum of reality made into a stereotype by our hopes for a promised land, or the loss of it. Maybe the negative image is as much the result of revenge on the small town for not having lived up to its mythology. And just maybe, some of us need to destroy the myth of the ideal small town to ease our urban discontent. After all, if Emerald City *turns out to be a dreadful place, then there is indeed no place like home.*

In terms of political culture, the smalltown belongs mostly to the frontier ethos. As settlements that provided essential trade services, markets or shipping points add regional farm to market road networks, their association is primarily with agricultural and pastoral hinterlands and wilderness. Towns are strongly associated with frontier colonialization as many of them were originally military outposts, railroad service points, or settlements that provided services for extractive industries like mining, trapping and forestry. The pioneer, or the frontiersman, became an American icon of rugged individualism and, as a denizen of territory yet to be fully integrated into the nation state, tended to be anti-government and anti-regulation of economic behaviors, and was in territorial competition with native peoples. The yeoman farmer, cowboy, and prospector took on heroic dimensions in the vastness and the westward expansion of America as celebrated in the frontier thesis of historians like Frederick Jackson Turner, and extended into the Caribbean, Central America and the Western Pacific in the policies of Pres. Theodore Roosevelt. The frontier was influential in establishing in the American political representative system the importance of land ownership above that of the single voting individual, a feudalistic residue that retains its political disequilibrium and contentiousness in the form commonly referred to as the "rural/urban divide," leaving the rural side of that equation primarily formed principally by social conservatism, laissez-faire capitalism, and Caucasian Christianity."

Okay, I admit it, I will need to purge my politics from any of this stuff I might use in my final draft. Just wanted to let you know what a good dose of American Midwest small town has done to my thinking. Putting Muncie in my rearview mirror tomorrow morning. Marius.

Marius, satisfactorily-exhausted, clicked "send" and picked up his mobile phone.

"Ahlaan eaziziun," Marius said when he heard Jazmeen's accented voice answer the phone.

"And hello to you, too, my dear," she repeated back to him in English. It thrilled him to hear her voice, now stronger, still with its sibilant elisions, but now with the return of that little lilt at the end of sentences that had been absent during the time of her sickness. "Where are you, Marius?" She asked.

"First tell me how you are," he insisted.

"I am fine. I had my check-up with the hepatologist the other day and he said my labs looked good, and there were no signs of rejection. I had a slight temperature the other day, but it must've been something else, and it went away. I felt good enough that Chamsi and I went to the beach for a long walk. She even let me drive the car. I think I am going to be okay, *inshallah.*" The reflexive "god willing" still occasionally popped up in her speech. "Oops," she added, "That's from living with Chamsi's family."

Marius laughed. "Hey, I still curse with 'goddamnit' and 'Jesus Christ'. They are old habits," he said to put her at ease.

She giggled. "You still should control your language, Marius. You are a professor, and you influence the way your students think and speak."

"I will try to clean up my act by the time I reach California . . . *inshallah.*"

"I will make no prayer," she said, "just a wish. Now, will you tell me where you are?"

"Yes, I'm in Indiana, in a place you probably never heard of. I'm a little bit outside of a middle-sized city called Muncie. I wanted to stop here because it is a little bit famous in American urban sociology because of some studies that were done back in the first part of the 20th century by a sociologist couple named Lynd. They studied the place twice, first in the

1920s, and then later at the end of the 1930s, so they could do a comparison. They used a different name for the town, calling it "Middletown," to indicate that they were looking to discover some characteristics that were characteristically American. I read the studies when I was an undergraduate."

"But that was years ago was it not?" she asked.

"Yes, it was, for America at least. And I expect the place has changed a good deal since the Lynds wrote "Middletown in Transition" in the 1930s. It just seemed appropriate for my drive-over America pilgrimage that I make a stop at the place that was supposed to be the most representative of this country." It flashed through Marius's mind how it was that this girl who came from a country whose history began in Mesopotamia, a place that historians referred to as the "cradle of civilization." For her, a long time ago was not measured in years, or even centuries, but millennia. Middletown, or Muncie, or whatever you call it, did not even register on the temporal scale of Iraq.

"Just don't stay too long. I need to see you," she said. The tone of the second sentence, and a verb 'need' caught his attention.

"Is there something amiss, something you haven't mentioned?"

There was a hesitation in her reply. "Oh, maybe nothing really, just things easier to speak with you about when we are together."

There was something, and Marius was a little more nervous. He was tired and wanted to go to sleep, but now he knew there was something that might keep him up if he didn't pursue the matter further.

"Like what? Can you just give me an idea?" he inquired.

There was a hesitation again. She regretted bringing it up, and tried to be vague about it. With all the separation since his having to leave LA, and the chance he took with his career for her, she did not want to become another obstacle to his finishing his work.

"Maybe it's just a woman thing, or an Arab thing, or a Muslim—I mean the *former* Muslim—thing."

Now Marius was more nervous. "You had better give me some idea of what is going on, *habibti*," he said. Gods were always lurking, patient for their chance, confident that the needs of human credulity would provide the opening they needed for adoration and obedience. He had feared not being there to provide vigilance, the rationality, and the protection from the metaphysical pitfalls that all faiths laid in the paths of those who wandered in the land of doubt.

"It is just that I feel, I don't know quite how to say it, that I owe something."

"Owe something?"

"That I must pay, or give back, in some way . . . for *it*."

Marius could feel his ears heating up. It was what happened to him whenever he became fearful. "You mean, when you say 'it,' the . . . ?"

"Yes, the organ, that's what keeps me alive now. What is the reason?"

Marius looked up at the ceiling. There were dead bugs, some of them large moths that could be seen in the frosted bowl of the ceiling light. There was also discernible water stain in the outdated "popcorn" ceiling. He felt remote, incapacitated. "There is no reason, and you don't owe anyone anything, my dear girl," he said firmly.

"Then why do I feel that there must be a reason?" she pleaded in a way that indicated to him that she must be more bothered by the matter than she had let on.

"Because that's how you have been brought up to look at things, that there is some higher purpose or plan in all of this." Marius knew already how ridiculous this line of thinking could go. He had run through it all himself many times before, how the mind yearned to connect dots. Dot one: Muslim girl falls under the thrall of the American atheist teacher. Dot two: Muslim girl is seriously injured in attempted honor killing. Dot three: American teacher is forced to leave city and ends up in small-town on other side of the country. Dot four: American teacher becomes involved in thwarting terrorist attack on high school. Dot five: terrorist survives in coma. Dot, Dot, Dot. It all fits together, like it was *supposed* to happen that way, like the way Clarence connected the dots for George, liked the way he was supposed to discover Zu-Zu's petals and that bell was supposed to ring at the end of the movie that neatly connects with that opening celestial sequence. Except this was not a movie narrative and, all of life was not made up of dots that were like movie scenes, they were not pre-connected by some invisible guiding hand, by some scripture, or script. Not at all. There were choices, there were forks in the roads, there were myriads of dots, like particles randomly caroming in a cloud chamber.

He was going to have to start a new beginning with Jazmeen, a new phase that was not walking into the happily ever after. That's how movies work, but not life. Like George Bailey, after Clarence gets his wings, George is going to have to figure out how to be happy tomorrow now that he has accepted the way he has connected—chosen—his dots. And like it or not, he might not have that much prediction, or direction, on his path through that cloud chamber of life.

Marius had encountered this line of thought many times as his dissertation had mingled with his existential ruminations. How many times had he considered Einstein's dictum that "God does not play dice with the universe?" Of course not. More like pinball, one can activate the flippers and nudge the machine—just don't "tilt." But, for him, God, Allah, or any other deity has nothing to do with it. Now, he felt a desperation to somehow fashion a comprehensible response to

Jazmeen for the putative "debt" she now felt she owed for having escaping the death penalty for entertaining the most fundamental human doubt. The thought tormented him, that she possibly could have allowed the doubt to become its own indictment of apostasy and justification for her suffering.

"I am very fatigued now, Jazmeen, but this is something that we need to discuss further," he said wearily. "Let me say this. What we did was a choice that I made, Jazmeen. It was not something that was preordained by some power that was greater than me. I was not doing something that was fulfilling some prophecy or divine plan. I was doing what I needed to do—and what I saw the opportunity to do—to save the life of someone that I love. I will take all responsibility for that, for the conception and execution of it, and I feel no regret for it. Fate, Kismet, Karma, Lady Luck, whatever anyone wants to call it, put those circumstances before me and it was I who decided to act as I did. I am no puppet of any God."

"I understand, Marius. I did not mean to upset you with my silly thoughts. It is that just so much has happened that has been difficult for me to explain to myself. Chamsi has been wonderful to me, but more of a sister than a guy in these sorts of questions. I do not wish to burden her with any of it. And I have tried to withhold these thoughts until you have returned because you are the keeper of my heart and my soul, if I have one. That is why I miss you so. Come as soon your work allows, *habibi*."

"Keep well, my dear. It won't be long. Good night."

He was sound asleep in less than a minute.

———

Marius crept along the classroom building hallway. The floor felt cool and smooth, and the light glancing in from the doorway at the end highlighted the slight undulations in the shiny linoleum. Mr. Gaffney came by pushing his floor polishing machine that whirred and left swirl marks on the surface. Marius thought nothing strange about it when Gaffney caught his eye and motioned with a turn of his head back toward the corner with the intersecting hallway.

Marius crept further along the wall to where he could hear some metallic sounds and some unintelligible muttering. Mr. Gaffney was now down the corridor about thirty feet or so, and was now polishing a circle around a still body in a coagulating pool of its own blood. The spinning polisher caught some of the edge of the blood, flinging it in splatters against the student lockers and over the custodian's shoes. Gaffney proceeded as though this were nothing unusual.

Still crouching, Marius approached the corner with the intersecting hallway where he could now hear some metallic clattering and more frustrated mumbling. As quietly and surreptitiously as possible he stretched his head around the corner. There, seated on the floor, was the shooter, outfitted entirely in black like a ninja, struggling to get a fresh magazine into his automatic rifle. It would not snap in place. Marius even thought for moment that maybe the problem was that there was a setting on the gun, like perhaps the safety, that was in the wrong place.

Suddenly, the ninja noticed him, quickly turning his head upward, but Marius only got a partial view of his eyes that were obscured by the black *balaclava* covering his face. The ninja tried one more attempt to insert the magazine as he swung the gun around, and Marius knew that if it loaded into the gun it was "game over" for him. The only remaining option was to go on offense and, in an instant, he turned the corner and leapt on the ninja.

With his superior weight, and coming from above, Marius was quickly able to engage his opponent from behind, pinning the arm that held the rifle, and sliding his other arm around his neck to secure a chokehold. The ninja immediately released the firearm and began clawing at Marius's hands and arms, twisting his body and thrusting out his legs to try to release the pressure on his throat and carotid artery.

Marius released his grip on the ninja's arm and secured it to his own to wrench up the pressure. His opponent struggled mightily, but Marius could sense that the lack of oxygen was weakening him. He held tight, listening to the gasps and gurgles until the ninja's body fell limp. Still he held on, for how long he didn't know, but supposing that it was the appropriate thing to do to finish the ninja off.

The body remained limp and there was no sign of respiration when the sheriff's deputy tapped Marius on the shoulder and told him that it was safe to release his chokehold. "Looks like you might have saved the government some legal expense," the deputy said, holding two fingers against the ninja's neck to detect a pulse. "Let's have a look at this bastard." The deputy grabbed hold of the top of the balaclava and roughly yanked it up off the ninja's head.

Skeins of thick, silky black hair tumbled over her beautiful face, and her the large, mahogany eyes stared pleadingly up at Marius.

Marius awoke with a shudder, breathing hard, rubbing the fatigue in his arms. The haunting image of those eyes still staring at him.

"Fuck!" Marius knew the dream. It had tormented him twice before, but each time he had been taken in by it, as though it came as a message he neither comprehended nor heeded. He flipped on the bedside light and looked at his watch. It was 4:15 am, 2:15 on the West coast.

He lay there, unable to sleep, staring up at the dead moths in the overhead light globe, thinking. Did Jazmeen express those doubts and concerns for a reason? Was there some existential reason behind that phone call? Were there's some dots he was supposed to connect? He wracked his brains with these thoughts. "And why this fucking dream—again?" he hissed through clenched teeth.

"Fuck it. The only reason that matters is the reason *I* give it." he said aloud, pulling on his pants. He stuck his hands in the pockets and pulled them out empty—no Zu-Zu's petals. He laughed at himself. "And fuck you, Clarence. Find somebody else to get you your wings."

He was checked out and was on the road, at speed, westbound, by 4:45.

It was in mid Iowa, at one of those non-major chain restaurants that Marius favored, off the main highway, with a neon sign that simply said "Eat Here" that he pulled into with the anticipation that he might have a fantastic homemade meal, or be pulling over 40 miles down the road and rushing into a field with explosive diarrhea. These eateries were the sorts of places that, owing to movies like the *Postman Always Rings Twice*, *In the Heat of the Night*, *Five Easy Pieces*, *Diner*, and dozens of others he could call to mind, he formulated his sense of what was essentially Americana, and he could not resist checking out where film lore met empirical reality. There was a long-haul 18-wheeler in the smaller truck parked in the gravel—a good sign by some folklore—and his mind was already conjuring an exquisite meat loaf in the tasty gravy, or maybe the best damned BLT with a side of fries that he would remember all the way to the California border. As he made sure his stuff in the back seat was well covered with a blanket, and the doors and trunk were locked, he found himself softly singing Tom Waits' *Invitation to the Blues*: "Well she's up against the register with an apron and a spatula/ Yesterday's deliveries, tickets for the bachelors /She's a moving violation from her conk down to her shoes/ Well, it's just an invitation to the blues," despite the rural ambience.

The truckers sat one stool apart from each other along the counter. One of them was in conversation with the counter girl whose fresh, Midwestern, corn-fed looks did not fit Waits' lyrics. The other was hunched over his coffee, flipping through an automotive magazine. Marius removed the laminated menu from between the ketchup bottle and the heavy sugar dispenser and began browsing it when he heard a man's husky voice coming through the serving window into the kitchen. "I just finished making my fresh tuna salad. You won't find better in three states."

Marius made no answer, unsure they were addressed him. But the counter girl looked down at him and said, "He means you, sir. He thinks you look like a tuna sandwich."

The trucker laughed. "Don't feel insulted, man," he said looking down the counter at Marius. "He thinks I'm Swedish meatballs."

"Sounds good to me," Marius said.

"It'll be on a fresh Kaiser roll," the voice from the kitchen said, "Unless you have some issue with Germany. It goes best."

"Agreed. Can you recommend a good Gewürztraminer to go with it?" Marius answered, joining the jocular spirit."

"Sorry, that young lady behind the counter drank the last case yesterday," the voice said. "Coffee's fresh."

"He's my uncle," the counter girl said, serving Marius's meal. "We don't get too many new faces since we are off the main road. "So he knows he can risk offending you, because you probably won't be back anyway. But it's just good fun. Where are you headed?"

"LA."

She waited till he looked up and could catch his eye. "Got a girlfriend there?"

Marius swallowed his coffee and looked like he had to think about it. "Did when I left."

"I think you will," she answered with a fetching smile. "If she's a smart girl."

"Thanks," Marius responded, noticing for the first time, as she slipped his bill underneath his plate, the tattooed face of Jesus on her inner forearm.

When he checked out at the cash register, the girl asked him if he enjoyed his sandwich.

"Tell your uncle it's the best tuna salad I have ever had. There were some subtle spices in there I couldn't identify, but they made all the difference."

"That's his little secret," she replied, again with that fetching smile. "Come back and have another sometime, Mr. Tuna Salad," she said with a suggestive inflection that reminded him of Violet in *It's a Wonderful Life*.

Marius smiled and turned as he went through the door. "Ya never know," he said, now thinking again of the Waits lyrics, "and I will ask to be served by . . . ?"

"Ask for Peach Cobbler."

Marius got into his car smiling, thinking that he just might have received an "invitation to the blues." As he buckled his seat belt, his mobile rang. It was Chamsi, and he felt a little upward movement of his tuna fish sandwich. He didn't waste a moment. "She okay?"

"Yeah, she's fine, physically at least. She told me of the conversation you had with her the other day—I hope you don't mind that, Marius, we are like close sisters now—and I think she's working over a lot of what you said. I'm sure you will be getting into that subject more when you get back. Where are you anyway?"

"Iowa, land of corn and quite good tuna salad sandwiches, which is now not settling too well in my digestive tract. What is your take on what she's feeling?"

"It's very strange for her, Marius, having a foreign organ in her body keeping her alive. And on top of that, an organ that came from a mass killer. And since her religious conversion—

If I can call it that—she just doesn't have all that stuff to help process what her brothers did to her, but now have to deal with the way we saved her life. There's no gods or prophets or scriptures, to fall back on to assure her that she did the right thing. And then you told her that there wasn't any reason or metaphysical explanation for your being out there in that small-town, and everything that happened. Instinctively, I think she wanted to find some reason of fate, or destiny or something to put it in place rather than it seeming like we were just seizing a target of opportunity and playing God."

Those last words caused Marius's stomach to constrict. "Good ole God. Always hanging around. Nothing he likes better than showing up at an atheist party like a drunk puking all over your bathroom, fucking things up. He was just tattooed on the forearm of my waitress."

"It's a lot of mental energy to keep things in perspective, Marius. And she is very new to it all. It's a lot for me to process, too. I've had dreams replaying that transplant."

"Right now I'm feeling very helpless, Cham, out here in the middle of nowhere. But let me say this much right now, and I'm hoping it can hold it until I get back there. I don't care which way you go with this. It doesn't matter if you believe in God. It doesn't matter because even if you believe he exists, he doesn't do his job. He lets shit happen. Even if you want to believe he's a good God, he lets religions proliferate in his name, whichever one he chooses—probably because he has the biggest ego in the universe and he loves being worshipped. And he lets those religions use him, exploit him for the money and the power selling all the bullshit they have created about him . And he really doesn't do anything about it. And so, we get all of the wars, the oppression, the enslavement, and the kind of thing that happened to Jazmeen. And the kind of thing that happened to Khalid—from a guy who fucking doesn't show up. And why? Because he was never there in the first place.

"But if you *don't* believe that God exists, as I don't, and therefore you don't believe that there is some supreme controlling manager that is responsible for all that happens in the universe, that doesn't mean that you have to surrender all agency, that you have to sit back and accept everything that happens as just part of some divine plan. Fuck no, because there is no plan, because there is no god. So even if things happen for no reason at all, it doesn't mean that they are not consequences even if they are without some divine meaning, that we should not act upon them.

"So if I acted like God in the face of the circumstances that befell me, so what? What is that old bromide? If life hands you lemons, well then make lemonade. If you want to call that acting like God, then I defy you to get through life without taking some agency and responsibility. I'll be damned if I was going to wait around for God, Allah, Yahweh, or whoever, to get off his ass and answer some prayers for Jazmeen, or some hapless school kids who were being shot by some crazy bastard who might well think he's a divine messenger. I might be a guy who was—if you want to put it that way—acting like a god. But at least I fucking showed up. *She will not be forsaken.*"

It was quiet on both phones. After a while, Chamsi spoke: "I'm sorry if I upset you calling about this, Marius. You need to concentrate on your driving. I didn't mean to accuse you of acting like a god. But I hope you don't mind if I still think that you are an angel."

Marius guffawed.

"Did I say something funny, Marius?"

"Sort of, Cham. Just let me know if you hear any bells ringing."

"What the hell are you talking about, Marius?"

"Don't you know? Bells. Every time one rings, an angel gets his . . . Never mind, it just means that I would be able to get home sooner."

Acknowledgements

It's a Wonderful Life (1946, RKO Radio Pictures)

"Invitation to the Blues" Tom Waits, *Small Change* (1972)

"Volare", Songwriters: Domenico Modugno,
Francesco Migliacci
Lyrics © Downtown Music Publishing

About the Author

Sebastian Gerard is a former university professor who has traveled, lectured and taught in China over the past quarter century. He was a Visiting Professor at the University of Paris and a Fulbright Scholar of American film and urbanism to universities in Hong Kong in 2000. Among his fiction publications he is author of *The River Dragon's Daughters: A Novel of Four Women of the Yangtze in Interesting Times.* He lives in Southern California and writes non-fiction under another name and has won awards for his print and broadcast journalism.